MILK OF
HUMAN
KINDNESS

A DISH FIT
FOR THE GODS

AT ONE
FELL
SWOOP

TRUTH
WILL OUT

LAY IT ON WITH
A TROWEL

HOIST
WITH HIS
OWN
PETARD

Shakespeare for Grown-ups

Also by E. Foley and B. Coates

Homework for Grown-ups
Advanced Homework for Grown-ups
Homework for Grown-ups Quiz Book

E. FOLEY & B. COATES

SHAKESPEARE FOR GROWN-UPS

Everything you Need to Know about the Bard

SQUARE PEG

Published by Square Peg 2014

2 4 6 8 10 9 7 5 3 1

First published in Great Britain in 2014 by
Square Peg
20 Vauxhall Bridge Road,
London SW1V 2SA

A Penguin Random House company

Penguin
Random House
UK

www.penguinrandomhouse.com
www.vintage-books.co.uk

A CIP catalogue record for this book
is available from the British Library

ISBN 9780224098557

Penguin Random House supports the
Forest Stewardship Council® (FSC®), the leading international
forest-certification organisation. Our books carrying the FSC label
are printed on FSC®-certified paper. FSC is the only forest-certification
scheme supported by the leading environmental organisations,
including Greenpeace. Our paper procurement policy can be
found at www.randomhouse.co.uk/environment

MIX
Paper from
responsible sources
FSC® C016897

Typeset by Palimpsest Book Production Ltd, Falkirk, Stirlingshire
Printed and bound by GGP Media GmbH, Pößneck, Germany

For Lola, Barnabas,
Iris and Joseph

Contents

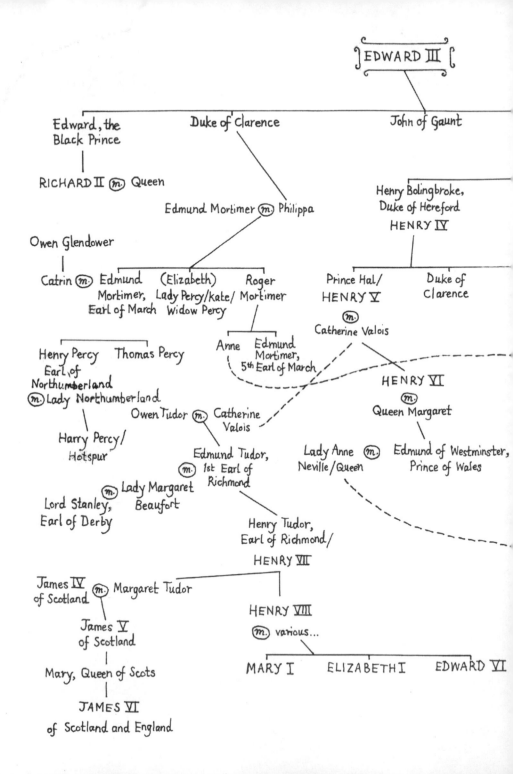

Duke of York ⓜ Duchess of York   Duke of Gloucester ⓜ Duchess of Gloucester

John Beaufort, 1st Earl of Somerset   Henry Beaufort, Bishop of Winchester   Thomas Beaufort, Duke of Exeter   Aumerle/ 2nd Duke of York   Earl of Cambridge ⓜ Anne Mortimer

John Beaufort, 1st Duke of Somerset   Edmund Beaufort, 2nd Duke of Somerset

Prince John, Duke of Lancaster/ Duke of Bedford   Humphrey, Duke of Gloucester ⓜ Duchess Eleanor of Gloucester

Richard Plantagenet, 3rd Duke of York ⓜ Duchess of York

Henry Beaufort, 3rd Duke of Somerset   Edmund Beaufort, 4th Duke of Somerset

ord/Earl Rivers   Lady Grey/ Queen Elizabeth ⓜ John Grey   ⓜ Edward Plantagenet, Earl of March — EDWARD IV   George Plantagenet, Duke of Clarence   Richard Plantagenet/ Duke of Gloucester/ RICHARD III ⓜ   Edmund Plantagenet, Earl of Rutland

Marquis of Dorset   Lord Richard Grey   Prince Edward/ Edward, Prince of Wales — EDWARD V   Richard, Duke of York   Lady Anne Neville/ Queen

A Family Tree of the Characters in Shakespeare's History Tetralogies

INTRODUCTION

William Shakespeare is without question Britain's greatest literary hero. His work has spoken to countless generations, nationalities and cultures, and to men, women and children alike. His plays have been translated into every language under the sun and performances of them can been seen from Afghanistan to Zimbabwe. But how much do you really know about the man and his wondrous words?

For many of us, our first experience of Shakespeare can be intimidating and (whisper it) a little wearisome. And if you have a bad start with the Bard, chances are that will affect your grown-up encounters with him too. Do you find yourself dozing off during *The Winter's Tale*? Does all that thumb-biting in *Romeo and Juliet* perplex you? Find it hard to stomach the jokes in *The Taming of the Shrew*? Lost by the language of the famous monologues from *King Lear* and *Othello*? Worry not, you aren't alone. And although today every schoolchild will encounter Shakespeare's work at some point in their English lessons, the majority of UK adults will only be properly familiar with one or two plays at most. In fact, a recent poll showed that 5 per cent of 18- to 34-year-olds think Shakespeare's most famous play is *Cinderella*, and 2 per cent from the same group think the man himself is a fictional character. That's why this book is essential reading for anyone who feels they should know more about our greatest poet, or, indeed, anyone looking to revive their acquaintance with him, or even just help their children with their homework.

As well as taking an in-depth look at the most-loved, -studied and -performed plays, we will take you on a journey through the different genres Shakespeare made his own – the Comedies, Histories and Tragedies – and we'll show you how to decode his enigmatic sonnets. We'll also show you that there is much to be treasured and enjoyed in his less familiar works.

We don't claim to be Shakespeare scholars; we are ordinary readers who were curious to learn more about our greatest national poet, and we became passionate about passing on the most interesting facts we discovered. The aim of this book is to give a solid understanding of Shakespeare's genius and to arm you with the tools you need to enjoy him with confidence and insight. In addition, we'll peruse some of the more perplexing problems that have agitated academics over the years: Did Shakespeare really write his plays himself? What exactly is the First Folio? What would it have been like to see one of his plays at the time of its first performance? What does 'hoist with his own petard' actually mean? Who might the sonnets' Dark Lady be?

Between these covers you will find nuggets on a broad range of topics including the historical context of Shakespeare's writing; his personal life, contemporaries and influences; his language and poetic skill; the key themes of his oeuvre; his less well-known works and characters; his most famous speeches and quotations; the phrases and words that he invented, and much more.

The world is a far richer place thanks to this glove-maker's son from Stratford and his unparalleled influence over our imaginations and language. His 'eternal summer shall not fade . . . So long as men can breathe or eyes can see' and we hope that by the time you finish this book you are as filled with admiration and enthusiasm for his work as we are.

'Brevity Is The Soul Of Wit'
All Shakespeare's Plays In One Sentence Each

Obviously a close reading of the plays will richly reward any student of Shakespeare, but we understand if you need a quick cheat's guide. We've set out each one in a sentence so you can always be ready to impress with extensive knowledge of the whole back catalogue of Will's works.

COMEDIES

The Tempest

The magician Prospero shipwrecks the enemies that originally ousted him from Italy, but when Ferdinand, the son of his arch-rival Alonso, falls for his daughter Miranda he finally faces them down and learns to forgive.

The Two Gentlemen of Verona

Proteus, who loves Julia, is friends with Valentine, who loves Silvia, but their friendship deteriorates when Proteus gets Valentine outlawed in order to pursue Silvia himself, much to the dismay of his page Sebastian who is actually Julia in disguise, until, after much trouble, everyone ends up with their original beloved.

The Merry Wives of Windsor

Falstaff's cynical seduction of two wealthy women goes awry when they find out about each other and decide to return the compliment by making him a laughing stock.

Measure for Measure

In the Duke of Vienna's absence, his frosty deputy Angelo resurrects arcane fornication laws but is busted trying to blackmail a nun into sex by the Duke in disguise as a friar.

The Comedy of Errors

Separated in a shipwreck as babies, friends Antipholus and Dromio of Syracuse head to Ephesus to search for their twin brothers, the helpfully named Antipholus and Dromio of Ephesus, leading to much confusion for wives and friends until their parents appear and sort everything out.

Much Ado About Nothing

In Sicily, Claudio and Hero are cruelly tricked and parted while Benedick and Beatrice fight and fall in love before deceptions and disguises are uncovered by a hapless nightwatchman and harmonious order is restored with marriages and jigging.

Love's Labour's Lost

The King of Navarre and three friends inconveniently swear off women for three years just before a beautiful princess and her ladies arrive for a visit, inspiring all of them to break their oaths after many love-letter mix-ups and other shenanigans.

A Midsummer Night's Dream

Mistaken administering of love juice results in Titania, Queen of the Fairies, falling for the ass Bottom, while two sets of couples get confused in the woods, before the natural order of things is restored.

The Merchant of Venice

Antonio makes a risky deal: putting up a pound of flesh as collateral against a loan to fund his friend Bassanio's pursuit of Portia, and when the money-lender Shylock calls in his debt, Portia, dressed as a man, successfully fights Antonio's case in a court of law with an ingenious defence.

As You Like It

The exile of brothers, dukes, fathers, daughters, cousins and clowns to the benign bubble of the Forest of Arden leads to disguise, gender-bending and, finally, happy marriages for all.

The Taming of the Shrew

Stroppy Katherina stands in the way of her more pliable sister Bianca's marriage, so Bianca's suitors persuade fortune-hunter Petruchio to marry her and embark on a campaign of mental cruelty that 'tames' her and leaves everyone content and happily married.

All's Well that Ends Well

Orphan Helena is determined to have her man Bertram – even if he doesn't want her – and tricks him into impregnating her by pretending to be Diana (who he does fancy), a tactic that makes him appreciate Helena and vow to be a good husband to her.

Twelfth Night, or What You Will

Twins Viola and Sebastian lose each other after a shipwreck and, believing each other to be dead, become the servants of amorous Illyrian nobles, but after much disguise-inspired confusion and a yellow-stocking-themed subplot, they are finally reunited.

The Winter's Tale

King Leontes' jealous madness leads to the demise of his children, and the death-by-grief of his wife, but happily many years later it is revealed that his wife and daughter are actually both alive and all are reconciled.

Pericles

Pericles competes for a wife and then loses her and his newborn daughter in a shipwreck before, many years later, reuniting with them after his wife has become a priestess and his daughter, Marina, a virginal prostitute.

The Two Noble Kinsmen

Friends Palamon and Arcite fall out over their love for Emilia but an unbiddable horse means Palamon eventually gets the girl.

HISTORIES

King John

King John is threatened by an angry nephew, the King of France and a cardinal, and is finally murdered by a malcontent monk.

Richard II

Proud, long-serving King Richard is finally undone by ambitious Henry Bolingbroke, his own vanity and a penchant for land-grabbing.

Henry IV, Part 1

Henry Bolingbroke is now King Henry, but his complete enjoyment of his reign is undermined by worries about his wayward son Hal and his associations with the drunkard Falstaff, and the rebellion of Henry Percy, gloriously nicknamed Hotspur, who's eventually killed by Hal.

Henry IV, Part 2

Hotspur's father avenges his son's death by threatening to cause civil war, news that makes Henry's health decline, until on his deathbed he makes up with his errant son Hal who rejects his pal Falstaff and prepares to accept the crown as a more sensibly named Henry V.

Henry V

Henry decides to start his reign with a rather punchy request to rule France, which is rejected, but after glorious victory at Agincourt, Princess Katherine of France marries him and the countries are bound together.

Henry VI, Part 1

Young Henry struggles to live up to his heroic father despite dealing successfully with Joan of Arc (although less successfully with his own dastardly dukes).

Henry VI, Part 2

Henry fails to control his nobles: cue War of the Roses.

Henry VI, Part 3

Henry loses his throne, regains it, soliloquises on a molehill, loses the throne again and is stabbed to death by the future Richard III.

Richard III

Hunchback ubervillain has his brother drowned in barrel of wine, his nephews (the 'Princes in the Tower') murdered, poisons his wife, is surprised when people start to turn against him, and then gets killed in battle by the future King Henry VII after inconveniently losing his horse.

Henry VIII

Henry meets and falls in love with the beautiful Anne Bullen at one of Cardinal Wolsey's parties, ousting his current wife, crowning Anne as Queen and allowing Cranmer, the Archbishop of Canterbury, to predict great things at the birth of their daughter Elizabeth.

TRAGEDIES

Troilus and Cressida

Troilus (Paris and Hector's brother) falls in love with Cressida (the daughter of a Trojan priest) and after a single night of passion loses her to the Greeks waiting outside the city's walls – cue much teeth-gnashing and revenge.

Coriolanus

Martial hero Coriolanus saves Rome from Volscian invasion, is persuaded to run for consul by his manipulative mother, banished when the people turn on him, dissuaded from enacting revenge on his former home by his family, and finally murdered by those vexing Volscians.

Titus Andronicus

Roman general Titus is infuriated when his arch-enemy and former captive, Tamora, Queen of the Goths, marries the emperor: murder, rape, mutilation, cannibalism and infanticide leave pretty much everyone dead.

Romeo and Juliet

Unsupportive relatives ruin young lovers' bliss, leading to a fatal fake suicide mix-up.

Timon of Athens

Generous playboy Timon gets into debt and leaves Athens to make his home in a cave, whereupon he discovers mounds of gold, and dies after realising his only true friend is his servant Flavius.

Julius Caesar

Worthy Roman Brutus, concerned about his dictator friend's political intentions, gets caught up in a conspiracy that ends with him stabbing a disappointed Caesar before being driven to suicide by his rival Mark Antony's superior oratory and tactics.

Macbeth

The Thane Macbeth receives a prophecy from three 'weyard sisters' that he'll be King of Scotland, and his murderously ambitious wife helps him to achieve his dream, but at the very worst price.

Hamlet

Listless student prince Hamlet, traumatised by his villainous uncle Claudius' fratricide, is inspired by the ghost of his father to feign insanity, sending his girlfriend Ophelia loopy and resulting in a catastrophic poison-and-fencing bloodbath.

King Lear

Old King Lear makes a terrible mistake in trusting his bad daughters and exiling his truest child, Cordelia, before going mad on a stormy heath and dying with Cordelia's expired body in his arms.

Othello

Moorish Venetian general Othello skips off to Cyprus with his beloved wife Desdemona and apparent best friend Iago, who makes it his mission to destroy their lives using only a handkerchief and a lot of insinuation.

Antony and Cleopatra

Mark Antony, one of Rome's three leaders, neglects his duties in favour of a passionate affair with Egyptian Queen Cleopatra, incurring Caesar's wrath and resulting in their bloody double suicide, by sword and, more inventively, by asp bite.

Cymbeline

British King Cymbeline, encouraged by his evil Queen, banishes his daughter Imogen's secret husband Posthumus, and annoys the Romans, but thankfully Imogen resists various ensuing attempts on her life and it all gets sorted out in the end.

THE LIFE AND TIMES OF WILLIAM SHAKESPEARE

'The web of our life is of a mingled yarn'
What we know about Shakespeare's life

Tantalisingly, we know very little about William Shakespeare's life. His thoughts on love, marriage, politics, children, death, sin, temptation and sexuality were never recorded, apart from in his works of course, which are open to endless interpretation. Despite the best efforts of archivists and scholars, Will remains an enigma, a blank canvas on which countless biographers have painted their own vivid and often fanciful pictures. Despite how familiar you may feel you are with the Bard's visage, there are only a handful of portraits of him in existence and historians still squabble over which are most likely to be accurate. The one above is the Chandos portrait from the National Gallery in London, attributed to painter John Taylor, which was said to have been originally in the possession of writer William Davenant, Shakespeare's godson (and, as rumour had it, according to John Aubrey's *Brief Lives*, his illegitimate son).

So what *do* we know about Shakespeare? There is a record of his baptism at Holy Trinity Church in the market town of Stratford-upon-Avon on 26 April 1564, and, given that in Elizabethan times children were typically baptised between two and four days after their birth, many people hedge their bets and take our national poet's birthday to be 23 April, which is also, rather conveniently, St George's Day. His father, John Shakespeare, was a glove-maker (and, pleasingly, a municipal ale-taster), and his mother, Mary Arden, was the daughter of a well-known and respected landowner. Shakespeare was probably educated at the King's New Grammar School, where he would have been coached extensively in the rigours of Latin and rhetoric: you can see him flexing those classical muscles in the plays where certain characters use magnificent rhetoric and persuasion to manipulate the action – think of Iago in *Othello*, Lady Macbeth in *Macbeth* and Portia in *The Merchant of Venice*. Older boys spoke Latin in class, and they would have had a good knowledge of classical texts and mythology.

We don't know what Shakespeare did after school – this is the first example of his 'lost years', where Shakespeare simply disappears from the record books – but it's likely that his father's financial difficulties (of which there *is* a record) prevented him from going to university, and Will probably spent his teenage years as an apprentice in his father's glove-making business. It's easy to speculate how frustrating this might have been for a young man with such an intense literary gift, but then again maybe he loved it. Many critics fall into the trap of assuming it's possible to guess Shakespeare's thoughts and opinions from our idea of what *we* would like the author of such brilliant plays and poems to be like. Some seventeenth-century accounts of the 'lost years' have it that he was forced to do a runner from home after being caught poaching deer from Sir Thomas Lucy's nearby estate at Charlecote. Again, there's an appeal to the idea of Shakespeare as a kind of proto-Danny the Champion of the World, but there's evidence that the deer park was only instated at Charlecote in the seventeenth century, so the sums don't quite add up.

Shakespeare married Anne Hathaway in 1582 when she was twenty-six and he was eighteen. The age gap was unusual, but even more unusual was Shakespeare's youth when he got hitched. The age of consent was twenty-one, so his father would have had to agree to the match. Perhaps this is explained by the fact that Anne was three months pregnant when they tied the knot; their first daughter Susanna was born in 1583, followed by twins Judith and Hamnet eighteen months later in 1585. Their marriage has been the subject of huge speculation – did Anne ever accompany her famous husband to London and witness the literary life he led there? Was theirs a union of mutual adoration, or one dogged by ill-temper and drudgery? It was certainly a long marriage, but we have no way of knowing if it was a happy one – even Shakespeare's last will and testament fails to set the record straight in any convincing way (see page 16).

After the record of his twins' birth there is another long 'lost' period, lasting right up to 1592, all the more frustrating because it's during this time that he left Stratford for London, and made the transition to successful actor, playwright and part-owner of a theatre. Many theories abound: taking as evidence a preoccupation with the ocean and storms in his plays (think *The Tempest, Othello, Twelfth Night*, etc.), some wonder if he went to sea, possibly spending time in Italy. Or perhaps he went north, working as a tutor for a

The coat of arms purchased by Shakespeare

Catholic family, before meeting the Lord Derby's Men – a company of actors – and travelling south with them to the bright lights (or at least flaming torches) of London. Or did he become a player in the Queen's Men – another acting company – and begin to ply his trade with them? We'll never know for sure, but the next concrete placing of Shakespeare is a bit of a battering in print, in Robert Greene's *Groatsworth of Wit, Bought with a Million of Repentance* (1592) (see page 16).

By the end of the 1590s, Shakespeare was a wealthy man, probably one of the first British writers to accumulate a stash of cash from the proceeds of his literary endeavours by taking shares in the theatre which performed his plays (records show he made a bit on the side from some illegal malt-hoarding and tax evasion too – he appears to have been a canny businessman). He broke the mould by securing for himself a percentage of box-office takings and was able to buy a flashy house, New Place in Stratford, and his status was so elevated that he was permitted to purchase a coat of arms bearing the motto 'Non sanz droict', or 'Not without right'.

In the late summer of 1596 Shakespeare's son Hamnet died at the age of eleven, from unknown causes. His daughters Susanna and Judith went on to marry and have children: Judith had three, but they all died young, and Susanna's daughter Elizabeth died childless, ending the line.

By 1613, Shakespeare was spending more and more time in Stratford, and had stopped writing plays – again the reason why he ceased writing remains a mystery. The fact that he signed his will in March 1616 probably means that his health was failing. The following month, close to his birthday, he died and was buried in the Holy Trinity Church. His will offers up another enigma: Anne Hathaway, his wife of thirty-four years, is mentioned in just twelve devastatingly brief words, 'I gyve unto my wief my second best bed with the furniture.' Much has been made of this apparent slight, and of course in modern times we might feel a touch

Robert Greene's 'upstart crow'

Robert Greene was a playwright who was about four years older than Shakespeare, and an established member of London's literary scene when Shakespeare arrived on it. He was part of a group known as the University Wits along with other well-educated writers like Christopher Marlowe, Thomas Lodge, George Peele and Thomas Nashe. A heavy drinker and gambler, womaniser and liar, he was also in possession of a monster ego. A fun chap to be around then, and certainly one with a chip on his shoulder about young William's accelerating success in his milieu.

It's not entirely clear why Shakespeare bothered Greene so much, but probably his audacity in believing he could move from being a provincial, lower-class actor to competing with the establishment playwrights rankled with this snooty, and less significant, writer. Shakespeare had not gone to Oxford or Cambridge

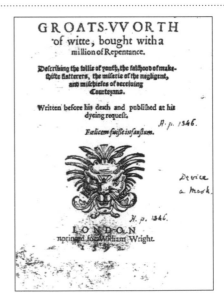

University, as most of his contemporary playwrights had, and even though he was writing his way into the history books as one of the most brilliant minds this

aggrieved to be honoured after all those years of wedlock with a dodgy bed. But in fact it's all about context. One theory is that the best bed would probably have been reserved for guests, and would have been considered an heirloom – i.e. an item reserved for heirs, not wives. Clearly the wondrous wordsmith didn't see his last will and testament as the place for anything more enlightening or flowery about his marriage. The inscription on his grave is a dream for conspiracy theorists – like an English Tutankhamun it offers up a curse on whoever disturbs his remains, prompting some to speculate there may be a hidden manuscript buried with the Bard.

....

country has ever produced, he was still just a man from the provinces. It also appears that Shakespeare did not throw himself into the gentleman poets' scene with the gusto they might have wanted; he wasn't a big drinker – according to John Aubrey's *Lives*, he was a man who 'wouldn't be debauched' – and he had his head screwed on when it came to finances. Greene, on the other hand, died penniless and bitter at the age of thirty two in September 1592 (with Marlowe pursuing him towards his Maker the following year), leaving behind enough unpublished work for a printer named Henry Chettle to produce a posthumous pamphlet entitled *Greene's Groatsworth of Wit, Bought with a Million of Repentance* – essentially a moralistic fable which is revealed at the end to be autobiographical.

The passage we're interested in begins with a warning to the other members of his gang not to trust actors who mangle poets' words. And he goes on: 'Yes trust them not: for there is an Upstart Crow, beautified with our feathers, that with his Tyger's hart wrapt in a Player's hyde supposes he is as well able to bombast out a blanke verse as the best of you: and being an absolute *Johannes Factotum* [jack of all trades], is in his owne conceit the only Shake-scene in the countrey.' That lovely 'tiger's heart' metaphor is a direct lift from the first act of *Henry VI, Part 3*. As Stephen Greenblatt points out in his excellent biography *Will in the World*, Shakespeare got his revenge, with an effusive apology from publisher Henry Chettle: 'I am as sorry as if the original fault had been my fault, because myself have seen his demeanour no less civil than he excellent in the quality he professes', and a nice dig through Polonius in *Hamlet*: 'that's an ill phrase, a vile phrase, "beautified" is a vile phrase'.

> Good frend for Jesus sake forbeare
> To digg the dust encloased heare.
> Blese be the man that spares thes stones,
> And curst be he that moves my bones.

This, and the other gaps in his biography, opens the door for fans to look for clues in his work. Feel free to enjoy yourself conjecturing. But try not to be disappointed that we don't know more facts about Shakespeare the man; sometimes it's best not to get to know your heroes – it keeps the magic alive.

Why is Shakespeare called the Bard?

'Bard' is an ancient Gaelic term meaning poet. It initially referred to a minstrel who might travel from village to village reciting legends of chieftains and their triumphs. Shakespeare has been given the epithet because he is *the* definitive poet, and recognised not just in Britain but across the world as such (though Scots might disagree – Robert Burns is known as the Bard in Caledonia). It's assumed that he was first called the Bard by David Garrick (see page 283) during the celebratory Shakespeare Jubilee held in Stratford in 1769 in his snappily titled 'An Ode upon dedicating a building, and erecting a statue, to Shakespeare, at Stratford upon Avon' which read:

> Sweetest bard that ever sung,
> Nature's glory, Fancy's child;
> Never sure did witching tongue,
> Warble forth such wood-notes wild!

What was life like in Shakespeare's day?

Given how universal Shakespeare's work feels, it's easy to imagine he was just like us; that if we met him in the pub we'd have loads in common. However,

London in Shakespeare's day

it is important to remember that the times he lived in in were very different from ours. Here are a few facts to help you orientate yourself in his world.

- **Population** There were about four million people living in England in the late sixteenth century. The English population today is about 53.5 million.

- **Disease** Outbreaks of the deadly bubonic plague frequently wiped out whole communities. Stratford lost a sixth of its inhabitants in 1564.

- **Queen Elizabeth** Elizabeth's rule (1558–1603) is now considered England's golden age of stability and achievement, but things didn't always look so rosy for her. Her father murdered her mother, she was disinherited then reinstated in line for the throne, she changed the religion of her country, the Pope sanctioned her assassination, she endured serious internal and external plots to overthrow her, she failed to subdue the rebellious Irish, and her decision not to marry and

produce an heir created an atmosphere of anxiety and paranoia about
the succession, resulting in a ruthless international and domestic
secret-service network, reliant on torture.

○ **Cities** London was the third largest city in Europe after Paris and
Naples.

○ **Communities** The majority of people lived in the countryside and
depended on unreliable harvests. The biggest towns were London,
Norwich, Bristol, York, Salisbury, Newcastle, Exeter and Coventry.

○ **Feudalism** This period saw a significant change from a feudal hierarchy
that encouraged a powerful chivalric noble class to a centralisation of
power around the absolute monarch. Historians have identified this
period as one of transition from the ideals and practices of medieval
times to the beginnings of the internationally connected modern age.

○ **Religion** England had been Catholic up until 1533 when Henry VIII
broke with Rome in order to marry Elizabeth's mother, Anne
Boleyn. It was then Protestant until 1553 when Mary I reinstated
Catholicism. On Mary's death in 1558 Elizabeth returned the
country to Protestantism. Religion was central to the general
population's life so this was a very confusing time. Shakespeare's
sister was baptised a Catholic in 1558 but just six years later he was
christened a Protestant. There were still Catholic priests in hiding
around the country giving masses to those who secretly held on to
the old religion.

○ **Violence** Society was generally more violent than today. Many
citizens were armed, there was no real police force, there were public
executions, frequent rioting and brawling; popular pastimes included
bear-baiting and dog- and cock-fighting, and the severed heads of
traitors were displayed on the walls in the capital. The literary world
didn't exist in some rarefied bubble outside of this: Ben Jonson killed a
man, Christopher Marlowe was stabbed in the eye and Shakespeare

himself was named in a court record as having made a man fear for his life or 'bodily hurt'.

○ **Science** The general view at this time was still that the sun orbited the earth. However, it was a period of great scientific endeavours, with Galileo, Descartes, Francis Bacon and William Gilbert all making important contributions. There were also radical developments in philosophy and ethics from intellectuals like Machiavelli and Montaigne.

○ **Europe** At the start of Elizabeth's reign, Protestant England was surrounded on all sides by Catholic nations – Ireland, France, Scotland (until 1560) and the Spanish-controlled Low Countries. This was an uncomfortable position, particularly after 1572 when thousands of members of the previously tolerated Protestant population in France were slaughtered in the St Bartholomew's Day Massacre.

○ **Alcohol** Much of the population was probably tipsy most of the time – water was unsafe to drink so people drank beer instead. Happy days.

○ **Foreign Policy** The old adversary France was replaced as English Enemy Number One by Spain, ruled by Elizabeth's brother-in-law, Mary's widower, Philip II. Spain tried to invade in 1588. The destruction of the Armada was a source of national pride but there was great anxiety about new threats.

○ **Family** People generally married in their twenties – Shakespeare bucked the trend by getting hitched in his late teens. Marriages were usually arranged by parents and there was little emphasis on privacy in domestic life. Wives and children belonged to, and obeyed, the man of the house. Girls did not generally go to school. The firstborn son inherited everything. Because children were so important to property rights, virginity and chastity were extremely important standards for noblewomen.

○ **War** The Protestant Reformation and the rise of powerful nation states led to Europe becoming a hotbed of conflict. The tensions leading to the Thirty Years War (1618–48) were ramping up, resulting in a devastating and vast conflict that would see all the major European powers set against each other, battling over religion and influence.

○ **Gangs** Nobles had groups of men who served them and hung around with them. These 'retainers' wore special clothing, a bit like gangs now, to show whom they supported. There were frequently fights between rival groups, as at the beginning of *Romeo and Juliet*.

○ **Empire** The English maritime explorations that were just beginning at this time set the country on the path towards the massive British Empire and the nation's involvement in the slave trade. The state of Virginia in America is named after Elizabeth's persona of the Virgin Queen.

○ **Food** Potatoes were a new and exotic food, brought to Europe by Spanish conquistadors from Peru, and people didn't drink coffee or tea or eat chocolate.

○ **Race** There were Moors (North Africans of Arab-Berber descent) in London (helpfully anti-Spanish), and Elizabeth had a few black servants on her staff. However, in 1596 and in 1601 she issued edicts expelling 'Negroes and Blackamoors' because of fears they were using resources and taking away jobs from the English – reasoning that has familiar echoes today. There were barely any Jews in England since their expulsion in 1290. However, London was extremely cosmopolitan because of trade. People were suspicious of foreigners but not racist in the modern sense.

○ **Terrorism** In 1605 the country was stunned by the attempted Catholic attack on Parliament by Guy Fawkes.

○ **Class** The middle class was starting to become a force to be reckoned with and the possibility of social mobility had only just taken root. Merchants and workers in the wool trade were gaining more and more power due to their economic success. However, England was a very hierarchical country and the monarchy encouraged the population to view this hierarchy as divinely ordained. There was even a law prescribing which classes could wear certain fabrics and colours.

○ **Calendar** England was on a different calendar to the rest of Catholic Europe who adopted the Gregorian calendar in 1582. (England didn't until 1752.)

○ **Legitimacy** Illegitimate children were regarded as morally inferior. They couldn't inherit or marry.

○ **Church** Everyone had to regularly attend (Protestant) church services, or face fines (and be regarded with suspicion).

○ **London** London was growing at a breakneck rate but still had a population of about 300,000 people, which is approximately the population of the Borough of Lambeth today. (London's total population is currently over 8,000,000.)

○ **Succession** Elizabeth died in 1603 without ever naming her successor to the throne. James I was just the most obvious and well-supported choice.

○ **King James** King James I's mother, Mary Queen of Scots, was executed in 1587 for involving herself in Catholic plots against Elizabeth.

○ **Scotland** James's accession brought the governments of England and Scotland under one rule, although they remained separate countries until 1707.

○ **Sewers** The main sewer in London was the Thames, which was filled with stinking rubbish, human and commercial waste, while still being used as an important travel artery and a source of water. There was only one bridge – London Bridge – which was populated with houses and shops.

○ **Language** The English language was rapidly expanding. There were no fixed grammatical rules and the same words were often spelled in many different ways.

○ **America** When Shakespeare was born, Europe had been aware of the existence of America for just seventy-two years. Columbus had landed in America in 1492.

○ **Witchcraft** Belief in witchcraft was prevalent and women suspected of being witches were persecuted. James I even wrote a book about them and involved himself in witch trials.

○ **Regicide** This was a time of great power for the British Crown but James I's son, Charles I, would end up being executed by his people in 1649 and England would become a republic until 1660.

○ **Puritans** Just twenty-six years after Shakespeare's death, the politically ascendant activist Protestants called Puritans would close all the theatres. In 1648 they would destroy them and any remaining actors would be arrested and flogged. The theatres would remain closed until the 1660 restoration of the monarchy.

○ **Life Expectancy** Surviving childhood was a difficult business, and average life expectancy was around the mid-forties. Many women died in childbirth and medical care still revolved around the idea of the four humours (see page 232), bleeding patients being a popular treatment.

○ **Printing** The first book to be printed in English had only been made in 1473, less than a century before Shakespeare's birth. People didn't see many visual images in their day-to-day lives, particularly after the Reformation, when artworks were removed from churches.

Queen Elizabeth I and Shakespeare

Overcoming a tricky start in life – she was banished from her father King Henry VIII's court at the age of two and a half – by the time Elizabeth and Shakespeare's paths crossed she was firmly entrenched as the titan of royalty we recognise today.

She was wickedly clever, fluent in both French and Italian, and enjoyed translating the classics and composing her own sonnets. She was a keen patron of the arts, and under her reign there was a remarkable flowering of English literature, particularly in drama – as well as Shakespeare, other literary giants such as Marlowe, Donne, Spenser and Kyd found their voices. Though Shakespeare is thought of as an Elizabethan writer, the queen was in fact in her late fifties when the Lord Chamberlain's Men were performing at court, and though it's true he spent more years of his writing career under Elizabeth's rule, he was in fact more prolific during her successor James I's reign. Elizabeth died in 1603, and there is a suggestion that her death and the end of the golden age is alluded to in Sonnet 107, which mentions the eclipse of the 'mortal moon'.

There is no evidence that Shakespeare and Elizabeth actually met but it is not beyond the realms of possibility, as Shakespeare's plays were performed at her court many times. Understandably, in fictionalised accounts of Shakespeare's life, particularly on film or television, the temptation to eavesdrop on what these two magnificent figures from English history might have said to one another is irresistible, so it has become a common misconception that they were acquaintances.

Women in Shakespeare's Time

For a nation ruled by a woman considered second in authority to God, the status of women in Elizabethan times was shockingly lowly. Most, aside from a very few of noble birth, were not afforded an education. Even those lucky ones were being trained for a life at home: they learned fruit preserving and bookkeeping rather than Plato and Pythagoras. And if a girl did manage to gain a good education, there was nowhere for her to exercise that learning, because women were not allowed to enter the professions: there were no female actresses, doctors, lawyers or priests,

Elizabethan Shepherdess

though they could become spinners or weavers if they wanted. They had no vote. The duty of women, whether rich or poor, was to their husbands; in effect they belonged to them. Petruchio's words about Kate in *The Taming of the Shrew* are full of the language of ownership: 'She is my goods, my chattels; she is my house, / My household stuff, my field, my barn, / My horse, my ox, my ass, my any thing'. Women were expected to bring a dowry to marriage – goods, money or land – also known as a marriage portion. A good woman was expected to be kind, patient, chaste, humble, soft and pliant, and since outer appearance was seen to correlate directly to inner status, they had to pay attention to their looks, Elizabethans particularly prizing roundness of hips and paleness of skin. Which makes it all the more extraordinary that Shakespeare created and gave prominence in his plays to women who are complex, confident, capable of manipulation and merriment, often with the lion's share of lines. Rosalind, Portia, Katherina, Lady Macbeth, Beatrice, Juliet, Cleopatra, Viola and Titania are as unforgettable as any Hamlet, Lear or Othello.

How innovative was Shakespeare?

It's hard to imagine now, when English literature studies have revolved around him for so long, but Shakespeare's genius did not develop out of a firmly established literary tradition of English theatre. The medieval miracle, mystery and morality plays (see page 45) that were popular in his childhood were very different from the sophisticated drama he and his contemporaries produced. Their radical reimagining of what drama could and should be was part of the burgeoning of the arts across Europe, which was inspired by classical models and commonly known as the Renaissance. Shakespeare was in the vanguard of those developing the new form.

○ The Earl of Surrey had only introduced blank verse to England with the 1557 publication of his translation of some of Virgil's *Aeneid*.

○ The same year saw the first publication of the sonnet form in English, first developed by the poet, and favourite of Anne Boleyn, Thomas Wyatt.

○ The first permanent theatre in England was built in 1576 by James Burbage. The lack of competition is evident in his choice of name: The Theatre.

○ Plays were not seen as a serious literary enterprise. In 1612 Sir Thomas Bodley was collecting work for the new Bodleian library but told his staff not to bother with drama: 'haply some plays may be worthy the keeping, but hardly one in forty'.

Shakespeare's Globe

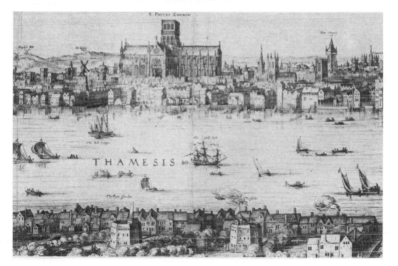

Engraving of Shakespeare's London showing the Globe Theatre

One of the great leaps forward of the English Renaissance was the creation of theatres as spaces in which sophisticated works could be performed. In medieval times, theatres simply did not exist. Actors were regarded as little more than vagabonds who travelled the country performing juggling acts or mimes from the back of open carts or at inn courtyards and the only alternative entertainments were the religious dramas presented on holy days. But by the late sixteenth century young men who had been educated at Oxford and

Cambridge began to put into practice in London the fruits of a classical education; drama developed rapidly, borrowing plots from legend and classical texts, introducing elaborate time frames, multiple roles and featuring protagonists with complex psychological profiles. In 1576 James Burbage built the Theatre in Shoreditch and it was here that the careers of Shakespeare, Thomas Kyd and Christopher Marlowe really began to take off. This didn't mean that drama became respectable: like many forms of popular entertainment it was considered by many to be vulgar, and plays were often criticised for promoting immorality and sedition. Theatres were located mainly in the red-light district, along with the bear-baiting and dog-fighting rings. Shakespeare was part of the Lord Chamberlain's Men (founded in 1594), later renamed the King's Men after the ascension of James I to the throne in 1603. They performed at the Theatre, the Curtain and then the Globe. The other main performing troupe in London was called the Admiral's Men, but history remembers them as a footnote – after all, they didn't have Shakespeare.

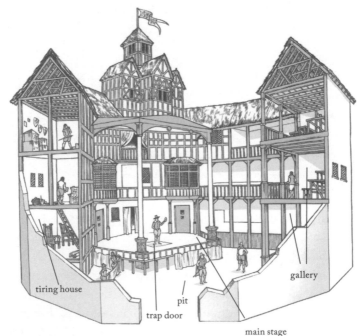

tiring house

gallery

pit

trap door

main stage

An Elizabethan theatre

By 1598 the lease on the Theatre had expired and the Lord Chamberlain's Men were in dispute with the owners of the land it stood on. James Burbage had died in 1597 and the venue had been vacant since his death; then one wintry night in December, Richard Burbage, James's son, led the Men to dismantle the Theatre and move the valuable building materials across the river to a new site in Southwark. It wasn't exactly theft: Richard knew his father had a clause in his contract with the owners of the Theatre, stating that while they owned the land, the theatre itself belonged to the company, but it was an audacious act. By the end of the summer of 1599 the rebuilt Globe Theatre was up and running, probably opening with a production of *As You Like It*. Profits were shared between the five or so 'housekeepers' of the company, who, along with Shakespeare, included William Kempe, Augustine Philips, John Heminges and Thomas Pope, though personnel changed over the years.

The Globe was vast: it could hold audiences of around three thousand and was extremely popular. Historians have estimated that about 20 per cent of the population of London regularly visited the theatre. As new plays were put on almost every afternoon there was plenty to keep people coming back. The design of the Globe followed existing venues for bear-baiting, and was loosely based on the layout of the inn courtyards and marketplaces where players had plied their trade in the 1570s. It was a twenty-sided polygon, as close as you could probably get to an 'O', comprised of a wooden outer building around a paved courtyard into which the stage jutted. Many of the audience paid the low entrance fee of a penny to stand in the courtyard, or 'pit'; these spectators were known as the groundlings. For those deeper of pocket there were three tiers of covered galleries. On each side of the stage, at the back, was a door, through which actors would enter and exit, and behind those doors was what we now call the dressing room, but in Shakespeare's day was called the 'tiring house'. Two posts at the front of the stage held up a cover to protect the actors, their very few props and costumes from the rain. No such luck for those standing in the pit. In the cover was a trapdoor through which characters could be lowered from the heavens, and underneath there was a trapdoor in the stage too, through which a

ghost, like King Hamlet, might appear. There was also a balcony that ran
the length of the stage for those scenes that required an upper window.
Because a large part of the audience were standing so close to the action,
drinking beer and eating hazelnuts, and the plays were performed in daylight, there was a less formal atmosphere to that found in theatres today.

Audiences enjoyed the elaborate costumes, but there was minimal set
dressing and no atmospheric lighting, so the words and the performances
had to be incredibly powerful. Since acting was considered a dishonourable
profession, women were prevented by law from becoming actresses, so
female roles were played by young men or boys right up until the 1660s when
the moral stigma receded. Cleopatra ironically refers to this practice in
Antony and Cleopatra when she says 'I shall see / Some squeaking Cleopatra
boy my greatness...'

It's mind-boggling how successful the theatres were, and how busy
someone like Shakespeare – as writer, part-owner and actor – must have
been: most companies performed five different plays in a week, and Shakespeare even performed in others' plays – he's named as a principal in a 1598
performance of Ben Jonson's *Every Man in His Humour*, around the time he
was probably writing *Henry IV, Part 2* and *Much Ado About Nothing*.

The Globe burnt to the ground in 1613, when, during a performance of
Henry VIII, a cannon used for special effects accidentally set light to the
thatched roof; amazingly no one was injured aside from one man whose
breeches caught fire but who managed to extinguish the flames using a bot-
tle of ale. It was rebuilt the following year – with a tiled roof – and thrived
until theatres were outlawed by England's Puritan administration in 1642.

The Globe was reconstructed for modern audiences in 1997, in a project
spearheaded by the American actor Sam Wanamaker. Faithfully using
Elizabethan building methods, it was a task that took ten years to complete.
It's not perfect, since there is no surviving architectural drawing of the original Globe, but it describes itself as the 'best guess' of the original. It's a truly
magical experience taking in a play there – as if the breath of Shakespeare
himself tickles at the back of your neck.

In 1596 James Burbage had invested in an indoor theatre called Blackfriars, which was also used for performances by the Lord Chamberlain's Men. It was in the heart of London and, while smaller than the Globe, it was not at the mercy of the harsher elements of the English weather. By all accounts it was a more sedate affair than its sister across the river, with spectators entirely seated, and evening performances conducted by candlelight. In fact, because of nimbyism on behalf of Blackfriars residents, the theatre didn't open until 1608, when the Lord Chamberlain's Men had become the King's Men, and James Burbage was dead; his legacy was realised by his son, with Shakespeare another shareholder in the venue.

Other, less famous, Elizabethan theatres

NEWINGTON BUTTS, ELEPHANT & CASTLE

It's extraordinary to think that where today the grim grey Elephant & Castle estates and roundabout loom over the London Borough of Southwark, in Renaissance times stood one of the earliest great Elizabeth theatres: Newington Butts. In those days the site was part of rural Surrey, and plays were performed there between 1576 and 1595, including Marlowe's *The Jew of Malta* and Shakespeare's *Titus Andronicus*.

CURTAIN THEATRE, SHOREDITCH

Little is known of the Curtain Theatre, so called because it stood on land called Curtain Close, but we do know that the Lord Chamberlain's Men performed there between 1597 and 1599, after they were forced to leave the Theatre. It is the theatre famously described as 'this wooden O' in *Henry V*.

ROSE THEATRE, BANKSIDE

Built by Philip Henslowe and used predominantly by the Admiral's Men, this is the theatre featured in the 1998 film *Shakespeare in Love*. It was erected in 1587 and staged performances of Marlowe's *Doctor Faustus, The Jew of Malta* and *Tamburlaine the Great*, Kyd's *Spanish Tragedy* as well as Shakespeare's *Henry VI, Part 1* and *Titus Andronicus*. It seems to have fallen out of favour by 1603. Marvellously, two-thirds of the Rose's foundations were rediscovered in 1989 during the demolition of an office block and it is now protected for future generations to learn from.

The Puritans and the theatre

The Puritans were a vociferous minority group of Protestants who wanted a return to a simpler, more morally strict and austere approach to life. They banned musical accompaniment from their own church services, so it's no great surprise that the theatre became an obvious target for their *froideur*; with its frivolity, rowdy crowds, costumes, transvestite actors, it was the very embodiment of art as a devilish distraction. One preacher called theatres 'idle places of intercourse'.

Their political influence was on the rise during Shakespeare's lifetime and they became gradually more powerful in Parliament. Queen Elizabeth did much to protect the theatres, as did her successor James, but during the English Civil War the Puritans took control of London and, denouncing the theatre and all associated with it as essentially Royalist, they ordered the closure of the theatres in 1642. The spoilsports. It took the restoration of the monarchy in 1660 for plays to once more be enjoyed.

Stage directions

There aren't a huge number of stage directions in Shakespeare's plays and most of them are brief and to the point, like the chilling '*He smothers her*' in *Othello* and '*Thunder. Enter the three Witches*' in *Macbeth*. Because of the textual history of the plays (see page 267) it is likely that the stage directions that do appear in the versions that have come down to us were not written by Shakespeare but added by the editors and performers who prepared the plays for publication. There is also a limit to what we know about how the plays were performed, so the famous direction in *The Winter's Tale*, 'Exit, persued by a bear', where Antigonus is about to meet his end at the claws of a bear remains somewhat opaque – would there really have been a trained bear onstage, or an actor dressed as a bear chasing him? Or would this direction have been fulfilled using props or some other method?

There are few directions involving interactions with scenery as Elizabethan theatres were pretty bare and unadorned. The stage's three entrances allowed for directions like '*Alarum as in battle. Enter Martius and Aufidius at several doors*' in *Coriolanus*. (An 'alarum' was a call to arms indicating a battle scene.) The trapdoor leading to the space under the stage allowed the actor playing Hamlet to carry out the direction '*Leaps into the grave*', and the balcony above the stage would have been used in '*Enter Cleopatra and her maids aloft, with Charmian and Iras*', and where '*Juliet appears above at a window*'.

We can't be sure how directions like '*Storm and tempest*' in *King Lear* were carried out but sound effects were certainly used. The sound of thunder was created with drums or by rolling a bullet over a sheet of metal. Music was clearly played at certain points, particularly in the late plays, like *Antony and Cleopatra*: '*Music of the hautboys is under the stage*', and *The Tempest*: '*Enter Ariel, invisible, playing solemn music*'. Entrances of important characters were often accompanied with trumpet blasts, as in *Timon of Athens*: '*Trumpets sound. Enter Alcibiades with his powers*'. Royal characters' entrances are often prefaced by a '*flourish*'. A flourish was a trumpet fanfare with drums to indicate a royal character coming onstage. (A sennet is the same but without drums, and a tucket is another kind of trumpet fanfare.) A cannon was also sometimes used for sound effects, as we know from the fate of the Globe (see page 30). Blood and gore were also not a problem for the props directors in those days as pig's blood was often used and props were created to fulfil directions like '*Enter a Messenger, with two heads and a hand*' in *Titus Andronicus*.

Despite the lack of detailed stage directions in the plays, if you listen carefully you'll notice that Shakespeare gives a lot of guidance to his actors through the speeches themselves – even using the metre of his verse to show where pauses in conversations should be by using **short lines**. Conversely, sometimes he splits the pentameter between two speakers to show characters that are in tune with each other finishing each other's lines or to add pace to a conversation. The following tense exchange between Macbeth and his wife after he's murdered Duncan makes up one line:

LADY MACBETH
> Did not you speak?

MACBETH
> When?

LADY MACBETH
> Now.

MACBETH
> As I descended?

> (ACT II, SCENE 2)

Censorship

Secular plays were a new and hugely popular art form in Shakespeare's day so it is unsurprising that the state soon got wise to the fact that it needed some control over them. The theatre was an extremely effective medium for influencing large gatherings of people and the authorities wanted to make sure that dangerous political and moral messages were not being spread.

From 1599 all the way up to 1968 a licence had to be obtained before a play was performed. The Lord Chamberlain's office was responsible for issuing this and from 1608 a civil servant with the great (though disappointingly misleading) job title of the Master of the Revels controlled the licences. Plays were submitted to the Master who would then ask for cuts of anything that could be considered seditious. Queen Elizabeth had given strict instructions 'that they permit none to be played wherein either matters of religion or of the governaunce of the estate of the common weale shall be handled or treated'. Scholars believe the deposition scene in *Richard II* was removed from later versions of the play because of this kind of sensitivity. Profanity was also outlawed but sexual jokes and subject matter do not appear to have been a problem.

From what we can gather Shakespeare's plays didn't suffer much at the hands of the censors. He did spend much of his career working under royal patronage so doubtless had a clear idea of what would be acceptable. The consequences of speaking too freely could be harsh: Ben Jonson was imprisoned for something in his now-lost 1597 satirical play *The Isle of Dogs* during Elizabeth's rule and again in 1605 for the anti-Scottish material in *Eastward Ho* which was judged offensive to James.

Shakespeare has actually suffered more censorship since his death than in his lifetime. In the nineteenth century he was famously bowdlerised by the eponymous Thomas Bowdler and had all his saucy bits removed, and school texts still sometimes gloss over the racier references in the plays.

How do you spell 'Shakespeare'?

Shakspere, Shaksper, Shakesspere, Shakspear, Shakysper, Shakespeer and Shakspeyre. In Tudor times individuals appear to have chosen whatever spelling of their names they felt like on that particular day. William's signatures on the documents that survive show his name in different abbreviated versions and spelled in different ways, and the quartos (see page 268) of his plays also show printed variations, with several using hyphens. However, his dedications to the Earl of Southampton in his poems *Venus and Adonis* and *The Rape of Lucrece* both go with 'Shakespeare', as does the First Folio, which, although published after his death, was put together by close friends and colleagues with posterity in mind. Critics in the eighteenth and nineteenth centuries preferred fewer 'e's but nowadays 'Shakespeare' is accepted as the standard. Spelling in general was not consistent in Elizabethan and Jacobean times so it was not unusual for names to appear in different forms, even on published material: Sir Walter Raleigh's name was spelled Rawly, Ralegh, Rawlegh, Raulie, Raleigh, Rawleighe and Rawlye in different contemporary documents.

Was Shakespeare really Shakespeare?

The short answer to this is, yes. Because we know so little about Shakespeare's life, and what we do know doesn't match up with our idea of a literary genius, various theories have developed which posit that a lower-class, teen-dad, money-lending, tax-dodging, non-graduate from Warwickshire couldn't have put together plays that rejoice in such magnificence of language and breadth of experience. Henry James, Malcolm X, Sigmund Freud, Mark Twain, Charlie Chaplin and Orson Welles have all doubted that the Shakespeare from Stratford was the Shakespeare we know as the great playwright, and there have been countless books written on the subject of who really wrote the plays, either using the name Shakespeare as a pseudonym or the man Shakespeare as a front. Those who believe in alternative candidates are known as Anti-Stratfordians or Anti-Shakespeareans. However, the available evidence supports the idea that Shakespeare, the actor-playwright-poet always acknowledged by his contemporaries as the author of the plays, whose name is printed on many of the earliest editions of them, did indeed write them. In addition, there is no direct evidence that anyone else did.

The interest in finding documents about Shakespeare's life only really picked up in the late eighteenth century, just as his star started to shine most brightly. Sadly, only a very few have ever been found, mostly dealing with financial and business matters, and this led to a slew of forgeries, biographical interpretations of the work and conspiracy theories by those desperate to fill in the blanks.

One of the reasons that Anti-Stratfordians get so much airtime is because everyone loves mysteries, secrets and codes. And Shakespeare is so superhumanly good that people – especially other writers as it happens – can't believe he could be an ordinary man. However, the fact that there are so many candidates as alternative authors shows that the evidence for any of them being Shakespeare is, well, pretty shaky. Below, we round up a few of the most popular theories and contenders.

Anti-Stratfordian	Pro-Stratfordian
Shakespeare wasn't educated enough to produce such erudite works.	Most scholars believe Shakespeare had an ordinary grammar-school education and internal evidence in his work supports this. But such an education and his evident wide reading would have supplied him with enough learning to write everything attributed to him.

Anti-Stratfordian	Pro-Stratfordian
Shakespeare didn't have enough experience of travel, nobles and court life to write about them with such accuracy.	Shakespeare had a marvellous imagination. Writers don't just write about what they have experienced. In any case, Shakespeare lived in London where he would have had access to books about, and travellers from, abroad, and he did visit court and noble houses as part of his work as an actor and playwright.

Equally, the plays contain evidence that their author was intimately connected to the theatre company he wrote for: he sometimes substitutes the actor's name for a character's name. This makes it unlikely that the writer was a noble himself.

The geography in the plays isn't perfect – his colleague and contemporary Ben Jonson is reported to have said: 'Shakespeare in a play brought a number of men saying they had suffered shipwrack in Bohemia, where there is no sea near by some hundred miles.' |
| Stratford Shakespeare was only interested in money and there is no evidence that he was a writer. | Most of the documentary records that have survived about Shakespeare are about business but this doesn't mean that's all he was interested in. And, in fact, it is false to say that writers are not interested in their livelihoods – man cannot live on art alone.

His will does have additions leaving money to colleagues in his theatre company, and Jonson refers to him as the 'swan of Avon' in the First Folio. |
| He didn't leave any books in his will so he clearly wasn't very well read. | It was common practice for books to be listed in a separate document called an inventory. Books were expensive and few people owned many but there is no reason to suppose he wouldn't have had access to books from libraries, bookshops, school and friends, as well as his own. |
| His name is hyphenated on some title pages, a common indicator of a pseudonym. | Spellings of names were not standardised at this time, and neither were typesetting conventions. |

Anti-Stratfordian

Baconian Theory

The plays were written by
Francis Bacon (1561–1626). The
works reflect the life of a
philosopher, scientist and
adviser to Queen Elizabeth and
King James more than
Shakespeare's. Bacon was clever
and his published philosophy
matches that of the plays. He
also hid his name and his secret
lineage in them in cipher.

Group Theory

The plays were written by
Francis Bacon and a team of
secret collaborators, or started
by the Earl of Oxford and
finished by other playwrights.

Pro-Stratfordian

This theory only developed in the nineteenth
century – no one before that seems to have had any
doubts about Shakespeare's authorship.

Computer analysis of verbal habits in the work
doesn't match it with Bacon's writing.

As discussed above, the writer of the plays didn't
need to be as much of an intellectual as Bacon was in
order to write them.

If you try hard enough you can find all sorts of
hidden codes but none of the Baconian ciphers have
been convincing.

There's no evidence Bacon was a great poet. He was
also pretty busy writing many philosophical and
scientific works under his own name.

The idea that Bacon would have hidden his
authorship of the plays in order to avoid the shame of
dabbling in a common art form, and that he would
have used the plays to secretly proselytise a republican
message and tell readers that he was actually
Elizabeth I's secret son, is far more complicated than
the simple idea that the person who everyone thought
wrote the plays, wrote the plays.

See above. Computer analysis shows that the plays
(bar those we know were co-authored, see page 271)
were written by one man with individual tics.

The evidence of collaboration with writers like
Fletcher etc. undermines the notion of a secret
author – this secret author would have had to have
secretly worked with all of these writers.

Anti-Stratfordian	Pro-Stratfordian

Anti-Stratfordian

Oxfordian Theory

The plays were written by Edward de Vere, 17th Earl of Oxford (1550–1604). The plays reflect the life of an adventurous courtier and he was also a poet.

Pro-Stratfordian

This theory only arose in the 1920s. It's the most popular alternative-author theory at the moment.

Look at the date of his death. Twelve plays had their first performances after 1604. That they were written earlier is not borne out by the texts, which show Shakespeare's more complicated late style and mirror the style of other Jacobean playwrights.

The lack of evidence linking Oxford with the plays does not necessarily point to a conspiracy to cover up his authorship. It's more likely there is no link. Contemporary accounts refer to the two writers as separate people.

The theory that the poems and plays reflect Oxford's secret relationship with Queen Elizabeth (Dark Lady) who gave birth to their son, Henry Wriothesley (Fair Youth), the third Earl of Southampton (the Prince Tudor Theory), is not supported by any evidence.

The theory that the poems and plays reflect Oxford's secret relationship with his own mother (Queen Elizabeth) who gave birth to their son, the Earl of Southampton (the Prince Tudor II Theory), is also not supported by any evidence.

Computer analysis of the work doesn't match it with Southampton's writing.

Anti-Stratfordian	Pro-Stratfordian

Marlovian Theory

The plays were written by Christopher Marlowe (1564–93). He was the first master of blank-verse drama and there are similarities between his writing and that of the Shakespeare plays.

Marlowe died in 1593. There's lots of evidence to support this, which makes it more likely to be true than the theory that he faked his own death due to his work in the Elizabethan secret service and then continued writing under the pen name, Shakespeare.

Computer analysis of the work doesn't match Marlowe's writing, although scholars do agree that Marlowe heavily influenced Shakespeare.

Elizabethan Theory

The plays were written by Queen Elizabeth I (1533–1603). She was very well educated and had lots of relevant experience – and the plays support Tudor rule.

Are you kidding? Don't you think she had enough to do? Plays were censored and playwrights relied on patronage so most plays were likely to be pro-regime. And, once again, look at the date she died.

The most important thing to remember is that the best creative artists are just that – creative. Shakespeare's amazing imagination allowed him to inhabit the worlds of kings, murderers, Egyptian queens, Roman soldiers, spirits, fairies, weavers, witches, young lovers, old men, fools, Frenchmen, Jews, Moors, Danish students, nursemaids, noblewomen, twins and ancient Greeks. As the great man said: 'The poet's eye, in a fine frenzy rolling, / Doth glance from heaven to earth, from earth to heaven; / And as imagination bodies forth / The forms of things unknown, the poet's pen / Turns them to shapes, and gives to airy nothing / A local habitation and a name' (*A Midsummer Night's Dream*).

WILL'S WORDS: SHAKESPEARE'S LANGUAGE AND STYLE

Before Shakespeare:
Mysteries, miracles and moralities

Although a trailblazer in many ways, Shakespeare didn't spring fully formed from nowhere. He changed the face of English drama but he was also working with material and conventions from the past. Before the development of the recognisable theatre of the sixteenth century, there were other kinds of drama available to the public which it's fair to assume the young William would have witnessed.

The **mystery plays** of the Middle Ages developed out of tenth-century church services and had chiefly biblical concerns at their heart, in particular stories about the Creation, Fall and Redemption. Originally they were performed in Latin by members of the clergy as part of big festivals like Easter, Corpus Christi, Pentecost and Christmas, but eventually ordinary folk got involved, mixing in a bit of street slang and moving them from the vestry to the marketplace.

A cycle of mystery plays would cover the Bible from Adam and Eve right through to Judgement Day, with different workers' guilds taking on a different story which they performed on a wagon with a curtained stage. Once one 'story' had been performed, the wagon would pack up and move on to another place where the previous story in the cycle had just been performed – so over the course of a day, or several days, a large city would be able to watch an entire cycle.

The major English mystery cycles were held from around the mid-fourteenth century until the late sixteenth century in York, Coventry, Chester and Wakefield, each consisting of between twenty-five and nearly fifty episodes. While the writing and characterisation was pretty crude, performers did go to town on special effects and costumes to represent the fires of Hell and the serenity of Heaven.

Miracle plays grew from the mystery plays, turning the spotlight onto stories of saints and divine miracles, as well as appearances and interventions of the Virgin. The most famous were the French *Miracles de Notre-*

Dame, a cycle of forty-two plays. Most English miracle plays were destroyed when Henry VIII banned them for being too Catholic after he broke with Rome in 1533.

The origins of the medieval and early Tudor **morality plays** lie in the miracle and mystery plays – this time the drama lies in the presentation of allegories, with personifications of different moral facets who try to force the main protagonist to choose a life of good over evil. The king of morality plays is probably *Everyman* (1500), which features Everyman, Beauty, Strength, Knowledge, God, a Messenger, Death, Fellowship and Good Deeds. God, believing humans are too obsessed with earthly possessions, sends Death to summon Everyman, who realises no one will go with him except Good Deeds.

One can trace the direct influence of the character of Vice from the morality plays on Iago, Richard III and Falstaff, and their influence can also been seen in how the struggle between good and evil plays out in many of the Tragedies, but it's still jaw-dropping to think that after this one-dimensional representation of the human condition, barely a hundred years on Shakespeare was dealing with the complex psychological forces at work in *Othello*, *Macbeth* and *Hamlet*.

Shakespeare's Influences

Its streets may have run with stinking rivers of effluvia and excrement, its pubs the location for murderous brawls, but if you were an aspiring playwright in the late sixteenth century, then London was the very best place on earth to be. Yes, Shakespeare was inspired by the classic fables and poetry he'd learned at school, the plays demonstrate an intimate knowledge of Aristotle, Ovid, Seneca and Plutarch (see page 176), but he was also surrounded by an extraordinary array of contemporary literary lions, perfecting and honing their ferocious skills just as he was starting out. Christopher Marlowe, in particular, Shakespeare's exact contemporary, is known to have been a huge influence, with his tormented protagonists and audacious use of blank verse. Who knows, if he hadn't been killed in a drink-soaked fight in Deptford, maybe Shakespeare would have spent his life in Marlowe's literary shadow. We know that collaboration was common, but imagine how good your solo efforts would have to be if you were trying to outclass the likes of Thomas Kyd's *The*

Spanish Tragedy, Christopher Marlowe's *Tamburlaine the Great*, George Peele's *The Old Wives Tale*, John Lyly's *Euphues, The Anatomy of Wit*, and Ben Jonson's *Every Man in His Humour*. You'd probably have to be as good as Shakespeare.

Shakespeare's language

'His language is starlight and fireflies and the sun and the moon. He wrote it with tears and blood and beer, and his words march like heartbeats.' It's not just Shakespeare's plots, characters and universal themes that make him so beloved. Orson Welles's passionate quote goes down on bended knee to celebrate the Bard's command of language and poetry. Shakespeare was both a dramatist and a poet and his genius was to combine his exceptional skills in both disciplines. He coined hundreds of new words and phrases and he is celebrated for his great soliloquies and speeches. Just think: one man gave us Hamlet's 'To be, or not to be', Henry V's 'Once more unto the breach', Macbeth's 'Is this a dagger which I see before me', Mark Antony's 'Friends, Romans, countrymen', Orsino's 'If music be the food of love' and, Jaques' 'All the world's a stage'. In Shakespeare's time the lack of stage sets would have meant that even more attention was given to the language. In fact, in the opening scenes of *The Taming of the Shrew* the lord who hires the actors to perform the main action describes a member of the audience who 'has never heard a play' before, rather than 'never *seen* a play' before.

Most of Shakespeare's plays are a mixture of **verse** and **prose**. Plays such as *King John* and *Richard II* are entirely in verse, *Julius Caesar* has barely any prose, and others such as *Much Ado About Nothing* and *The Merry Wives of Windsor* have a great deal. Usually prose is employed for comic or light scenes and often for common characters' speech – as well as for characters who appear to be mad. Generally, the more formally poetic the language is, the more noble the speaker or subject, or the more emotionally intense the scene. Sometimes prose is used subtly to mark out contrasts or differences in relationships – for example, Hamlet usually addresses his best friend Horatio in verse but his false friends Rosencrantz and Guildenstern in prose. Equally Henry V is most definitely a noble character prone to high-falutin verse speeches, but in his intimate flirting scene with Princess Katherine they speak prose.

Shakespeare is most famous for his **blank verse** but there are other styles within his plays too – Romeo and Juliet speak a **sonnet** (see page 248) to each other when they meet, Ophelia sings **songs**, as do other characters like Desdemona in *Othello*, Feste in *Twelfth Night*, Amiens in *As You Like It*, Ariel in *The Tempest*, and Balthasar in *Much Ado About Nothing*, who sings the famous 'hey nonny nonny' song.

Academics have traced a progression in Shakespeare's blank verse from the regular metre and phrasing of the earliest plays, with lots of end-stopped lines, through to a higher frequency of irregular and manipulated lines in the later plays, powerfully conveying the sense or emotion of the scene. Lady Macbeth's anxious speech as she waits for Macbeth to return from murdering Duncan is a good example. Notice also the hard consonant sounds of 'k's and 't's and the mono- and disyllabic words which add to the sense of panic:

> Alack! I am afraid they have awak'd,
> And 'tis not done: th'attempt and not the deed
> Confounds us. Hark! I laid their daggers ready:
> He could not miss 'em. Had he not resembled
> My father as he slept, I had done't.
>
> (ACT II, SCENE 2)

Critics have also observed a progression in Shakespeare's exposition within his speeches – moving from the direct rhetorical outlining of plot or thought in the earlier plays to much more fragmented, impressionistic speech in the later plays which more accurately reflects the workings of the human mind.

A quick guide to useful poetry terminology

Metre is simply the official term used to describe poetic rhythm – the magic ingredient which sets verse apart from prose. Poets often use particular patterns and rhythms for their works, above and beyond the innate beats and musicality of the way we speak.

English words all have different patterns of stress – you naturally say one syllable of the word 'postman' with more emphasis. 'Postman' is generally pronounced with a stress on the first syllable '**post** man' rather than on the second syllable 'post**man**'. The number and pattern of stresses in a line of poetry define its metre.

Lines of poetry are divided into **feet**. Each foot is a particular pattern of stressed and unstressed syllables that is then repeated a set number of times in the line. An **iambic pentameter** is a line of five feet (the word pentameter comes from the ancient Greek meaning 'five measures') where each foot is a specific pattern of one unstressed syllable followed by one stressed syllable called an **iamb**. Dimeters have two feet, trimeters have three, tetrameters have four and hexameters have six. Other common types of feet are trochees (stressed, unstressed), spondees (stressed, stressed), anapaests (unstressed, unstressed, stressed) and dactyls (stressed, unstressed, unstressed).

'Shall **I** | com**pare** | thee **to** | a **summ** | er's **day**?' from Sonnet 18 is a perfect iambic pentameter. Shakespeare's greatest talent was for blank verse: the official term for unrhymed iambic pentameter.

Blank verse sounds natural as it closely resembles the rhythms of ordinary speech but it is also easy to memorise because of its repeated patterns of stress. It is often referred to as replicating the rhythm of a heartbeat. This metre was relatively new to English poetry, having been introduced by the Earl of Surrey in his translation of Virgil's *Aeneid* around 1540. Before the 1560s plays were written entirely in rhyme but Marlowe brought blank verse to the fore.

Shakespeare didn't just stick to this regular metre line after line, however. Sometimes he added odd feet of different types into an otherwise ordered pattern for emphasis or surprise and sometimes he disrupted the rhythm by adding extra syllables or dropping them altogether. His earlier plays have lots of **end-stopped lines** – where the line of verse ends with a full stop or other punctuation mark showing that the end of the character's thought has coincided with the pattern of the poetry. This can sound rather neat and regular and in his later plays sentences often run on into the middle of verse lines (a poetic device called **enjambment**) or have an extra unaccented syllable at the end (a **feminine** or **weak ending**). He also sometimes arranged patterns of rhyming words at the ends of certain lines, most commonly rhyming two lines in a row to make a **rhyming couplet**, as in this example from *Hamlet*: 'The time is out of joint. O cursèd spite, / That ever I was born to set it right!' He particularly used this effect in **capping couplets** to end scenes.

Shakespeare clearly enjoyed language in and of itself as he frequently indulged in **wordplay**. He – and the Elizabethan audience – was particularly fond of **paronomasia** (punning). Some of the most famous examples are Mercutio's dying words 'Ask for me tomorrow and you shall find me a **grave** man', Richard III's 'Now is the winter of our discontent / Made glorious summer by this **son** of York' and Beatrice's 'The Count is neither sad, nor sick, nor merry, nor well; but **civil**, Count; civil as an orange, and something of that jealous complexion.' (This plays on the homophonous 'civil' and 'Seville'.) His wordplay is also often bawdy as in Hamlet's exchange with Ophelia: 'Lady, shall I lie in your lap? . . . Do you think I meant **country matters?**' and the dialogue between Pompey and Mistress Overdone discussing Claudio's arrest for fornication in *Measure for Measure*: Pompey: 'Yonder man is carried to prison.' Mistress Overdone: 'Well! What has he **done?**' Pompey: 'A woman.'

Shakespeare's love of larking about with language is also evident in the many **neologisms** he coined. Some have counted that he came up with around two thousand new words, or forms of words, in his works, although it is worth remembering that many of these may have been in currency but simply not recorded in print before. Some of the best are 'addiction', 'gloomy', 'radiance', 'eyeball', 'barefaced', 'flowery' and 'swagger'.

He also enjoyed using many different **rhetorical devices**. As well as the common emphatic sound effects of **alliteration** (repetition of the first letters of words), 'Beauty's effect with beauty were bereft' (Sonnet 5), **anaphora** (repetition of the same word), 'Mad world! mad kings! mad composition!'(*King John*), **assonance** (repetition of the same vowel sounds), 'For men so old as we to keep the peace' (*Romeo and Juliet*), and **consonance** (repetition of the same consonants), '. . . a poor player, /That struts and frets his hour upon the stage' (*Macbeth*), Shakespeare also used more complicated figures of speech. *Hamlet* features many **hendiadys**, more than sixty, in fact. Hendiadys is the expression of a single idea by two words joined with 'and' when, instead, one could be used to modify the other. Often it takes the place of an idea more straightforwardly expressed with an adjective and a noun, e.g. 'grace and favour' instead of 'gracious favour', 'nice and warm' instead of 'nicely warm'. Examples include Hamlet asking the Ghost why his sepulchre 'Hath op'd his ponderous and marble jaws'; Horatio explaining how Fortinbras 'by law and heraldry' forfeited his lands; Laertes telling Ophelia to regard Hamlet's affection for her as 'a fashion and a toy in blood'. This device gives equal emphasis to both words where normally the adjective would be secondary, and also allows the playwright to link seemingly unrelated words for dramatic effect. Critics have argued that the frequency of this form in *Hamlet*, which can complicate the meaning of the phrases, reflects the difficulty the hero has in seeing things clearly and establishing truth, and the play's preoccupation with duality.

In a similar way Shakespeare was fond of using **antithesis** (a device in which an opposition or contrast of ideas is expressed), **oxymoron** (a figure of speech where apparently contradictory terms appear in conjunction) and **paradox** (a seemingly self-contradictory statement that may in fact be true) in his plays to create tension and illustrate the gap between appearance and reality. Juliet's speech on discovering that Romeo has killed Tybalt includes several examples:

> O serpent heart, hid with a flowering face.
> Did ever dragon keep so fair a cave?
> Beautiful tyrant! fiend angelical.
> Dove-feather'd raven, wolvish-ravening lamb!
> Despisèd substance of divinest show!
> Just opposite to what thou justly seem'st!
> A damnèd saint, an honourable villain!
> O nature what hadst thou to do in hell,
> When thou didst bower the spirit of a fiend
> In moral paradise of such sweet flesh?
> Was ever book containing such vile matter
> So fairly bound? O, that deceit should dwell
> In such a gorgeous palace!

> (ACT III, SCENE 2)

Some of Shakespeare's most memorable quotations illustrate his technical command of rhetoric. Antony's 'Friends, Romans, countrymen, lend me your ears' from *Julius Caesar* is a brilliant example of **synecdoche** (a figure of speech in which a part represents the whole), and Richard II's 'I wasted time, and now doth time waste me' is often used to illustrate **chiasmus** (the inversion in a second phrase of the order of words in the first).

However, the field in which Shakespeare truly excelled in creating unparalleled poetry and drama was in his **imagery**. His **similes** and **metaphors** are often heart-stoppingly original, thought-provoking and illuminating. Revel in a few of his greatest hits below:

Romeo describing Juliet's beauty:

> O, she doth teach the torches to burn bright.
> It seems she hangs upon the cheek of night
> As a rich jewel in an Ethiop's ear;

Viola telling Orsino about her father's daughter's secret love in *Twelfth Night*:

> She never told her love,
> But let concealment, like a worm i' th'bud
> Feed on her damask cheek: she pin'd in thought,
> And with a green and yellow melancholy
> She sat like Patience on a monument,
> Smiling at grief.

Claudio musing upon the pickle he's in in *Measure for Measure*:

> The miserable have no other medicine
> But only hope.

And of course the famous Sonnet 130, 'My mistress' eyes are nothing like the sun' (see page 257) which plays with the idea of hackneyed similes in romantic poetry.

The importance of the little words 'thou' and 'you'

Many people think that 'thou' and 'you' are interchangeable in ye olde language of Shakespeare but in fact they have different connotations. 'Thou' is an informal and singular form of address, much like the French 'tu'. 'You' is the formal term that is used when addressing more than one person and as a mark of respect, for example when talking to a social superior in the very hierarchical Elizabethan world. It is also used by nobles speaking to each other. 'You' equates with the French 'vous'.

Shakespeare carefully selects these terms in several places in his plays to indicate subtle shifts in relationships and attitudes. In *Twelfth Night*, Sir Toby Belch encourages Sir Andrew Aguecheek to address Cesario as 'thou' three times in his letter of challenge to him in order to annoy him. In *Othello*, Othello calls Iago 'thou' but Cassio 'you'. This could be taken to mean either that Iago is a more intimate friend of Othello's and therefore the 'thou' is complimentary, or that Othello sees Iago as inferior to Cassio. Interestingly, Ariel and Caliban both call Prospero 'thou' and Lady Macbeth stops calling Macbeth 'thou' and moves to 'you' as the play develops. In *King Lear*, when Kent is remonstrating with the king for his bad decision about Cordelia he says, 'What wilt thou do, old man?' but reverts to the respectful form later in the play. In a similar way, you can see Lear's abandonment of the royal 'we' in the final scene of the play as representative of his calamitous fall and new-found humility.

Shakespeare's changing critical response

Other writers on Shakespeare

Samuel Pepys on *A Midsummer Night's Dream:* 'the most insipid, ridiculous play that I ever saw in my life.'

Thomas Rymer on *Othello:* 'a warning to all Good Wives that they look well to their Linnen.'

Voltaire: 'Shakespeare is a drunken savage with some imagination whose plays please only in London and Canada.'

Milton: 'sweetest Shakespeare, Fancy's child, / Warble his native wood-notes wild.'

Alexander Pope: 'If ever any Author deserved the name of an *Original*, it was *Shakespeare*.'

Samuel Johnson: 'Perhaps it would not be easy to find any author, except Homer, who invented so much as Shakespeare . . . The form, the characters, the language, and the shows of the English drama are his.'

Samuel Taylor Coleridge: 'Our myriad-minded Shakespeare'

Elizabeth Barrett Browning: 'There Shakespeare, on whose forehead climb / The crowns o' the world; oh, eyes sublime / With tears and laughter for all time!'

Charles Dickens: 'It is a great comfort, to my way of thinking, that so little is known about the poet. It is a fine mystery, and I tremble every day lest something should come out.'

George Bernard Shaw: 'With the single exception of Homer, there is no eminent writer, not even Sir Walter Scott, whom I can despise so entirely as I despise Shakespeare when I measure my mind against his.'

T. S. Eliot: 'probably more people have thought *Hamlet* a work of art because they found it interesting, than have found it interesting because it is a work of art. It is the *Mona Lisa* of literature.'

Robert Graves: 'The remarkable thing about Shakespeare is that he is really very good – in spite of all the people who say he is very good.'

Jeanette Winterson: '[Shakespeare] sums up the creative process, which is not concerned with originality of source but originality of re-making.'

Howard Jacobson: 'Only a fool would think he has anything to add to Shakespeare.'

Imagine inviting Shakespeare into a university library and showing him the miles of shelving devoted to the books and journals that have been written about him. No doubt he'd be amused – and baffled – by some of the angles of approach. Literary criticism takes many forms and doesn't just mean speculating on the true message of a text, or how its effects are achieved; it can also be a way of taking entirely modern concerns and using them to draw enlightening conclusions from past works. There are numerous, not necessarily discrete, schools of thought that often interplay with one another. Below we have prepared a quick overview of some of the most popular that have been used to interpret Shakespeare's work and some terminology you may come across in your travels through the thorny undergrowth of lit crit.

The Contemporary Response to Shakespeare

Shakespeare was clearly very popular in his own time but he was not regarded as the towering, incomparable god of literature he is today. The 'university wits' who dominated the literary scene at the time scorned his lack of learning (see page 16). His most popular plays, based on the number of reprints each achieved, were *Hamlet, Richard III, Pericles* and *Henry IV, Part 1*.

Biographical Criticism

Biographical criticism is concerned with uncovering truths about the author from his works and interpreting those works in the light of his life. For example, some critics have theorised on the impact the death of Shakespeare's eleven-year-old son Hamnet in 1596 might have had, particularly on the plays that were written around this time or that deal with parents and sons, like *Hamlet*.

Feminism and Gender Studies

Feminist literary criticism examines the representation of women and explores the use of female stereotypes and ideas regarding femininity, masculinity, family and romantic relationships. Gender studies and queer theory are closely related to feminist theory with different emphases. The cross-dressing in the Comedies is an example of a subject of interest to all of these approaches.

Marxist Criticism

Marxist theory is the application of socialist thought to literature. In particular, it is concerned with the social and economic context of literature, not only that portrayed but also that in which it is made. Marxists envision a class struggle taking place which will eventually lead to the overthrow of capitalism. Plays like *Coriolanus* and the Histories are of particular interest to Marxist critics as they show tension between patricians and plebs and nobles and commoners.

New Criticism

This early-twentieth-century school of theory advocated close reading of texts without reference to their biographical or historical context or the reader's response. The Russian Formalists developed similar ideas in the early 1900s, focusing on analysing the literary devices used in texts. Their work became influential in the Western world in the 1960s. Some new-critical approaches to Shakespeare have focused on his imagery (e.g. interesting clothes imagery in *Macbeth*), word choice (e.g. the use of the word 'honest' in *Othello*), and use of irony and wordplay.

New Historicism and Cultural Materialism

New historicism developed in the USA in the twentieth century and looks at texts in the light of their historical context and also investigates what literature tells us about history. New historicists reject psychoanalytical readings of Shakespeare as they argue that the entire concept of an individual self was different in the Early Modern period. The related British school of criticism is known as cultural materialism. A new-historicist approach would posit that understanding the tumultuous religious events in England preceding *Hamlet*'s composition would enrich a student's understanding of the role of the Ghost in the play.

Performance Criticism

Performance criticism seeks to put Shakespeare back in the theatrical rather than literary context by analysing particular stagings of the plays.

Post-Colonialist Criticism

Post-colonial theory looks at Shakespeare's work in the light of the history and effects of colonisation, and also in the ways in which Shakespeare has been used to endorse such colonisation. Post-colonial critics have particularly focused on *The Tempest* where the interaction between coloniser and colonised is dramatised and which draws on source material from real colonisers.

Presentist Criticism

Presentist criticism openly imposes modern ideas and concerns that can be anachronistic into its interpretation of historical literary works. Readings of *Othello* focused on our ideas about racism and *Twelfth Night* focused on homosexuality would fit into this category as Shakespeare would not have had the same conception of those issues as we do now.

Psychoanalytical Criticism

Pyschoanalytical interpretation of literature explores the unconscious of the characters, makers and societies that produce literature. It connects to the popular character-based criticism of the nineteenth century that focused on the motivations and personalities of Shakespeare's human creations. Sigmund Freud was fascinated by Shakespeare and it was a follower of his, Ernest Jones, who wrote about the influential theory that Hamlet suffered from an Oedipus complex. Jacques Lacan was another celebrated psychoanalytical critic interested in *Hamlet* who developed Freud's theories with his own ideas, which fed into structuralism.

Reader–Response Criticism

In a reaction to new criticism, reader-response criticism foregrounds the reader's or audience's response to a play rather than the author's intentions or an objective interpretation, and analyses why works can produce different reactions from different readers. According to this school of thought the meaning of a text is constructed by the reader rather than the author.

Structuralism, Post-Structuralism and Deconstruction

Structuralism came to prominence in the mid-twentieth century and its central idea is to interpret texts with close attention to their constituent parts in the light of semiotics (the study of signs and symbols in communication). It posits that all language and literature is part of a system of signs and that this 'structure' is composed of elements that are defined by their relationship to other elements, rather than referring to concrete reality. Structuralists are interested in ideas such as genres (e.g. the elements that make *As You Like It*, *Much Ado About Nothing* and *Twelfth Night* comedies), and recurring narrative structures and binary oppositions in texts (e.g. black/white, male/female, solid/melt; Hyperion/satyr; heaven/earth; break/hold).

The French linguist Ferdinand de Saussure is commonly regarded as the founder of this school of thought, and it was developed in the 1950s by critics such as Roland Barthes and Michel Foucault. There is some blurring of the boundaries between structuralism and post-structuralism, which is seen to have followed it and which includes the work of critics like the philosopher Jacques Derrida who argued that there is no stable and absolute meaning to be found in language or texts. Derrida's theories are also known as deconstruction.

* * *

One of the astonishing things about Shakespeare's works is how open to interpretation they are: one can 'read' the plays in a myriad of ways and doubtless critics will continue to find new ways of dissecting them far into the future. For us, though, their power lies in their beauty and humanity, which make them as rewarding today as they must have done centuries ago. A+, Mr Shakespeare!

Phrases that Shakespeare invented

We need to say it again: Shakespeare's impact on everyday speech is extraordinary. He introduced around 1,700 words to the English language and a multitude of phrases. You probably find yourself quoting him more often than you realise. Here are some of the expressions that have entered English idiom thanks to him.

○ **'A dish fit for the gods'** This comes from *Julius Caesar* and is spoken by Caesar's eventual murderer Brutus, who is describing how his friend should be elegantly and respectfully killed rather than butchered. Think about that next time you use this to praise your mother-in-law's Sunday roast.

○ **'All of a sudden'** This phrase is so commonplace it seems odd to think that it comes from *The Taming of the Shrew*, where one of the characters is understandably marvelling at how his master has fallen in love at first sight: 'I pray, sir, tell me, is it possible / That love should of a sudden take such hold?' Shakespeare's Comedies would be considerably longer if all his characters were subject to the same doubts.

○ **'As luck would have it'** This comes from *The Merry Wives of Windsor* in a scene where the aspiring seducer Falstaff is detailing his escape from Mrs Ford's house in a laundry basket at the arrival of her husband: 'As good luck would have it, comes in one Mistress Page; gives intelligence of Ford's approach; and, in her invention and Ford's wife's distraction, they conveyed me into a buck-basket.'

○ **'At one fell swoop'** This is part of Macduff's heartbreaking speech in *Macbeth* lamenting the murder of his wife and children: 'All my pretty ones? / Did you say all? O hell-kite! All? / What, all my pretty chickens and their dam / At one fell swoop?' This phrase is an element of the metaphor Macduff uses of a bird of prey, the kite, killing his chickens. The word 'fell' at this time meant 'fierce'.

○ **'Brevity is the soul of wit'** These words are spoken by Polonius to Gertrude and Claudius in *Hamlet*. He uses the phrase to explain why he's cutting to the chase and telling them he thinks Hamlet is mad without too much preamble. Polonius is considered a foolish old duffer by Hamlet but he does have several sensible lines that have made their way into common discourse, such as 'Neither a borrower nor a lender be' and 'To thine own self be true'.

○ **'Discretion is the better part of valour'** Falstaff again, this time in *Henry IV, Part 1*, explaining how his tactic of playing dead on the battlefield has saved his life more effectively than any dramatic heroics. If you don't know Falstaff already you are probably getting a good sense of his character just from the context of the two phrases he is responsible for in this section.

○ **'Hoist with your own petard'** This is Hamlet expressing his amusement at getting his friends Rosencrantz and Guildenstern killed instead of him: 'For 'tis the sport to have the enginer / Hoist with his own petar'. A 'petar', or 'petard', was a sixteenth-century explosive device for breaching fortifications so this phrase refers to the engineer of a bomb being blown up ('hoist') by his own explosives.

○ **'The dogs of war'** A vivid image taken from Mark Antony's speech in *Julius Caesar* predicting the bloody conflict that will follow his friend's assassination: 'And Caesar's spirit, ranging for revenge, / With Ate by his side, come hot from hell, / Shall in these confines with a monarch's voice / Cry "Havoc!" and let slip the dogs of war'. Incidentally, the first use of the word 'assassination' ever recorded is in Shakespeare's *Macbeth*.

○ **'Fair play'** This phrase, which is now overly used as a stand-alone concession of the acceptability of an action, as well as a definition of something being carried out in a just and fair manner, originates in *The Tempest* where Miranda accuses her lover Ferdinand of cheating at chess but admits she doesn't mind: 'Yes, for a score of kingdoms you should wrangle, / And I would call it fair play.'

○ **'Good riddance'** This comes from *Troilus and Cressida* where Patroclus expresses his delight at seeing the back of the unpleasant Thersites after Thersites has just called him Achilles' bitch ('I will hold my peace when Achilles' brach bids me, shall I?'). The word 'riddance' was used more widely in Shakespeare's time and you could wish someone different kinds of riddance. In *The Merchant of Venice* Portia wishes the Prince of Morocco a 'gentle riddance'.

○ **'Lay it on with a trowel'** This useful phrase originates in *As You Like It* where Celia and the jester Touchstone are larking about and making fun of the courtier Le Beau.

○ **'Love is blind'** This crops up in several of Shakespeare's plays, including *Two Gentlemen of Verona*, *Henry V* and *The Merchant of Venice*.

○ **'Milk of human kindness'** This is part of a speech by the ambitious Lady Macbeth where she castigates her husband for not being ruthless enough to climb the Scottish political ladder: 'Yet do I fear thy nature, / It is too full o'th'milk of human kindness / To catch the nearest way.'

○ **'Wild -goose chase'** This comes from a line of Mercutio in *Romeo and Juliet* but doesn't quite mean what we might expect. Mercutio uses the phrase to refer to the fact that he and Romeo have been trading witticisms and one-upping each other in turn, a pastime clever, smart-arsed young men still enjoy today. He likens this badinage to a type of horse race familiar at the time called the 'wild-goose chase' where one rider leads a group of others on an elaborate course which they have to copy.

A short Shakespearean dictionary

There's no questioning the genius of Shakespeare's way with words, but it is also true that there is a huge difference between our language and his, and for some this can be an obstacle to enjoyment of the works. Many books have been written containing exhaustive Shakespearean glossaries – there is even one dedicated entirely to his use of sexual language – so here we've put together a (by no means all-encompassing) selection of our favourite Elizabethan archaisms. Let us insculp your minds and passy-measure you through the language of the Bard with a quick guide to some of the more zany Shakespearean words and phrases.

WORD	DEFINITION	WORD	DEFINITION
aery	nest	chopless	lacking jaws
agate	dwarf, midget	clapper-claw	to assault
anters	caves	dastard	cowardly
aroint thee	be gone	dew-bedabbled	adorned with dew
atomies	very small figures	doubty-handed	excellent in combat
bawcock	a splendid fellow	facinerious	wicked
bootless	useless	fap	drunk
brock	badger	feater	neatly
broken sinews	stretched nerves	firk	to beat
bruit	echo	fustilarian	aged smelly lady
busky	bushy	gallimaufry	a hotchpotch
cacodemon	evil spirit	geminy	a couple or pair
caitiff	wretched thing		

WORD	DEFINITION	WORD	DEFINITION
gibingly	in a mocking way	**lily-tincture**	very pale-skinned
gorbellied	great of girth	**loggats**	a game involving throwing sticks
hedge-pig	hedgehog		
hysterica passio	hysteria	**loose-wived**	cuckolded (cheated on by your wife)
immure	wall	**malapert**	cheeky or saucy
implorator	one who implores	**malkin**	wench
incarnadine	turn red	**malmsey-nose**	red-nosed
insculp	to engrave		
jackanapes	an idiot or buffoon	**mammer**	stammer
jadery	exhibiting jaded behaviour	**maugre**	in spite of
		moonish	capricious
jauncing	romping, rough-riding	**mummer**	a miming actor
jennet	Spanish horse	**napless**	ragged
keech	an agglomeration of solidified fat	**nether-stock**	a stocking worn on one's shin
kibe	chilblain	**nook-shotten**	of an awkward shape
kicky wicky	girlfriend or wife		
kissing comfit	a delicacy to sweeten the breath	**nuncio**	messenger
		nyas	a young hawk
knotty-pated	blockheaded, dull-witted	**obloquy**	public condemnation
		oeillade	an amorous glance (or ogle)
ladder-tackle	rigging		
lazar	leper	**open arse**	medlar fruit (from its shape)

WORD	DEFINITION	WORD	DEFINITION
oppugnancy	opposition	**quiddity**	subtlety
orison	a prayer	**quosque**	how much longer
owlet	a young owl	**rabbit sucker**	baby bunny
paddle	to fondle	**racker**	torturer
palter	prevaricate, quibble	**raisins of the sun**	sun-dried grapes
passy-measures	slow dance	**rampallian**	a ruffian or scoundrel
patchery	trickery	**resty-stiff**	seized up (limbs)
pedascule	pedant (diminutive)	**sarcenet**	flimsy
pestiferous	pernicious	**scambling**	rough, turbulent
pettitoes	feet	**scrimer**	swordsman
pickthank	sycophant	**scurvy-valiant**	contemptible
pillicock	penis (slang)		
piss o'th' nettle	to be in a bad mood	**sennight, seven-night**	a week
poltroon	a coward	**shelvy**	sloping
popinjay	chatterbox	**shrike**	shriek
puke-stocking	dark-coloured stockings	**silly-ducking**	over-elaborate bowing
		smirched	stained
pumpion	pumpkin	**smutch**	to make dirty
quean	a badly behaved girl or woman, hussy or prostitute	**sowl**	drag roughly
		sprag	alert
queller	killer	**stillitory**	distilling space

WORD	DEFINITION	WORD	DEFINITION
swashing	swaggering	varletto	rogue
tabor	a little drum	verdour	vigour
tallow-face	of a waxy complexion	vesper	evening
tardy-apish	behind the curve	vinewed	decaying
termagant	savage	waggish	playful
thraldom	servitude	wall-eyed	with a menacing stare
thrasonical	boastful	wanny	pale
tisick	consumption of the lung	wawl	yell
		whelm	drown
Tom o'Bedlam	lunatic	whoo-bub	hubbub
tripe-visaged	loose of jowl	Winchester-goose	inflamed or swollen groin as a result of venereal disease
troll-my-dame	ball game a bit like miniature bowling	wonder-wounded	awestruck
twink	a wink of an eye		
unheedy	reckless	wrong-incensed	on fire with rage
unsinewed	weak		
unsmirched	spotless	yesty	frothy
urchin-snouted	with a hedgehog-like nose	younker	fashionable young fellow
		zir	colloquialism of sir
vantbrace	armour for the forearm	zounds	God's wounds

THE COMEDIES

'This fellow's wise enough to play the fool'
The Comedies

Shakespeare's comedy plays don't quite resemble what we think of as classic humour pieces in the twenty-first century; it's essential to change one's perspective when looking at the group as a whole. Firstly, and rather counter-intuitively, the defining feature of a comedy play is not humour. The key characteristic is that it centres on an opposition or conflict between two groups: the young rebelling against the old, for example, or court life versus country life. Just as the Tragedies often feature a comic interlude, the Comedies will often have a serious or sombre subplot – see the opening scenes of *As You Like It*, for instance. And more often than not they focus on compli-cated family relationships and the convoluted entanglements of romantic love. Not all the Comedies will fit the formula perfectly, but some common characteristics that usually feature in Shakespearean comedy are:

- the movement of the play from conflict to a resolution of conflict, with complications and obstacles along the way, ending in a celebratory happy ending

- love and marriage

- mistaken identities

- a complex, multi-stranded plot, frequently involving disguise and doubles or mirrors

- stock characters: the fool, the old man, the smart servant

- very comedic language with lots of punning, wordplay and elaborate insults

- an inversion of the normal order of things

- arguments between families, but no deaths

The Comedies reflect a broad range of human relationships, so there is always a delicate interplay between the light and the dark. Some plays are very difficult to classify – *The Merchant of Venice* falls under the Comedy heading, and it's true that it ends on a note of celebration and resolution, but at its heart is a deeply tragic figure: Shylock loses everything dear to him, including his religion. This blending of tones is part of what makes seeing a Shakespearean comedy such a thought-provoking and fulfilling experience.

* * *

A Midsummer Night's Dream
High Jinks And Love Potions
In The Enchanted Woods

Bottom and the mechanicals, ACT III, SCENE 2

With its frantic pace, naughty fairies, careless humans and whimsical title, *A Midsummer Night's Dream* has long been a favourite with audiences, and in particular with children. For many it's the first Shakespeare play they come across. Written around the same time as *Romeo and Juliet* it shares some themes with its darker sister – star-crossed lovers driven apart by interfering parents, moments of love at first sight, and the play-within-a-play that takes place at the end is a dreadful performance of Ovid's *Pyramus and Thisbe* (which Shakespeare drew on for *Romeo and Juliet*). The fact that the world's greatest literary genius was still able to poke fun at himself by parodying heavy-handed romances is, in our opinion, yet another reason to love the man.

In Athens, Theseus, Duke of Athens, and Hippolyta, Queen of the Amazons, discuss their forthcoming wedding, due to take place in four days (Act I). They have previously fought each other in battle, but Hippolyta has been militarily defeated, whereas Theseus is romantically slain: he's deeply in love with his bride-to-be. Egeus arrives to beg help with a problem he's facing. Alongside him are his daughter, Hermia, and the two men vying for her hand, Lysander and Demetrius. Egeus wants Demetrius to be his son-in-law – in fact if he doesn't get his way, he wants his daughter executed. But Hermia is in love with Lysander. Theseus suggests that there is another option: Hermia might become a nun. Faced with these choices, rather unsurprisingly, Hermia and Lysander decide to run away, and arrange to meet in the woods the following night. But before they leave, they tell Helena, who is madly in love with Demetrius, of their plan. Miserable, jealous Helena decides to tell Demetrius of the lovers' plot.

The enchanted forest is a popular location that night. A bumbling, chaotic, ego-riven group of amateur actors meet to discuss their latest dramatic offering: Quince, Flute, Snout, Starveling and Bottom plan to stage a performance of *Pyramus and Thisbe* to celebrate Theseus's wedding, and the forest offers them the perfect place to practise in peace. And Oberon and Titania, the quarrelling King and Queen of the Fairies, play out their marital woes in the forest too (Act II). Titania accuses Oberon of taking a fancy to Hippolyta, while Oberon accuses Titania of the same for Theseus. He'll forgive her, though, if she hands over the young human boy she's chosen as her chief page. Titania refuses outright: 'Not for thy fairy kingdom.' As punishment, Oberon tells his lieutenant fairy, Puck, that he's going to trick her with a love potion or 'juice' while she's asleep, which will work by forcing her to fall in love with whatever she first comes across upon awaking, 'Be it on lion, bear, or wolf or bull'. While Puck is off gathering the herbs for the love juice, Oberon spots Demetrius and Helena arguing. Helena's pleas for love fall on Demetrius's cruelly deaf ears, so Oberon decides to kill two birds with one stone and drop some love juice onto Demetrius's eyes, too. Upon awaking and spying Helena he'll return the love she is so desperate for.

Hold tight, here's where it gets confusing. Oberon squeezes the potion onto a snoozing Titania, and instructs Puck to find Helena. Meanwhile Hermia and Lysander are lost. They decide to gather their strength and have a sleep, and Puck mistakes them for a slumbering Demetrius and Helena and drips the magic juice into Lysander's eyes. As Puck leaves, Demetrius and Helena come running into the sleeping pair, Lysander awakes, sees Helena and falls deeply in love. She thinks he's taking the mick. But it's deadly serious, for Hermia in particular. Now the sight of Hermia makes Lysander feel physically ill.

As Titania sleeps nearby, the performers wander in to begin their rehearsal (Act III). Bottom is vocal as ever, insisting on rewrites. Puck sneaks up on them, and decides to have some fun; he gives Bottom an ass's head. The rest of the cast flee in fright when they see him, and his weird braying and singing wake Titiana who falls instantly in love. Bottom appears to take the entire thing in his stride and heads off with Titania and the four fairies she has instructed to treat him as a king. Oberon is mightily tickled that his wife has fallen for an ass called Bottom, but when he sees Hermia and Demetrius arguing and realises Puck has picked the wrong Athenian to juice, he's not quite so pleased. Happily, as Hermia runs off Demetrius picks this moment for a nap, so while Puck rushes to find Helena, Oberon puts juice in Demetrius's sleeping eyes. He wakes as Lysander and Helena appear, so now the tables have turned and Helena has both men infatuated with her. Hermia arrives and laments the loss of Lysander's love, but Helena is still furious. Now she thinks all three are teasing her, in the most spiteful way. As Hermia is insulted by both men she begins to think maybe she's been the victim of a plot engineered by Helena. Lysander and Demetrius decide to fight a duel, leaving Hermia alone and bewildered.

Puck finds the entire situation hilarious, but Oberon is angry, and orders Puck to sort it out by giving Lysander the antidote. Puck imitates the men's voices and draws them apart. Lysander, finding himself alone in the woods, decides it's time for a nap, as does Demetrius, and then Helena wanders in and lies down to sleep too. Puck wants the full house, and is delighted when Hermia turns up and also has a kip. Puck squeezes the antidote potion onto Lysander's eyes. Titiana and Bottom come along and nod off as well (Act IV), making a glorious sleeping tableau. Oberon arrives and reveals that Titania has given him the human boy he wanted, and he now plans to release her from the spell. Titania awakes and tells him of a horrible dream she's had in which she was in love with an ass. Now Puck removes the ass's head from Bottom without waking him. Oberon, Titania and the fairies dance off in newly found happiness leaving the five humans slumbering. Theseus, Hippolyta and Egeus then arrive on the scene and with a blast of the trumpet wake the two young pairs of lovers . . . groggily they recount their adventures and harmony is restored: Demetrius loves Helena, Lysander loves Hermia. Bottom wakes up after they've all left, completely confused. But he's reunited with the other players and they prepare for their moment in the sun at the Duke's wedding feast (Act V).

As the aristocrats look on, amused and entertained, but perhaps not quite in the intended way, the am-dram troupe perform a truly hopeless version of *Pyramus and Thisbe*. The players and the royals go to bed, and Oberon, Titania and the fairies enter the house to lay a blessing on the heads of all the sleeping lovers, with Puck delivering a final epilogue bidding the audience a sweet goodnight.

KEY THEMES

The Nature of Love

LYSANDER
> Ay me! For aught that I could ever read,
> Could ever hear by tale or history,

The course of true love never did run smooth;
But either it was different in blood –

HERMIA

O cross! too high to be enthrall'd to low.

LYSANDER

Or else misgraffed in respect of years –

HERMIA

O spite! too old to be engaged to young.

LYSANDER

Or else it stood upon the choice of friends –

HERMIA

O hell! to choose love by another's eyes.

LYSANDER

Or, if there were a sympathy in choice,
War, death, or sickness did lay siege to it,
Making it momentany as a sound,
Swift as a shadow, short as any dream,
Brief as the lightning in the collied night,
That, in a spleen, unfolds both heaven and earth,
And, ere a man hath power to say 'Behold!',
The jaws of darkness do devour it up:
So quick bright things come to confusion.

(ACT I, SCENE I)

In *A Midsummer Night's Dream*, the concept of love is tricky; in the name of love, the characters display foolishness, capriciousness, cruelty and irrationality. In the enchanted forest, love really does make men and women mad. Even in the opening lines there is tension. In theory, the older sets of lovers – Theseus and Hippolyta and Oberon and Titania – ought to be present as examples of grown-up love (think about Beatrice and Benedick in *Much Ado About Nothing* or Orlando and Rosalind at the end of *As You Like It*). But it's not so simple: Theseus and Hippolyta's union is born of war.

Theseus is now smitten, and willing the days to pass until they are wed, but Hippolyta's position is not so certain. She's virtually silent in the face of Theseus's impassioned proclamations, and as he waxes lyrical she remains tight-lipped. The arguments, oscillations and spats that disrupt the union of Oberon and Titania are clearly not a great advertisement for the benefits of long-term monogamy and marriage either.

Lysander's famous lines above describe a key theme of the play – that love always offers up a bumpy ride for those lucky (or unlucky) enough to fall under its spell. Lysander notes that in all the books he's read, and as history over the years has shown, the course of love has never run smooth. Social standing, or age, or guardians stand in the way, and even if lovers can overcome those obstacles, then war, sickness or death can interrupt love's true path, so it can be as fleeting as a shadow, and almost before you know you have it, it's gone. Even the play-within-a-play, *Pyramus and Thisbe*, reminds us of the darkest tragic consequences of love – the two young lovers end up dead.

The irrationality of love is at the heart of the play; love is seen as a kind of madness or spell, as symbolised by Puck's love juice, which mimics that intensity and speed with which people seem to fall head over heels in real life too. Titania and Bottom's union takes this idea of love as a kind of cosmic joke to the extreme: the idea of this beautiful Queen of the Fairies besotted with a pompous ass has tickled us for generations. In the end, though, marriage symbolises harmony for all, as the fairies dance and sing their way through the slumbering palace, blessing each union in turn.

Nature and Chaos

TITANIA

> These are the forgeries of jealousy:
> And never, since the middle summer's spring,
> Met we on hill, in dale, forest or mead,
> By paved fountain or by rushy brook,
> Or in the beached margent of the sea,
> To dance our ringlets to the whistling wind,

But with thy brawls thou hast disturb'd our sport.
Therefore the winds, piping to us in vain,
As in revenge have suck'd up from the sea
Contagious fogs; which falling in the land,
Have every pelting river made so proud
That they have overborne their continents.
The ox hath therefore stretch'd his yoke in vain,
The ploughman lost his sweat, and the green corn
Hath rotted ere his youth attain'd a beard;
The fold stands empty in the drowned field,
And crows are fatted with the murrion flock;
The nine-men's-morris is fill'd up with mud,
And the quaint mazes in the wanton green
For lack of tread are undistinguishable.
The human mortals want their winter here;
No night is now with hymn or carol blest.
Therefore the moon, the governess of floods,
Pale in her anger, washes all the air,
That rheumatic diseases do abound.
And thorough this distemperature we see
The seasons alter: hoary-headed frosts
Far in the fresh lap of the crimson rose;
And on old Hiems' thin and icy crown
An odorous chaplet of sweet summer buds
Is, as in mockery, set: the spring, the summer,
The childing autumn, angry winter, change
Their wonted liveries, and the mazed world,
By their increase, now knows not which is which.
And this same progeny of evils comes
From our debate, from our dissension;
We are their parents and original.

(ACT II, SCENE I)

Here Titania levels harsh accusations at her husband Oberon, telling him that every time she and her fairies have attempted to meet, 'To dance our ringlets to the whistling wind', Oberon and his gang have disrupted their sport, and this in turn has led to a fundamental breakdown in the very fabric of nature. Using language heavily laden with symbols of the natural world, she describes how the weather has turned – actually the very seasons have changed, frosts have spread over the roses, and ice wears a garland of flowers as if playing a cruel joke. It's a disaster for the humans: they can't play in their mazes because the treads have become invisible, and, slightly less frivolously, their crops are failing. And it's all down to them: 'We are their parents and original.' Only their reconciliation can bring about the natural balance of things again, and in fact the play can be read as a series of journeys from chaos to order. Egeus complains that his daughter has been bewitched by rhymes from Lysander, in 'faining voice verses of feigning love', and he wants to restore social order by invoking the ancient rule of Athens that states she belongs to her father, and he can dispose of her as he will. And when the humans find themselves in the woods, away from their strictly ordered society, chaos ensues, but all to the good – it's as if the turmoil is a necessary evil from which true tranquillity can be born.

KEY SCENE

In the 'what fools these mortals be' scene (Act III, Scene 2), Shakespeare's lampooning of love reaches its absolute zenith. While Oberon delights in the irony of Titania falling for an ass, his laughter turns to horror as he realises the havoc Puck has sown on the human relationships in the forest. As Helena attempts to shake off Lysander's advances, and Hermia pleads with Demetrius to explain what he's done to Lysander, Puck muses that this is the way love always goes – 'Then fate o'er-rules, that, one man holding troth, / A million fail, confounding oath on oath': for every man holding true to love's promises there are a million more who break their vows. Amid the conflict and chaos, Puck stands back giggling at the craziness of human beings – 'what fools these mortals be!' – before intervening with his love juice to restore peace and harmony.

KEY SYMBOL

The **moon** 'like to a silver bow / New bent in heaven' is referred to countless times throughout the play – three times in its opening lines alone. This is partly for practical reasons: Shakespeare's plays were primarily performed during daylight hours, so to create the atmosphere of an enchanted evening he presses the point home through repeated mentions of the silvery orb. But it's heavily symbolic too, and its symbolism shifts and changes as the characters and scenes demand. It is first introduced as a symbol of chastity as Theseus laments it delaying his wedding night and the conjugal bliss he imagines will take place. But as well as chastity it can also represent desire; Lysander's wooing of Hermia has happened by moonlight, and they plan to elope by the light of the moon, and all the characters chase each other through the sylvan setting by the light of the moon too. And if you think we're overstating how significant the connection between the moon and the play is, chew on this: three of Uranus's moons (discovered from the late eighteenth century onwards) are named after the most important fairies in *A Midsummer Night's Dream* – Oberon, Titania and Puck.

Much Ado About Nothing
Doubles, Deception And Honour

'Come, bind them: – thou naughty varlet!' ACT IV, SCENE 2

Much Ado About Nothing was probably written in 1598 or 1599, just as the new Globe Theatre was taking shape in Southwark. It's quite a difficult play to categorise, containing as it does elements of both comedy and tragedy, but as an introduction to the works you could do worse than to start with *Much Ado*. There is real, cruel, malignant deception alongside playful bouts of disguise and trickery; there are serious points about honour and shame alongside musings on love and relationships; there are no deaths, and the play ends with love triumphing and multiple marriages. It was written before the great tragedies *Othello*, *Hamlet*, *Lear* and *Macbeth*, but the epic themes explored in those later works are present here too: sexual betrayal, infidelity and deception.

In Elizabethan times the 'Nothing' of the title had a double meaning: 'nothing' was pronounced exactly as 'noting', and at the time 'noting' also meant gossip, rumour and overhearing. There's a slightly ruder pun at work here too: 'no thing' was slang for 'vagina' – a woman had 'no thing' between her legs. So the snappy title could mean 'A Great Big Fuss About Nothing', 'A Great Big Fuss About Gossip' and even 'A Great Big Fuss About Sex'.

PLOT SUMMARY

In Messina, Sicily, Governor Leonato is preparing to welcome his friend Don Pedro back from war. Don Pedro is Prince of Aragon and is accompanied by his treacherous bastard brother Don John, who has recently been involved in a thwarted rebellion against Don Pedro (Act I). Also in the visiting party are Benedick, a Lord of Padua, and Count Claudio, a Lord of Florence. Leonato's daughter is Hero, and his niece is Beatrice, who has been embroiled in a long-running war of words – 'a merry war' – with Benedick. The first misunderstanding occurs early on when Antonio, Leonato's brother, informs the Governor that Don Pedro has fallen in love with Hero, when in fact it is Claudio who has fallen for her, Don Pedro having only agreed to secure her hand by disguising himself as his shy friend at a masked ball that evening. Don John hears of these plans, and, along with his loyal servants Conrade and Borachio, sees a chance to use the information in whatever way possible to make life tricky for Don Pedro and Claudio.

At the ball (Act II) Don Pedro successfully woos Hero on Claudio's behalf and, despite dastardly Don John's efforts to cause mischief, a date is set for the wedding, in a week's time. Hero's hand in marriage secured, Don Pedro turns his attention to Benedick, and hatches a plan to make Benedick and Beatrice fall in love. This involves Benedick overhearing Claudio, Leonato and Don Pedro discussing how insanely in love Beatrice is with him. The plan is a huge success, Benedick enacts an immediate volte-face, and resolves to return Beatrice's love. In the meantime Don John and Borachio have dreamt up their own scheme involving Margaret, Hero's lady's maid, shouting her love for Borachio from Hero's window, tricking any onlookers into thinking it is Hero who is in love with Borachio, and, scandalously, that they are about to spend the night together.

Next it is Beatrice's turn to be tricked by 'Cupid's crafty arrow' (Act III): Hero and Ursula (another of Hero's maids) discuss Benedick's passionate and unrequited love for Beatrice and again the plan works: Beatrice too swears to love Benedick in return. The day before the wedding, Borachio and Conrade spring their trap, and Claudio is convinced of Hero's infidelity. Furious, he vows to humiliate her at the altar. However, Dogberry, the constable in charge of the night watch, has overheard Borachio's boasts about the thousand ducats he has earned from Don John for his deception. Dogberry arrests the pair, but his attempts to tell Leonato what has happened are frustrated by his own inarticulacy – with his over-elaborate language and fear of appearing like an idiot in front of his superior and boss, he manages to tie himself up in ever-tightening linguistic knots. The tension rises as Leonato rushes off to his daughter's wedding blissfully unaware of what is about to unfold.

As promised, at the altar Claudio denounces Hero (Act IV). Hero faints, and as she falls to the ground unconscious her desperately humiliated father Leonato prays that she is dead – the shame she will bring on her family alive is to him a fate worse than death. Claudio and Don Pedro leave, believing Hero has in fact shuffled off her mortal coil, and the Friar presiding over the wedding, who can tell that Hero is innocent, suggests that this may not be a bad thing: by faking her death, the family might extract some remorse from Claudio, and she may be able to build a new life elsewhere, where no one knows her past. Left alone, Beatrice and Benedick admit their love for one another, and Beatrice asks Benedick to kill Claudio in order to prove that he really does love her. At first he thinks she's joking, but when he realises she's deadly serious he agrees to carry out her wishes.

After a painfully inept trial during which Dogberry's malapropisms threaten to entirely untip the scales of justice, a confession is finally extracted from Borachio and Conrade. Leonato, with the slowly dawning realisation that his daughter has been terribly slandered, challenges Claudio and Don Pedro, who mock him. Leonato leaves just as Benedick arrives, and Claudio and Don Pedro try to engage him in their ridicule of the old man. Benedick is having none of it, and is really not joking as he challenges his old friend Claudio. He leaves, telling them both that he must 'discontinue their company'. Now the constables arrive with Borachio and he repeats his confession to Claudio and Don Pedro, who are devastated to discover Hero's innocence – they know they are to blame for her death. Deeply chastened, they apologise profusely to a still angry Leonato, who says that perhaps one way to soothe the wound is for Claudio to marry his brother's daughter, who is very similar in looks to Hero, and is now the brothers' only heir (Act V). At the wedding, the masked bride is revealed to be Hero, and Claudio is thrilled. And Beatrice and Benedick realise that they have each been tricked, but confess in front of all that they really *do* love each other. A messenger arrives with news that Don John has been arrested, but the play closes with Benedick suggesting that his punishment will wait – now is the time for dancing and celebration.

KEY THEMES

Rhetoric and Reality

BENEDICK

> What, my dear Lady Disdain! are you yet living?

BEATRICE

> Is it possible disdain should die, while she hath such meet food to feed it as Signior Benedick? Courtesy itself must convert to disdain, if you come in her presence.

BENEDICK

> Then is courtesy a turncoat. But it is certain I am loved of all ladies, only you excepted; and I would I could find in my heart that I had not a hard heart, for, truly I love none.

BEATRICE

> A dear happiness to women, they would else have been troubled with a pernicious suitor. I thank God and my cold blood, I am of your humour for that; I had rather hear my dog bark at a crow than a man swear he loves me.

BENEDICK

> God keep your ladyship still in that mind, so some gentleman or other shall 'scape a predestinate scratched face.

BEATRICE

> Scratching could not make it worse, and 'twere such a face as yours were.

(ACT I, SCENE I)

Benedick and Beatrice are without question one of Shakespeare's best-loved couples. Much ado is obviously made of Hero's supposed fornication, and indeed more lines are spent on Claudio and Hero, but the meat of the play lies in the complex and brilliantly rounded characters of Benedick and Beatrice. Charles I apparently even annotated his copy of the Second Folio with the words 'Benedick and Beatrice'. We know from the start that they are destined for each other – both names mean blessed – and it is in their extraordinary exchanges that their romance is played out. This first encounter is typical: full of wordplay and bickering, it is a real demonstration of verbal athletics. The conversation is peppered with insults – Benedick wondering how it's possible that 'Lady Disdain' can still be alive, Beatrice claiming that Benedick is so difficult to be around that 'courtesy itself must convert to disdain', i.e. that even his presence turns good manners into bad. By the end these two clearly intelligent beings are reduced to slightly infantile name-calling – Benedick imagining the face of a future husband scratched by her barbs, Beatrice claiming a scratched face couldn't be as ugly a visage as his (you can virtually hear them saying 'nah, nah, nah, nah, nah'). In fact, though, in this early parley they can already draw great parallels with each other. Crucially, both are committed singletons: Benedick, in his arrogant way, claims that all the ladies love him, but that he doesn't love a single person. Beatrice agrees she feels the same – 'I am of your humour'. They are linked by their powerful charisma and their sparring has an attractive inevitability about it. As in many of Shakespeare's sonnets, here is romantic love characterised by a sort of aloof and mocking disdain.

Language and Hierarchy

CLAUDIO

Out on thee, seeming! I will write against it.
You seem to me as Dian in her orb,
As chaste as is the bud ere it be blown;
But you are more intemperate in your blood

Than Venus, or those pamper'd animals
That rage in savage sensuality.

(ACT IV, SCENE I)

As in *As You Like It*, there's also a criticism at the heart of the play about courtly language as an expression of the conventions of a strict hierarchy, and a suggestion that this more formal language is less true and honest an expression of love. The unbendingly ordered world of the court at Messina allows plenty of scope for exploring the dangers of its self-imposed rules. This happens through language in the first instance: when Claudio falls for Hero his language immediately becomes inflated. As Benedick notes: 'He was wont to speak plain and to the purpose, like an honest man and a soldier; and now is he turned orthography; his words are a very fantastical banquet, just so many strange dishes.' And in Act IV, when Claudio dumps Hero at the altar, in his anger his language again veers to the over-elaborate; it's packed with classical allusions, to chaste Diana, and the more hot-blooded Venus. But more than that, it's perhaps also Claudio's adherence to a strict moral code that allows him to be so easily manipulated by Don John's lies: he simply can't conceive of another explanation to the events unfolding in front of him. His extreme reaction to her apparent transgression eventually leads to Hero's 'death'. Even when he's faced with truth he can only say to Leonato that his behaviour was down to a case of mistaken identity, and it's clear that he'd almost certainly act the same way again in the same circumstances. As always in Shakespeare, there's a deeply human sympathy at play here, and a lack of moral judgement; we're simply shown why characters might act in a particular way, within a given framework.

Doubles and Deception

The play is crammed with doubles and mirrors: Claudio and Benedick are mirrored in Hero and Beatrice, there are the brothers Don John and Don Pedro, and there are two marriage scenes that act almost as plays within a play. Each double sheds light on its counterpart: so Claudio and Hero are an example of the dangers of young, innocent, naive romantic love, whereas Beatrice and Benedick are older, wiser, more genuine. Good things and happiness come of their love, whereas the idealised love of Claudio and Hero breeds only bad: jealousy, anger and violence. Linked to this is the idea of deception and misunderstanding – the play is full of lies, and even where the deception is benevolent, the dangers are clear. Don Pedro's innocuous intention to woo Hero on behalf of Claudio is seized upon by his villainous brother Don John, for example, as an opportunity to humiliate Hero. The lies are a source of both the comedy and the tragedy. The 'noting' of the title is a red herring of sorts – in fact the play is about mis-noting, and misinterpretation.

KEY SCENE

Don John sees the seeds of his malevolent labour bear fruit in the **wedding scene** (Act IV, Scene 1). In high dramatic style, using shockingly bitter and vicious language, Claudio denounces Hero at the altar. Hero is shamed; but it's not just her that feels the force of Claudio's accusations, her family are humiliated too – with her father quickly turning on her: 'O, she is fall'n / Into a pit of ink'. While this scene spells disaster for Claudio and Hero's dreams of a happy ever after, conversely it marks a turning point for a deepening relationship between Beatrice and Benedick. It's the moment of Benedick's transition from arrogant bad boy, confirmed bachelor and one of the lads, to a man with sympathies towards the women of the play. Benedick has an epiphany of sorts – 'Surely I do believe your fair cousin is wronged' – and switches his allegiances. With a stroke of quite staggeringly bad timing he also chooses this moment to admit to Beatrice that he loves her. And as she then asks him to kill his best friend to prove it, we see Benedick faced with the ultimate test of his new-found loyalties. We leave the scene in suspense: everything in Hero's life is ruined and the immediate switch to the following court scene increases the dramatic effect.

KEY SYMBOLS

To Beard or not to Beard, that is the question. **Physical features** play a key role in the symbolism of the play. Claudio's lack of a beard relates to his naivety and inexperience, while in contrast Benedick's whiskers mark him out as a man of the world. Beatrice is a self-proclaimed beard-hater, and in Act II she tells Leonato, 'Lord, I could not endure a husband with a beard on his face! I had rather lie in the woollen.' Her rejection of beards symbolises her rejection of men in general, and it's very telling that Benedick's first act upon realising he is in fact horribly in love with Beatrice is to have a good old shave.

There are also many allusions to the idea of marriage as a form of **taming a wild animal**. In the opening act, Claudio and Don Pedro josh with Benedick, quoting the saying 'In time the savage bull doth bear the yoke' at him, meaning that it's inevitable that Benedick's wildness and savagery will be tamed by the yoke of marriage. Benedick responds by saying he would take the bull's horns and hang them on his forehead to mark him out as a cuckold (a man with an unfaithful wife). In the final scene, as Benedick is married to Beatrice, Claudio reminds him of the savage bull, but now the image of the yoked, tamed animal has been transformed into something quite different: 'Bull Jove' refers to the story from classical mythology of Zeus adopting the form of a white bull in order to carry off Europa. So the labouring farm animal becomes a virile and lusty image of sexuality.

Dogberry's malapropisms

Derived from the French term *mal à propos*, which means inappropriate, a **malapropism** is defined as a ridiculous misuse of words, and particularly substituting words for ones that sound the same but render the sentence meaningless. Dogberry is an expert at malapropism, which was later theatrically immortalised by Mrs Malaprop in Sheridan's play *The Rivals*. Dogberry is a wonderful dramatic device – not only is he there for the comedy of

course, providing light relief at the play's darkest hours, but also because his mangled verbosity almost prevents Borachio's betrayal being uncovered. His desire to appear intelligent and erudite in the elevated company of his master means he simply cannot explain to Leonato what he has uncovered. Here are some of the best examples of his confusion, with the correct word in brackets:

As You Like It
Courtship And Concealment
In The Forest Of Arden

1613 map of Warwickshire showing the forest of Arden

As You Like It was written sometime between 1598 and 1600, and was one of the first plays performed at the Globe. Shakespeare's main source was *Rosalynde, or Euphues' Golden Legacy* by Thomas Lodge, an Elizabethan pastoral

'Marry, sir, I would have some **confidence** with you, that **decerns** you nearly.' (conference, concern)

'First, who think you the most **desertless** man to be constable?' (deserving)

'Is our whole **dissembly** appeared?' (assembly)

'But truly, for mine own part, if I were as **tedious** as a king, I could find it in my heart to bestow it all of your worship.' (wealthy)

'Our watch, sir, have indeed **comprehended** two **auspicious** persons' (apprehended, suspicious)

'O villain! Thou wilt be condemned into everlasting **redemption** for this.' (damnation)

'Only get the learned writer to set down our **excommunication** and meet me at the jail.' (communication)

romance of 1590 which told of a golden age of men and women living in harmony with nature. Stuffed full of Petrarchan love poetry (Petrarch was an uber-romantic fourteenth-century Italian poet, about whom you can find out more on page 248), it was in essence a celebration of creamy old England – written just after the navy's glorious defeat of the Spanish Armada. *Rosalynde* was hugely popular, going through at least three editions by the time Shakespeare came to write his own version. In *As You Like It*, he compresses the timescale and injects a bit of fun into the proceedings, despite the rather bleak opening scenes which pit brothers against brothers and uncles against nieces. As the play develops it becomes a joyful explosion of humour, confusion, mockery, disguise and trickery.

PLOT SUMMARY

Hold tight, this is a slightly complicated storyline . . . The play opens in the court of Duke Frederick, father to Celia, uncle to Rosalind (Act I). Duke Frederick has exiled his brother Duke Senior, Rosalind's father, with several of his lords to the Forest of Arden. Rosalind has been allowed to remain because she and Celia are exceptionally close – 'never two ladies loved as they do'. Orlando is the younger brother of Oliver, both sons of deceased Rowland de Bois. The brothers hate each other; Oliver believes his legacy and right to an education are being withheld from him, and after a quarrel he hatches a plan to kill Orlando by goading Charles the wrestler. In the presence of Duke Frederick, Celia and Rosalind witness the wrestling match which, against all expectations, Orlando wins. When the Duke discovers that Orlando is the son of a former enemy, he stalks off, in contrast to Rosalind's reaction when she discovers their fathers were friends. She presents him with her necklace as a token of her affection and Orlando immediately falls in love, and later Rosalind admits to Celia that she has also fallen for Orlando. Duke Frederick, feeling a touch threatened by Rosalind's growing popularity, sends her into exile, and a heartbroken Celia vows to go with her. They take the jester Touchstone too, and use disguise as a means of protection: Rosalind will dress as a man called

Ganymede, and Celia will be Aliena, a name to suit her present state, cast out from her life.

In the Forest of Arden, Duke Senior revels in the ease of life away from the devious plotting and back-stabbing of the court (Act II). Meanwhile Orlando is warned by his faithful servant Adam that Oliver has sworn to burn down his home. Orlando is stuck – he doesn't have the money to go elsewhere – until Adam offers to give him his life's savings, as long as he can come along for the ride to Arden.

Rosalind, Celia and Touchstone, in disguise, overhear two shepherds, Corin and Silvius, discussing Silvius's unrequited infatuation with a woman called Phebe. Rosalind recognises something of her own feelings for Orlando, and after Silvius has left, they approach Corin for food. He has none, and what's more his flock and cottage are for sale. Rosalind offers to buy the land and have Corin work for her. Meanwhile, the journey to Arden has left Adam on his last legs. Orlando vows to find food, whatever the danger, and approaches the Duke, sitting at a table heavily laden with a feast, with his sword drawn. The Duke is kind though – the forest is not a place from which civilisation has been banished. While Jaques, one of the Duke's men, makes his famous speech on the seven ages of man (see page 119), Orlando fetches Adam, and the Duke discovers Orlando is the son of his old friend Rowland.

Duke Frederick, realising that Celia and Touchstone have vanished along with Rosalind, suspects Orlando of playing a role in their disappearance (Act III), and orders Oliver to track them down. Orlando has been keeping busy in the forest by pinning love poetry in honour of Rosalind to trees – and worse, immortalising his dreadful ditties by carving words into their bark. Rosalind, not knowing who their author is, reads some verses out to Touchstone. Celia reveals that the author is Orlando, and Rosalind is keen to know if he realises she's in the forest too. Then she overhears Orlando discussing her with Jaques – and decides to trick him. As Ganymede, she presents herself as having the power to cure sick men of the madnesses of love. She offers to treat Orlando – he must come to her cottage daily and woo her as 'Rosalind'.

When Orlando fails to arrive at the agreed time, Rosalind is devastated: in private, at least, she's a woman in love who's been stood up. Corin offers to show her the true devastation of love: Silvius's hopeless wooing of Phebe. They watch on as Silvius pleads his case, and Rosalind steps in with a very cutting riposte to Phebe's heartlessness. In the old adage of treat 'em mean to keep 'em keen, Phebe is immediately attracted to the aloof Ganymede and while she can't concede to return Silvius's love, she does agree to soften her position by offering him 'neighbourly' love. She asks Silvius to take a letter to Ganymede. He obliges, delighted at least to be of use to her.

Jaques and Rosalind are getting to know each other by discussing the nature of melancholy when Orlando appears ready to woo 'Rosalind' (Act IV). There is wonderful banter between them – they are equals in wit and intellect. They undergo a mock wedding, making Celia increasingly uncomfortable, and when Orlando leaves, promising to return within two hours, Rosalind again emphasises to Celia how deeply in love with him she is. Then Silvius arrives with Phebe's letter – he thinks it'll be a telling-off, but it turns out to be a love letter. Rosalind sends Silvius packing with the instruction from Ganymede that he orders Phebe to love Silvius.

Now Orlando's brother Oliver arrives looking for Ganymede and Aliena, and as he pulls out a bloodied handkerchief he reveals he's been sent to explain why Orlando hasn't returned within two hours as promised. Orlando had come across a man lying under a tree, with a snake wrapped around his neck. On spotting Orlando the snake disappeared under a bush, scaring out a lioness, at which point Orlando realised the man was in fact his treacherous brother. Orlando made to leave twice, but his nature got the better of him and he returned to help, injuring himself in the process. Oliver has been converted to the good by his brother's willingness to save his life. Rosalind faints on hearing of Orlando's wounds, prompting Oliver to comment that 'you lack a man's heart'. Her mask is beginning to slip.

Oliver reveals to Orlando that he has fallen in love with Aliena – and they are due to be married in the morning (Act V). As Ganymede, Rosalind tells Orlando that a resolution is coming to his situation with Rosalind. And when Phebe approaches Ganymede, angry that the contents of her letter have been revealed, again Rosalind hints that the next day all will be resolved. The players are assembled and Ganymede makes Phebe swear that if she refuses to marry Ganymede, she will marry Silvius. She also extracts a promise from Duke Senior that if she can bring Rosalind before him, he will agree to her marriage to Orlando. Rosalind and Celia return dressed as themselves with Hymen, the Greek goddess of marriage, who has handily turned up. The couples are united: Orlando and Rosalind, Oliver and Celia, Phebe and Silvius (Phebe's had a rethink since she discovered Ganymede is in fact a woman), as well as Touchstone and the shepherdess Audrey. Finally Jaques de Boys – Oliver and Orlando's middle brother – arrives to tell the assembled crowd that Frederick has converted to a religious order and Duke Senior will be reinstated at court. Rosalind has the final say with a witty epilogue where she concedes it's unusual to let a lady have the last word.

KEY THEMES

The Court Versus the Countryside

Enter DUKE SENIOR, AMIENS *and two or three Lords,*
like foresters

DUKE SENIOR
Now my co-mates and brothers in exile,
Hath not old custom made this life more sweet
Than that of painted pomp? Are not these woods
More free from peril than the envious court?
Here feel we not the penalty of Adam,
The seasons' difference, as the icy fang
And churlish chiding of the winter's wind,
Which, when it bites and blows upon my body
Even till I shrink with cold, I smile, and say
'This is no flattery. These are counsellors
That feelingly persuade me what I am'.
Sweet are the uses of adversity,
Which like the toad, ugly and venomous,
Wears yet a precious jewel in his head;

And this our life, exempt from public haunt,
Finds tongues in trees, books in the running brooks,
Sermons in stones, and good in everything.
I would not change it.

AMIENS

Happy is your Grace,
That can translate the stubbornness of fortune
Into so quiet and so sweet a style.

DUKE SENIOR

Come, shall we go and kill us venison?
And yet it irks me the poor dappled fools,
Being native burghers of this desert city,
Should in their own confines with forked heads
Have their round haunches gor'd.

(ACT II, SCENE I)

The exiled Duke Senior here extols the virtues of their new life in Arden. He concedes that there are hardships, 'the icy fang / And churlish chiding of the winter's wind', but even as he suffers physically, he is happily aware of the freedom of life in the forest: 'our life exempt from public haunt'. The dangers they face in the forest are at least direct and honest, as opposed to the pomp and circumstance of the 'envious court', where the surface is celebrated, and danger and peril are far more pernicious.

As You Like It would have been recognisable to Elizabethan audiences as lying firmly within the pastoral tradition; there is a clear tension between the corrupt life at court, with murder, ambition and usurping brothers set against a more 'pure' natural order of things. Shakespeare's Forest of Arden is not a magical place – full of sprites and fairies, transformations and spells, like the forest in *A Midsummer Night's Dream* – instead we have here a more realistic depiction, where conditions can be harsh and people must work to set food on the table. Arden is celebrated as one of Shakespeare's most successful environments – a sort of hymn to an Elizabethan Good Life.

The forest appears to have some benevolent force: it is a place where love can blossom and bloom, and it can have a transformative effect on the most cretinous characters. As soon as bad brother Oliver arrives he witnesses Orlando's kindness, bravery and willingness to self-sacrifice in the lion and snake encounter and is immediately transformed to the good. And in the closing scenes Jaques de Bois (*bois* being the French for wood) reveals that the scheming Duke Frederick, arriving in Arden to put his brother 'to the sword', has encountered a holy man and immediately renounced life at court.

But as always in Shakespeare's work, things are not quite as simple as they might first appear: there are grey areas too. There are two distinct worlds in the forest: the cave where the Duke and his men live, and the world of agricultural labour which defines the lives of Corin and Silvius. Even as the Duke rhapsodises about the joys of a simple life away from the court, there is an irony at work – he ends with an expression of bloodthirstiness about killing deer. We learn that Jaques, the melancholy and downcast outsider of the play, believes that the Duke is as much a usurper of this realm as his brother was in his own, and while the exchange between Duke Senior and his lord is comically aimed at punctuating Jaques' pompous nature, the seed has nevertheless been planted in the audience's mind – is the Duke merely duplicating the corrupting conditions of court? There's more complexity to Corin and Silvius too. Yes, they can be read as pastoral literary archetypes, the old shepherd who attempts to counsel the younger one (Silvius's name even means 'of the wood'), but there's a shadow here too. Corin is acutely aware that his fortunes are tied to his master's. Other characters also challenge romantic ideas of the pastoral: Audrey the shepherdess is a bawdy, earthy, sometimes lewd mouthpiece of a different set of values.

The Language of Love

ORLANDO

> What were his marks?

ROSALIND

> A lean cheek, which you have not; a blue eye and sunken, which

you have not; an unquestionable spirit, which you have not; a beard neglected, which you have not – but I pardon you for that, for simply your having in beard is a younger brother's revenue. Then your hose should be ungartered, your bonnet unbanded, your sleeve unbuttoned, your shoe untied, and everything about you demonstrating a careless desolation. But you are no such man: you are rather point-device in your accoutrements, as loving yourself than seeming the lover of any other.

ORLANDO
Fair youth, I would I could make thee believe I love.

(ACT III, SCENE 2)

Rosalind, as Ganymede, is explaining, with the emphatic use of antithesis, to Orlando how to identify the 'marks' of a man in love. He would have sunken cheeks, which Orlando does not, eyes which betray sleeplessness, which again Orlando has not, 'a beard neglected', no, and a general appearance of dishevelment. Instead Orlando is rather 'point-device', in other words he looks so well put together that Ganymede accuses him of only being able to love himself. Orlando's reply is that he wishes he could persuade Ganymede how very much in love with Rosalind he is. This is a light-hearted expression of one of the play's key themes of love and language. Despite the many dramatic devices employed throughout the play – poetry, epilogues, songs, disguise – the real engine powering the action is the love story between Rosalind and Orlando. There's the sense right from the start that Orlando needs to find a way of expressing himself honestly before he can be worthy of Rosalind's love.

Rosalind is in love too, but she's a woman capable of very truthful and honest self-analysis, and recognises early on the madness of love. When overhearing Silvius's yearning for Phebe, she says, 'Searching of thy wound / I have by hard adventure found my own.' Orlando, on the other hand, has a journey to undertake in altering his literary register. It is telling that when Rosalind and Orlando first meet Orlando is literally struck dumb – 'What passion hangs these weights upon my tongue?' He then moves on to a conventional form of courtly love with the littering of the forest with some pretty awful love poetry dedicated to her. The trees of the forest groan under the weight of creakingly bad rhymes and unoriginal imagery like: 'From the east to western Ind / No jewel is like Rosalind.' Other characters in the play, especially Rosalind and Touchstone, prick this foolish bubble of romantic love, and in the passage above Rosalind's words are in straightforward prose rather than fancy poetry. But then, through the wonderful scenes in which Rosalind, as Ganymede, attempts to 'cure' him of love, Orlando begins to find his own voice. These exchanges have been recognised as some of the best in Shakespeare's plays and likened to intellectual jousting matches; there's an abundance of wit and wordplay, irony and insinuation, and mounting sexual tension, especially as we begin to understand that Orlando has seen through Rosalind's disguise. But by the final marriage scene, Orlando's language is pared back and beautifully simple – a true expression of heartfelt love: 'If there be truth in sight, you are my Rosalind.'

KEY SCENE

The **pact scene** (Act III, Scene 2) is where the lovers first meet in the forest and make a pact to keep meeting. Rosalind (dressed as Ganymede), Celia and Touchstone have been mocking the atrocious poems they've found pinned on trees, lamenting the poor bark that the mysterious versifier has ruined, as well as his awful way with metre – 'the feet were lame and could not bear themselves without the verse and therefore stood lamely in the verse' – when Rosalind discovers it is in fact her beloved Orlando who is the author. The bad poetry doesn't seem to dampen her feelings for him, but it's at this moment she vows to have some fun and 'speak to him like a saucy lackey'. Rosalind is in disguise, but there is an unmistakable flirtation and banter taking place when she and Orlando converse, leading some critics to surmise that Orlando knows Ganymede's true identity from the word go. It's possible they're both stringing each other along. 'Ganymede' promises that 'he' will 'cure' Orlando of his passion for Rosalind: 'I would cure you, if you would but call me Rosalind and come every day to my cote and woo me', setting in motion the play's romantic mission – the education of Orlando to make him into a worthy lover.

KEY SYMBOL

The **disguise** of Ganymede that Rosalind adopts in *As You Like It* is symbolically important. In Greek mythology, Ganymede was abducted by Zeus in the guise of an eagle, and taken to Olympus to serve as the cup-bearer to the gods. His myth served as a model for the common, and at the time socially acceptable, practice of erotic relationships between older men and teenage boys; and in the play this shape-shifting and gender-bending seems to allow Rosalind the freedom to move beyond the normal conventions of courtly love. The joke would have been intensified in Shakespeare's day by the fact that the actor playing Rosalind would be a young man pretending to play a woman pretending to play a man who is loved by both a man (Orlando) and a woman (Phebe). Head-spinning? Yes, but there is a great joyfulness and exuberance in the abundance and diversity of human relationships on offer in this play, and that's one of the reasons it is many people's favourite.

The critical response to *As You Like It*

We don't have a record of how popular *As You Like It* was in Shakespeare's day, but it's clear it took its place at the top of the table in the revival of the Bard's work, remaining to this day one of his most produced works. William Hazlitt was dazzled by the romance of the forest, saying 'The very air of the place seems to breathe a spirit of philosophical poetry; to stir the thoughts, to touch the heart with pity, as the drowsy forest rustles to the sighing gale'. New historicists, seeking to put the play in its social context, have focused on Orlando as a man suffering the consequences of primogeniture, explaining that the play is all about reinforcing the bonds of brotherhood. The happy ending occurs when Rosalind reveals herself as a woman and, with the words 'To you I give myself, for I am yours', she restores the natural hierarchy of men over women. But it's the feminist critics who've really taken this play to heart, for pretty obvious reasons. Despite the conventional ending, Rosalind is an assertive, powerful, transgressive woman who refuses to accept the idealised Petrarchan notion of womanhood, and it is she who closes the show.

Is Rosalind Shakespeare's greatest female role?

Rosalind has a massive one-quarter of the lines in the play, and without question she is the centre of *As You Like It*. Even the epilogue brings attention to her, and here's Shakespeare at his most postmodern – the young boy actor steps forward, Ganymede's mask slips, then Rosalind's, and then even the actor's, and by exploding the convention thus we have another wonderful celebration of the dizzying intricacies of human relationships.

Beautiful, passionate, loyal, intelligent, funny and feisty, Rosalind has been played by all the greats: it was in this role that Vanessa Redgrave first found fame and Helen Mirren and Helena Bonham Carter have also turned in stellar performances. One interesting testament to the power of Shakespeare's language was the story of Edith Evans's Rosalind at the New Theatre in 1937. The actress had originally been rejected by Lilian Bayliss of the Old Vic for not being attractive enough, but her Rosalind was so perfectly portrayed that critic Alan Dent said: 'In the end the audience was made one with Orlando.' There's some speculation that her passionate love affair with co-star Michael Redgrave (Vanessa's dad) as Orlando may have added an extra dimension to the proceedings. Cheek by Jowl produced an audacious all-male production with Adrian Lester taking the starring role on a blank white stage and winning a *Time Out* award for his portrayal of Rosalind. The *New York Times* said: 'his Rosalind burns with a thrilling compassion for the other love-addled inhabitants of Arden, providing the play with its essential heart and conscience'.

Shakespeare's most redoubtable women

Experts have long pondered Shakespeare's attitude to women, his sexuality, the misogyny demonstrated at times towards the Dark Lady of the sonnets, the condition of his long – and long-distance – marriage to Anne Hathaway, but what's definitely not in question is that he wrote marvellous parts for women. In Shakespeare's works, women are often the heart of the action, the character around whom the dramatic impetus revolves, getting the largest piece of the pie when it comes to the choicest lines. We're calling this section 'Most Redoubtable Women' – not heroines – because sometimes the most unforgettable dames can't properly be called heroines. So who is your favourite? Lady Macbeth with her horrifyingly dark sexual power? Rosalind, with wit and wisdom that one should aspire to? Or the steely innocence of young Juliet? Here are our favourites for you to consider.

Lady Macbeth in *Macbeth*

Murderous, ambitious, manipulative, dangerously charismatic, and prepared to fight for her husband's right to power at any cost, Lady Macbeth is probably the most infamous of Shakespeare's women. But her inability to escape the crushing guilt she feels, her descent into madness and eventual suicide are both moving and deeply shocking.

Best lines, hissed at her husband in an attempt to get him to man up:

My hands are of your colour, but I shame
To wear a heart so white.

(ACT II, SCENE 2)

Viola in *Twelfth Night*
Just one of Shakespeare's many gender-bending girls, Viola is probably the most likeable: bold, feisty and, crucially, true. In a play full of characters who can't seem to commit to one person or another, she knows whom she loves and never errs from the path. Despite finding herself at the centre of a sticky love triangle, she emerges triumphant – though we have to admit we're not quite sure exactly what it is she sees in the pompous narcissist that is Orsino.

Best lines, on the nature of cross-dressing:

This fellow is wise enough to play the fool,
And to do that well, craves a kind of wit.

(ACT III, SCENE I)

Rosalind in *As You Like It*
Another cross-dresser, Rosalind has to be one of Shakespeare's best-loved female roles. As Ganymede, she takes control of her unfortunate circumstances and heads into the forest to change her destiny. As legendary critic Harold Bloom pointed out, one of Rosalind's greatest attributes is her self-knowledge: she can be cynical about love, or romantic, but she is never deluded.

Best lines, when winding up the love-struck Orlando:

Love is merely a madness, and, I tell you, deserves as well a dark house and a whip as madmen do: and the reason why they are not so punished and cured is, that the lunacy is so ordinary that the whippers are in love too.

(ACT III, SCENE 2)

Beatrice in *Much Ado About Nothing*
Like Rosalind, Beatrice is another of Will's most quick-witted women. Her verbal bantering with Benedick is among the most lively, flirtatious and, occasionally, caustic you're ever likely to come across in literature. There's a vulnerability that her pride masks which is very appealing, as is her fierce loyalty to the (rather drippy) Hero. And her request of Benedick after Hero has been unceremoniously dumped is worthy of any Lady Macbeth.

Best lines:

BENEDICK
Come, bid me do any thing for thee.
BEATRICE
Kill Claudio!
BENEDICK
Ha, not for the wide world!
BEATRICE
You kill me to deny it. Farewell.

(ACT IV, SCENE I)

Cleopatra in *Antony and Cleopatra*
Cleopatra is an extraordinary character. A fierce lover, warrior, shrewd politician and propagandist, she refuses to bend to the will of any man, even in death. She has bewitched audiences and readers down the ages, and a fascinating modern prism through which to view her is that of celebrity. She is a woman who is hyper-conscious of her public image, and determined to play her role to its final conclusion.

Best lines, accusing Antony of betraying her with his own wife (this takes some real chutzpah):

> Why should I think you can be mine and true,
> Though you in swearing shake the thronèd gods,
> Who have been false to Fulvia? Riotous madness,
> To be entangled with those mouth-made vows,
> Which break themselves in swearing!
>
> (ACT I, SCENE 3)

Portia in *The Merchant of Venice*
At first glance, Portia's lot is a fairly desperate one, despite appearances. Yes, she's rich and beautiful, but she's pursued by a bunch of money-grabbing knaves who are only after one thing, and, worse, her choice in which of these knaves she has to marry has been set by her father from beyond the grave. By the end of the play, however, she has held her own in a male-dominated court of law and turned all expectations about cosseted wealthy women on their head: both Antonio and Bassanio owe her big time.

Best lines, in disguise while defending Antonio in court:

> The quality of mercy is not strain'd,
> It droppeth as the gentle rain from heaven
> Upon the place beneath: it is twice blest;
> It blesseth him that gives, and him that takes.
>
> (ACT IV, SCENE 1)

Juliet in *Romeo and Juliet*
Juliet's fate isn't quite as happy as Portia's, Rosalind's or Beatrice's, but along the way she does prove herself to be more than a match for the men around her. It is, after all, Juliet who proposes to Romeo, rather than the

other way round. And she is brave enough to abandon her family and all that she knows for a love she really believes in.

Best lines, spoken to Romeo in the orchard:

> O, swear not by the moon, th'inconstant moon,
> That monthly changes in her circled orb,
> Lest that thy love prove likewise variable.

(ACT II, SCENE 2)

Shakespeare's funny bone

A cracking sense of humour probably isn't the first thing that comes to mind when one summons up the spirit of the Bard, but in fact Shakespeare would have had his contemporary audiences rolling in the aisles, and even today, with a little background knowledge to help us illuminate the more arcane witticisms, it's easy to see where the laughter lies in his plays.

The first thing to say is humour isn't only present in the Comedies – it also has a role to play in the Tragedies and Histories. Shakespeare uses **comic breaks** to leaven the heaviest and most dreadful situations, give breathing space to an audience dealing with suicide, murder and betrayal. The gravedigger scene in *Hamlet* is a good example of this, and the drunken porter's scene in *Macbeth*. But these odd little vignettes don't just lighten the audience's load, they also, ingeniously, act as an intensifying agent: by allowing the audience to draw breath and remember what normal life and normal people are like, the terrible actions of magicians, generals, princes, kings and their wives are thrown into sharp relief.

Shakespeare was a big fan of wordplay and punning (see also page 48), which he often used to great effect in sexual innuendo. The bawdiness of Petruchio and Kate in *The Taming of The Shrew* is a good example.

Given that 'tail' in Elizabethan times was street slang for both 'vagina' or 'penis', this exchange between the two is enough to make a grown woman blush:

> PETRUCHIO
> Come, come, you wasp; i'faith, you are too angry.
> KATHERINA
> If I be waspish, best beware my sting.
> PETRUCHIO
> My remedy is then to pluck it out.
> KATHERINA
> Ay, if the fool could find it where it lies.
> PETRUCHIO
> Who knows not where a wasp does wear his sting? In his tail.
> KATHERINA
> In his tongue.
> PETRUCHIO
> Whose tongue?
> KATHERINA
> Yours, if you talk of tales, and so farewell.
> PETRUCHIO
> What, with my tongue in your tail? Nay, come again,
> Good Kate. I am a gentleman –
> KATHERINA
> That I'll try.
> [*She strikes him*]
>
> (ACT II, SCENE I)

Saucy man! No wonder she gives him a wallop.

Shakespeare also enjoyed scatological silliness, again depending on puns, and an Elizabethan audience's understanding of them, to get the point across. See, for example, the eternal punning on the pronunciation of

Ajax's name in *Troilus and Cressida* – 'a jakes' was a euphemism for a privy or loo. Another grubby example, in *The Comedy of Errors*, sees Antipholus and Dromio discussing a woman who is very fat – in fact they end up comparing her body to the very earth. They go on:

ANTIPHOLUS OF SYRACUSE
In what part of her body stands Ireland?
DROMIO OF SYRACUSE
Marry, in her buttocks: I found it out by the bogs.

Shakespeare's humour ranges from the farcical nature of plays like *A Comedy of Errors*, to the parodic *Pyramus and Thisbe* episode in *A Midsummer Night's Dream* and the buffoonery of a character like Sir Toby Belch in *Twelfth Night*, and from the sophisticated witty badinage of Beatrice and Benedick in *Much Ado About Nothing*, to the satire and sarcasm of the wise fools in plays like *King Lear* and *As You Like It*.

There are many very funny comic characters in the plays too, aside from the obvious ruffians, fools and clowns like Falstaff, Feste, Touchstone and Launcelot Gobbo. Mercutio in *Romeo and Juliet* is a dazzling comic creation: a great sceptic and puncturer of Romeo's overblown romantic aspirations. Even in death he's able to crack a joke: at the moment of the fatal blow, pondering the wound and punning on 'grave'. And when telling Romeo to fight his lovesickness he makes lewd innuendo about exactly how he believes his body might cure him of his desperate romanticism:

If love be rough with you, be rough with love.
Prick love for pricking, and you beat love down. –
Give me a case to put my visage in!

Other great comic creations to look out for are Bottom in *A Midsummer Night's Dream*, Dogberry in *Much Ado About Nothing* and Thersites in *Troilus and Cressida*. And if you need a joke about Shakespeare himself when discussing his use of comedy with your friends you need look no further than this classic:

> Shakespeare walks into a pub. The landlord says, 'Get out. You're barred.'

Will Kemp and his jigs

Will Kemp was a great comic actor, known for his slapstick genius. He was one of the shareholders of the Lord Chamberlain's Men along with Shakespeare, and is most associated with the roles of Dogberry in *Much Ado About Nothing* and Peter in *Romeo and Juliet* – in the quarto texts of both his name appears, probably in a slip of the hand, rather than the character's name. He was also a great jigger. Jigs were a key part of the Elizabethan theatre experience. It feels weirdly jarring to us, today, that a play like *Romeo and Juliet* could end with a vision of two young corpses immediately followed by a ribald song-and-dance, but that's what audiences expected and what people paid their good money for. Jigs fell out of fashion after about 1600, as the theatre became more intellectual, and the jig came to be regarded as a rather base form of humour.

Kemp parted company from the Lord Chamberlain's Men in 1599 in unknown but possibly acrimonious circumstances; we don't know the details of what caused the falling-out, but some point to a scene in *Hamlet* as a clue, in which the Prince says:

> And let those that play your clowns speak no more than is set down for them; for there be of them that will themselves laugh to set on some quantity of barren spectators to laugh too.

Perhaps Shakespeare was getting tired of the funny guy stealing all the limelight? Kemp was replaced by the more sophisticated comedic talent (but less good dancing) of Robert Armin, and scholars see this change in the company reflected in the comic roles Shakespeare created. Kemp certainly did not hang up his dancing shoes in the aftermath of his departure though. In early 1600 he undertook the grandly appointed 'Nine Days Wonder', rather brilliantly morris dancing from London to Norwich. What a man.

Shakespeare's problem plays

The categorisation of 'problem play' was dreamt up by the English writer Frederick Boas in his 1896 book *Shakespeare and his Predecessors*. Boas took the term from the moniker given to the work of the famously gloomy Norwegian playwright Henrik Ibsen, who was writing about difficult social issues and using characters to reflect and give voice to opposing points of view onstage. Boas used 'problem' to describe those plays that previous scholars had struggled to pigeonhole into the three genres of comedy, tragedy and history laid out in the First Folio. There is still some debate over which of Shakespeare's plays really are problematic, but most agree that the three below fit the bill (or rather, *don't* fit the bill, so to speak).

Play	Problem
All's Well that Ends Well	Originally classified as a comedy, and it's true that by the end of the play Helena ends up with her husband, but the fact that Bertram is deeply unlovable makes us worry about her particular 'happily ever after'. It has at its core a debate about the issues of marriage and fidelity.
Measure for Measure	Here's another ambiguous ending that means it's hard to call *Measure for Measure* a true comedy – we never actually 'hear' Isabella's response to the Duke's proposal. Again the play raises questions about the institution of marriage.
Troilus and Cressida	With elements of comedy, tragedy and history, this is one of the most baffling of Shakespeare's plays. It's an acidic attack on the weaknesses of human emotions, and a battle cry against the vagaries of war.

Some critics might add to this list *The Merchant of Venice*, *Antony and Cleopatra*, *Timon of Athens*, *The Winter's Tale* and even *Hamlet*.

The Merchant Of Venice
Love, Money And Justice In The City Of Trade

'Why dost thou whet thy knife so earnestly?' ACT IV, SCENE I

The Merchant of Venice was probably premiered in 1597 and was categorised as a comedy in the First Folio. The qualities that have made it one of Shakespeare's most popular plays – it is thought to have been performed more than any other bar *Hamlet* – have also led some scholars to classify it as a problem play (see page 106). It has strong elements of comedy, romance and indeed tragedy, as well as moments of gruesome high drama and suspense, but a merrily happy ending for almost everyone. The slipperiness of its moral message is evidenced by the fact that it has been used as a tool in the past by both the Nazis (broadcasting a version of it just after Kristallnacht in 1938) and by those seeking tolerance and equality. And we have in Shylock one of the Bard's most controversial characters – a role taken on by the greats: Henry Irving, John Gielgud, Al Pacino, Patrick Stewart and F. Murray Abraham.

PLOT SUMMARY

In Venice, wealthy merchant Antonio complains of melancholy (Act I). His friends tease him about the fact that his money is tied up in ships and trading ventures abroad, but that's not what's making him low. Perhaps it's anxiety about his best friend Bassanio, who has been trying to woo a woman who lives in Belmont. The object of Bassanio's desire is Portia, a beautiful, intelligent, very wealthy heiress, who, despite the obvious favours fortune has bestowed upon her, finds herself trapped in an impossible situation when it comes to choosing a suitor. In the meantime, Bassanio has borrowed money from Antonio to make himself appear worthy of her affections, but he has spent it, and he needs more, 3,000 ducats more, to be precise. We know Antonio's ready money is tied up abroad, but his good name still carries huge weight, so he instructs Bassanio to secure a loan from a moneylender, using Antonio's credit.

In Belmont, meanwhile, the details of Portia's dilemma emerge. Her father has left strict instructions in his will to potential suitors: to win Portia they must first choose from one of three caskets – one gold, one silver, one lead – and whoever finds her portrait inside secures her hand. If they choose incorrectly, they must vow never to bother Portia again or indeed ask any other woman for their hand in marriage, and they will also promise never to tell anyone which casket they have chosen. Portia has no control whatsoever over her choice of future husband, and frankly, as she discloses to her faithful maid Nerissa, the candidates so far have been pretty disappointing. The only man who has piqued her interest is a young man from Venice . . . who goes by the name of Bassanio.

Back in Venice, Bassanio negotiates with Shylock, the Jewish moneylender, who, it becomes clear, hates Antonio with a passion. They have history: Antonio has undercut Shylock's business in the past by offering credit without interest, and Shylock claims that Antonio has offended himself and all his fellow Jews with anti-Semitic insults. Shylock does offer the money though (which ironically enough he himself must borrow from another lender, Tubal), on condition of an unusual bond: if Antonio does not pay back the 3,000 ducats within three months, Shylock is entitled to a pound of Antonio's flesh. Bassanio is appalled and at first attempts to back out of the deal, but Antonio treats the whole thing with laughter, and signs his pact with Shylock.

In Belmont, various suitors prove their worthlessness to Portia (Act II). The pompous Prince of Morocco goes for gold, and the Prince of Arragon, dismissing the lead casket as 'base', chooses silver – their choices are wrong and they both prove themselves arrogant and dismissive of those around them. Portia is relieved, but as the arrival of Bassanio is announced she feels a mounting sense of anxiety – just as Antonio's bond carries a deadly forfeit, so the casket bond is pretty catastrophic for Portia and Bassanio too: if he chooses incorrectly he will leave Belmont forever.

In Venice, Shylock's daughter Jessica laments life in her father's hellish home, and reveals that she has planned to elope with Bassanio's friend Lorenzo, marry him and convert to Christianity. On the night of a masked ball, her father leaves her in charge of his house and his money, little knowing she's about to steal off into the night and rob him not only of her love, but also a good share of his jewels and wealth.

As Bassanio prepares to leave Venice for Belmont there are rumours that Antonio's ships are in trouble. Shylock's reaction to Jessica's elopement is full of fury – directed both at his child and, equally, at the loss of his money. Again, rumours abound that he will take his grief and anger out on Antonio and do his very best to enact the deadly bond.

The three months stipulated in Shylock and Antonio's agreement are nearly at an end (Act III), and as Shylock hears that Antonio's ships are indeed lost he can't help but show his delight. In Belmont, Bassanio has made the correct choice and snared his bride, his friend Gratiano has snagged Nerissa, and with the arrival of Lorenzo and Jessica the stage seems set for a big slushy love-in, but the couples' happiness is cut short with the arrival of a letter from Antonio in Venice, stating that he is in deep trouble: all of his business ventures have failed. Another Venetian, Salerio, gives an even more striking account of Antonio's situation: Shylock has demanded justice, and he wants his pound of flesh no matter what money Antonio repays. Portia insists her husband must return to Venice and do what he can – including using her own wealth – to secure his friend's safety. Portia and Nerissa each give their husbands a ring and make them swear not to give them up at any cost. They leave Lorenzo and Jessica in charge of the house in Belmont, claiming they are travelling to a monastery for a spell of contemplation while their husbands battle it out in the courts of Venice. In fact, Portia, full of gumption, has decided to take matters into her own hands, and will also travel to Venice disguised as a lawyer, with Nerissa as her clerk.

During the trial (Act IV), the Duke, presiding over events, appeals to Shylock's better nature, attempting to reason with him. Shylock shows no compassion, even when offered 36,000 ducats. He wants justice according to the letter of the law and he wants his pound of flesh. As he sharpens his knife ready to take the first cuts, Bassanio and his friends grow increasingly agitated. Portia arrives in disguise as Balthazar, a young lawyer from Padua, and initially she too tries, in a beautiful speech, to persuade Shylock of the virtues of mercy. When he refuses, she emphasises then that the 'strict court of Venice' and its rules must be obeyed, and to the letter. Just as Shylock is about to begin his butchery she intervenes: according to the law, Shylock must take his pound of flesh, and nothing more or less. If even a drop of Christian blood is spilled, he'll have his own forfeit: he'll lose his wealth as well as his life. Of course, faced with these impossible conditions, Shylock refuses, but as he prepares to leave, Portia steps in with further implications of the risk he poses to Christian blood. Since Shylock is a foreigner who has threatened the life of a Venetian, he must divide his wealth between the state and Antonio, and the Duke will decide whether he lives or dies. The Duke shows Shylock mercy, and Antonio insists that Shylock must sign a document stating that on his death, his wealth will go to the newly Christian Jessica and Lorenzo. In a final twist of the knife, Shylock must convert to Christianity too. He leaves a broken man: he has lost everything.

As Antonio and Bassanio leave the court triumphant they are determined to reward the brilliant young lawyer. Portia (as Balthazar) mischievously claims her only payment can be the ring on Bassanio's finger (which she of course has given him). Nerissa demands the same of Gratiano. Bassanio and Gratiano reluctantly agree.

The parties all return to Belmont, where Jessica and Lorenzo are mooning around in the moonlight (Act V). They are delighted when they hear they will inherit Shylock's cash. Portia and Nerissa make their husbands sweat a little, before revealing that they are in fact Balthazar and his clerk, so the ring bond has not truly been broken. Then news arrives that three of Antonio's ships have docked safely – he has been spared his money and his life.

KEY THEMES

Love and Money

BASSANIO

> In Belmont is a lady richly left,
> And she is fair, and (fairer than that word),
> Of wondrous virtues, – sometimes from her eyes
> I did receive fair speechless messages:
> Her name is Portia, nothing undervalu'd
> To Cato's daughter, Brutus' Portia:
> Nor is the wide world ignorant of her worth,
> For the four winds blow in from every coast
> Renownèd suitors, and her sunny locks
> Hang on her temples like a golden fleece;
> Which makes her seat of Belmont Colchos' strond,
> And many Jasons come in quest of her.
> O my Antonio, had I but the means
> To hold a rival place with one of them,
> I have a mind presages me such thrift,
> That I should questionless be fortunate.

(ACT I, SCENE I)

There are many types of love on show in *The Merchant of Venice*: romantic love, brotherly love, Christian love and, of course, the love of money, and throughout there is tension and conflict between them. We have love versus money, friendship versus greed. It's there in the two main locations of the play as well as in the characters – Venice represents trade and commerce, wealth and avarice, whereas Belmont represents peace, love, music and goodwill. The romantic relationship between Portia and Bassanio is central but the speech above, Bassanio's first words about his beloved Portia, demonstrates how much, in this play, economic realities come to invade romance. Bassanio's speech is laden with the language of finance: there is 'rich', 'undervalu'd', 'worth', 'thrift'. He even compares the object of his desire to Jason's Golden Fleece. Like the other Jasons pursuing her, Bassanio is on a quest, but is it a quest for money or love? Bassanio must borrow heavily in order to win the chance to demonstrate the purity of his love for Portia. Is it ever definitive that Bassanio is after Portia's riches or not? And does it matter? In Elizabethan times it was not considered unusual to marry for money.

Shylock is a stock hate figure, the type theatregoers of the time would have recognised as an archetype of evil. He is often held up as a symbol of greed, and is accused by the Christian characters of valuing his ducats more than the human relationships around him. But his reaction to his daughter's disappearance is murky; we're never sure if he's furious about losing her or if he's furious about the money she has taken. So is Shylock only interested in money? He is devastated by the fact that Jessica has sold his beloved wife's ring to buy a pet monkey – he wouldn't have given it up for 'a wilderness of monkeys'. And Bassanio and Gratiano give up their rings – symbols of everlasting love – with only a moment's hesitation. Does this mean they are generous or thoughtless? Ironically, in the key conflict surrounding the pound of flesh, Shylock is ultimately not motivated by money but by revenge – in fact he turns down the vastly inflated sums offered to him by Antonio's friends.

Justice and Mercy

PORTIA
> The quality of mercy is not strain'd,
> It droppeth as the gentle rain from heaven
> Upon the place beneath: it is twice blest;
> It blesseth him that gives and him that takes:
> 'Tis mightiest in the mightiest: it becomes
> The thronèd monarch better than his crown;

His sceptre shows the force of temporal power,
The attribute to awe and majesty,
Wherein doth sit the dread and fear of kings;
But mercy is above this sceptred sway;
It is enthronèd in the hearts of kings,
It is an attribute to God himself;
And earthly power doth then show likest God's
When mercy seasons justice: therefore, Jew,
Though justice be thy plea, consider this,
That in the course of justice, none of us
Should see salvation: we do pray for mercy;
And that same prayer, doth teach us all to render
The deeds of mercy. I have spoke thus much
To mitigate the justice of thy plea,
Which if thou follow, this strict court of Venice
Must needs give sentence 'gainst the merchant there.

SHYLOCK
My deeds upon my head! I crave the law,
The penalty and forfeit of my bond.

(ACT IV, SCENE 1)

Portia's soaring, beautiful words express an explicitly Christian view of justice and mercy. In almost worshipful language, Portia claims mercy is godly,
sent from heaven; it is strongest in the strongest beings, and suits a king even
better than the most ornate crown. Only God can make the final judgement, but by acting mercifully, we become closer to God. In contrast, the
short sharp shock of Shylock's brutal two answering lines expresses a more
Old Testament viewpoint – Shylock wants an eye for an eye and a tooth for
a tooth. But the issue of mercy is a far thornier one in the play than this
conversation might suggest. In Act IV Shylock has already picked apart the
hypocrisy of so-called gentle Christians who are also slave owners – 'You
have among you many a purchas'd slave, / Which (like your asses, and your

dogs and mules) / You use in abject and in slavish parts, / Because you bought them, – shall I say to you, / Let them be free, marry them to your heirs?' How does treating human beings like dogs or asses equate with the tender mercy that Portia describes in such lofty terms? And finally, when Shylock has lost his case and is given over to the justice of the court, do the Duke, Portia and Antonio really exhibit the very quality whose virtues they have been extolling? Portia has secured Antonio's life and fortune, but she demands more, that he 'shall have all justice, – soft no haste! / He shall have nothing but the penalty.' And while Shylock's life is spared, he has lost everything he holds dear. It's a strange kind of mercy for a man who has not committed any actual crime.

KEY SCENE

Aside from being the moment when the play's central theme of mercy is discussed at length, the **courtroom scene** is also one of the most charged and extraordinary in all of Shakespeare's plays. Here is terrible prejudice, extreme violence, pitiless revenge, set against moving friendship, generosity of spirit (and wallet), and dexterous intelligence (from a woman, no less). We know from the start that the court is deeply prejudiced against Shylock – the Duke makes this clear with his opening words about Antonio's opponent: 'A stony adversary, an inhuman wretch'; and Shylock takes a perverse glee in turning down first the staggeringly inflated sum of 36,000 ducats that Antonio's friends offer, and then even the offer of Bassanio's life for his friend's. Shylock's pleasure is evident too when he sharpens his knife, driving Gratiano to low insults, 'damn'd inexecrable dog!'. The tension mounts as the court awards Shylock his pound of flesh and Portia leaves it to the very last minute to save her husband's beloved friend from the jaws of death. The final image of Shylock, a ruined man with no family, fortune or faith, introduces yet another register of emotion in the audience: we have deeply conflicted feelings towards this figure of evil. It's a roller coaster of emotional highs and lows, and courtroom drama at its very best.

KEY SYMBOL

Portia's bond is just as strong as the one that threatens Antonio's life. In line with Shakespeare's interest in depicting interfering parents in his Comedies, her father has left strict instructions in his will that any suitor must choose between **three caskets** made from gold, silver and lead. The gold casket is inscribed with the words: 'Who chooseth me shall gain what many men desire'; silver says: 'Who chooseth me shall get as much as he deserves'; and lead says: 'Who chooseth me must give and hazard all that he hath.' Each suitor's choice symbolically reveals a truth about them, and shows them worthy or unworthy of Portia's hand. The arrogant Prince of Morocco (a man so taken with his own appearance that his opening salvo to Portia is concerned with his own complexion) is dazzled by the gold casket, but finds inside a scroll inscribed with the immortal lines:

> 'All that glisters is not gold,
> Often have you heard that told, –
> Many a man his life hath sold
> But my outside to behold, –
> Gilded tombs do worms infold.'

> (ACT II, SCENE 6)

The Prince of Arragon reasons that gold is an easy choice, and since he's a fine upstanding man, he'll not allow himself to mix with the 'barbarous multitudes'. Silver gives what its selector deserves, and the Prince of Arragon has a pretty high estimation of what he deserves, but he is also met with fairly damning words. His casket's scroll identifies him as an idiot, presenting him with a picture of a fool – his mirror self.

Bassanio chooses lead. He is a smart cookie. He knows that appearances can be deceptive, that 'the world is still deceiv'd with ornament' and that money-grabbing is not a good look. He plumps for unassuming, modest lead and gets his girl.

Elizabethan attitudes to Jews

Shylock

In 1290, King Edward I issued his Edict of Expulsion, expelling between 16,000 and 17,000 Jews from England and banning them from returning, a law which remained in force until 1656, when Oliver Cromwell repealed it. Officially, then, in Renaissance times no Jews lived openly in England. There were, however, some Marranos, Jews of Spanish descent who had been forced to convert to Christianity. The Queen's doctor, Rodrigo Lopez, was a Marrano who met a grisly end: he was hanged, drawn and quartered after being found guilty of attempting to poison the monarch. Jews were still a target of fear and loathing in the sixteenth century, demonised and caricatured, and Christopher Marlowe's play *The Jew of Malta*, performed ten years before *The Merchant of Venice*, would have done little to change public perception, featuring as it does that electrifyingly villainous character Barabas.

Shakespeare's play takes a more nuanced approach. There is endless debate about Shylock: undoubtedly he is the villain of the piece, but he is also the life force and central energy of the play, and there are subtleties and complexities to him too. The loss of his daughter to a Christian man is devastating to him and he eloquently expresses the common humanity between Jews and Christians with this moving speech:

> I am a Jew. Hath not a Jew eyes? hath not a Jew hands, organs, dimensions, senses, affections, passions? fed with the same food, hurt with the same weapons, subject to the same diseases, healed by the same means, warmed and cooled by the same winter and summer, as a Christian is? – if you prick us, do we not bleed? if you tickle us, do we not laugh? if you poison us, do we not die? and if you wrong us, shall we not revenge?

(ACT III, SCENE I)

As always with the Bard, there is no easy answer.

Shakespeare's best minor characters

Crab the dog

It's not all just about the headline roles in Shakespeare's plays. Often less central characters have important functions in moving the plot along, reflecting the main action and peopling the stage with interesting personalities. They even sometimes get the best lines. Rosencrantz and Guildenstern went on to get their own Tom Stoppard play and Falstaff has his own section in this book on page 139. This is a list of our other favourites.

1. **Crab** the dog from *The Two Gentlemen of Verona*

Although a non-speaking part, Crab is regarded by many as the highlight of this early play. 'The sourest-natured dog that lives' belongs to Launce, Proteus's servant. While Proteus and Valentine get carried away on flights of fancy about their great loves, Launce and Valentine's servant, Speed, undercut this high romance with a more prosaic view of life. Launce's descriptions of Crab's misdemeanours – stealing Silvia's food from her plate and pissing under the table – certainly do this, and the master's loyalty to his pet in always taking the blame – 'I have sat in the stocks for puddings he hath stolen' – is sweet to behold.

2. **Macduff** from *Macbeth*

The Thane of Fife is Macbeth's opposite. Despite the fact that Malcolm ends up on the throne, Macduff is the conventional hero of the play. 'Dear Duff' is crucial in the plot: he discovers Duncan's body, rebels with Malcolm, loses his wife and children to the tyrant and finally kills him. Being born by Caesarean section, he fulfils the witches prophecy that 'none of woman born / Shall harm Macbeth'.

3. Nurse from *Romeo and Juliet*

Juliet's nanny since birth, the Nurse is Juliet and Romeo's go-between and a rather silly adult who fails in her responsibility to keep her mistress safe. Her language is both affectionate – 'What, lamb! What, ladybird!' – and bawdy – 'I am the drudge and toil in your delight, / But you shall bear the burden soon at night' – and she is a down-to-earth, entertaining character in the earlier part of the play before lapsing into silence after Juliet's faked death. The close bond between her and her charge is broken after Tybalt's death and Romeo's banishment when she encourages Juliet to get on with life and marry Paris, despite being already married: 'I think you are happy in this second match, / For it excels your first'. She's a slightly darker character than history has remembered her: this betrayal of Juliet could be seen as the event that ultimately leads to her death.

4. Malvolio from *Twelfth Night*

As Olivia tells him to his face, her steward is 'sick of self-love' and tastes 'with a distempered appetite'. Malvolio is a Puritan like many of those who were endeavouring to shut down the theatres in Shakespeare's day. His contempt for the carousing Sir Toby inspires the drunken old knight and Maria the maid to make a fool of him. They trick him into thinking his mistress loves him and has written him a letter asking him to smile a lot and wear cross-gartered yellow stockings – things she actually hates. This letter also has a hidden naughty joke in it to make him appear even more ridiculous. When Malvolio says 'By my life, this is my lady's hand: these be her very C's, her U's and her T's, and thus makes she her great P's', there are a couple of double meanings present: the word 'cut' had the same meaning that our similar archswearword has now and 'p's' of course sounds the same as 'pees'. The joke goes somewhat too far when the conspirators imprison the steward in a dark room and try to make him believe he is mad. Never one for enjoying the riotous Twelfth Night spirit, he ends the play vowing revenge.

5. Jaques from *As You Like It*

Duke Senior's courtier, 'melancholy Jaques', revels in his own misery: 'I can suck melancholy out of a song, / As a weasel sucks eggs.' Not exactly a man of action, he is the cynical fly in the happy soup of Arden and is not interested in the amorous pursuits of the central characters. Fascinated by Touchstone, he sees himself as carrying out some of the functions of a fool: 'Invest me in my motley. Give me leave / To speak my mind, and I will through and through / Cleanse the foul body of th'infected world'. (Court jesters or licensed fools often wore patchwork outfits – motley – and had special licence to criticise their patrons and the court's faults with impunity.) Jaques has one of Shakespeare's most famous speeches, 'All the world's a stage . . .', also known as the Seven Ages of Man speech. However, the message of the speech, that life is pointless and we are helpless in old age, is undercut in the play by the arrival of Orlando's ancient loyal servant Adam who has saved his life. Jaques ends up renouncing the world, and the happy finale of the play, by going to live with Duke Frederick as a hermit.

6. **Puck** from *A Midsummer Night's Dream*

Puck, also known as Robin Goodfellow, is Oberon's fairy jester and the central instigator, mostly at his lord's command, of the action of the confused love plot and Titania and Bottom's enchanted affair. His enjoyment of mischief is clear – 'The wisest aunt, telling the saddest tale, / Sometime for three-foot stool mistaketh me; / Then slip I from her bum, down topples she' – but he also revels in beautiful verse. His 'Now the hungry lion roars . . .' speech is justly famous and his words to the audience end the play: 'If we shadows have offended, / Think but this, and all is mended, / That you have but slumber'd here / While these visions did appear.'

7. **Queen Margaret** from *Henry VI, Parts 1, 2* and *3*, and *Richard III*

Queen Margaret is an extreme character; York calls her 'She-wolf of France, but worse than wolves of France' and refers to her 'tiger's heart wrapp'd in a woman's hide!' Suffolk captures her on the battlefields of France in *Part 1*, and, despite his attraction to her, arranges her marriage to the king, which begins *Part 2*: 'Margaret shall now be queen, and rule the king; / But I will rule both her, the king and realm.' The two start an affair and plot against their rival Gloucester, but Suffolk is exiled and dies at the hands of pirates. Naturally, Margaret then carries his head around with her everywhere. She completely dominates her husband, eventually taking over resistance to the Yorkists and personally stabbing York to death on the battlefield. After her defeat, and the death of her husband and son, she takes on the role of enraged prophetess in *Richard III*. Richard calls her a 'hateful wither'd hag' but Margaret always gives as good as she gets: 'Thou elvish-mark'd, abortive, rooting hog', 'bottled spider', 'poisonous bunchback'd toad'. Her many dreadful curses on her enemies all come true.

8. **Emilia** from *Othello*

Emilia has the misfortune of being Iago's wife. She is also Desdemona's companion and Iago uses their closeness to steal Desdemona's handkerchief and plant it in Cassio's room. He also apparently suspects she has cheated on him with Othello. In this way she inadvertently brings the whole tragedy to fruition. Her values are more pragmatic than Desdemona's and she believes that the same rules in marriage should apply to women and men: 'Then let them use us well: else let them know, / The ills we do, their ills instruct us so.' She lies to Desdemona about not knowing where her handkerchief is, out of obedience to Iago, but exposes him after the murder, which leaves her desperate with grief. Iago seems to have been expecting her to cover for him and stabs her to death for telling the truth.

9. **Paulina** from *The Winter's Tale*

When Leontes goes mad and wreaks destruction on his family, 'that audacious lady' Paulina remains loyal to Hermione and bravely stands up to the king despite him calling her a witch: 'Thy tyranny / Together working with thy jealousies / (Fancies too weak for boys, too green and idle / For girls of nine), O, think what they have done / And then run mad indeed: stark mad!' After she loses her husband to the famous bear (see page 32) she stays with Leontes, persuading him against remarrying. She is then responsible, with a 'lawful' spell (or by bringing her out of hiding now the oracle has been fulfilled), for bringing the statue of Hermione to life to truly fulfil the happy ending and is married off to Camillo as a reward.

10. **Thersites** from *Troilus and Cressida*

Thersites is 'a slave whose gall coins slanders like a mint'. He has a fine turn of disgusting phrase and a sharp eye for stupidity and he takes no nonsense from anyone, calling his boss Ajax 'thou mongrel beef-witted lord!' He sees clearly that the Greek army are fools who 'war for a placket' (petticoat). Luckily for him he is a 'privileged man' in the role of the fool who can speak openly: 'wars and lechery; nothing else holds'.

The Romances

Romance is a nineteenth-century category ascribed to Shakespeare's later comic plays. It does not mean the plays are necessarily 'romantic' in subject, but rather links to the French medieval poetic genre of Romance which was characterised by chivalric concerns, adventures, magic and quests. We're talking more *Don Quixote* than Mills & Boon. Many scholars see the later works as significantly different from the lighter, more straightforward early Comedies and these plays are also sometimes known as the Tragicomedies. *Pericles*, *The Winter's Tale*, *Cymbeline* and *The Tempest* are the core Romances, with *Henry VIII* and *The Two Noble Kinsmen* also sometimes included.

The Romances tend to be more episodic and stylised than the early plays and share themes of loss, reunion and rebirth, redemptive parent–child relationships, emphasis on feminine virtues, and often include elements of tragedy, pastoral and masque (see page 129). They deal with potentially tragic subjects but end happily. The way different genre elements are mixed is exemplified in *Cymbeline*, which was actually categorised as a tragedy in the First Folio, despite its happy ending. It features a British king who rejects his good daughter like King Lear, a jealous husband who is deceived into thinking his wife has cheated on him and decides she deserves death like Othello, a pure woman taken advantage of in her bedchamber like Lucrece, lost children returned to their parents as in *The Winter's Tale*, mistaken identities and a woman dressing as a man as in *Twelfth Night* etc., a king with an ambitious wife like Macbeth, fake poison like Juliet's, the appearance of a classical deity as in *The Tempest*, and Roman soldiers going to battle as in *Julius Caesar* and the other Roman plays.

Critics have ascribed this mash-up of elements to various concerns. Satirical and tragicomic plays grew in popularity in the early 1600s, particularly the work of John Fletcher who collaborated with Shakespeare on *Henry VIII*, *The Two Noble Kinsmen* and *Cardenio*, and would take over from him as playwright for the King's Men. The masque form was also simultaneously being developed by writers like Ben Jonson. In 1608 the King's Men started performing in the indoor theatre at Blackfriars which had been used for performances of Fletcher's work, as well as that of Thomas Middleton and Francis Beaumont, and so had an existing, moneyed, audience with a proven taste for the sophisticated. This theatre also allowed for plays that ranged further in time due to the necessity of act breaks for trimming the candles.

Although the plays end with unity, their bitter-sweet tone does not allow the audience to come away feeling completely comfortable. There is no real contrition in *The Tempest*, beyond Alonso's; Posthumus does not seem worthy of Imogen in *Cymbeline*; and despite the wonderful drama of Hermione's statue coming to life in *The Winter's Tale*, her sufferings, and the deaths of Mamillius and Antigonus, don't feel adequately recompensed by her reunion with Perdita and Leontes. The world of the Romances is hopeful but not perfect.

The Tempest
Power And Magic On An Enchanted Island

The Tempest, ACT I, SCENE 6

The Tempest is thought to have been written in 1611 and it is Shakespeare's most celebrated Romance. There used to be a school of opinion that believed it was also Shakespeare's literary swansong, a farewell to the theatre life which had given him so much, but that he was about to leave forever. People thought Prospero was expressing the playwright's own intentions to give up writing in those captivating words 'But this rough magic / I here abjure'. However, we now know Shakespeare went on to write several more plays.

PLOT SUMMARY

The play begins with a shipwreck (Act I). Unbeknown to the nobles on board, the tempest has been created by someone they know, the magician Prospero. Prospero has lived with his daughter Miranda on an island since his brother Antonio, with the help of Alonso, the Duke of Naples, ousted him as Duke of Milan and cast them adrift in a leaky boat. Thanks to the help of a nobleman called Gonzalo, they survived and landed on the island, along with Prospero's beloved books.

After their arrival, Prospero freed the spirit Ariel who had been imprisoned in a tree by a now-dead Algerian witch called Sycorax. In return for this, Ariel pledged to serve Prospero. Prospero also keeps Sycorax's son, Caliban, as his slave. Caliban hates Prospero and accuses the magician of usurping his island. Prospero was originally benevolently disposed towards Caliban until he tried to rape Miranda.

Alonso, his son Ferdinand, his brother Sebastian, Prospero's brother Antonio, Gonzalo and the butler Stephano and jester Trinculo wash up on the island. They are separated, and when Ariel's music leads Ferdinand to meet Prospero and Miranda, the young people immediately fall in love. This is Prospero's intention but in order to make Ferdinand work for his daughter's affection he pretends not to believe he is the Prince of Naples and imprisons him.

On a different part of the island (Act II), Alonso is convinced that his son has drowned and Gonzalo's efforts to make everyone feel more upbeat fall on deaf ears. When Ariel casts a spell sending everyone except Antonio and Sebastian to sleep, Antonio encourages Sebastian to kill his brother and take his kingdom. Ariel wakes Gonzalo up in time to prevent this. Elsewhere, Caliban initially mistakes Trinculo for one of Prospero's spirits sent to torment him and hides under his cloak, where Trinculo joins him, attempting to shelter from the rain, causing confusion for the drunk Stephano who mistakes them for a strange island creature. Caliban is so impressed with the wine that Stephano shares with him that he decides to worship him and help him take the island from Prospero. Buying someone a drink can be a powerful gesture.

Back at Prospero's home (Act III), Miranda secretly gets engaged to Ferdinand and Prospero hears of Caliban's plot from Ariel. He also takes his revenge on Alonso, Sebastian and Antonio by presenting them with an illusory feast before making it vanish after Ariel has admonished them for their crimes. Alonso then repents his actions. After entertaining himself in this way (Act IV), Prospero agrees to Ferdinand and Miranda's marriage and arranges a masque performed by his spirits to celebrate. He and Ariel then scare Caliban, Stephano and Trinculo away with spirits in the form of hounds. Ariel brings Alonso's group to Prospero who forgives them (Act V). Alonso is glad about Ferdinand and Miranda's marriage and the news that the ship is ready to return them to Italy. Ariel brings along Trinculo, Stephano and Caliban and they are reprimanded. Finally, Prospero agrees to return to rule as Duke of Milan, frees Ariel and leaves the island and

Caliban behind. In the epilogue he tells the audience he has given up magic and only needs their applause to be set free from the spell of the play.

KEY THEMES

Power

PROSPERO

Dull thing, I say so – he, that Caliban
Whom now I keep in service. Thou best knowst
What torment I did find thee in: thy groans
Did make wolves howl and penetrate the breasts
Of ever angry bears. It was a torment
To lay upon the damned, which Sycorax
Could not again undo. It was mine art,
When I arrived and heard thee, that made gape
The pine and let thee out.

ARIEL

I thank thee, master.

PROSPERO

If thou more murmur'st, I will rend an oak
And peg thee in his knotty entrails till
Thou hast howled away twelve winters.

ARIEL

Pardon, master,
I will be correspondent to command
And do my spiriting gently.

(ACT I, SCENE 2)

Different kinds of power are explored in *The Tempest*. The first is political influence, as shown by Antonio and Alonso's usurpation of Prospero's dukedom, and Antonio and Sebastian's plotting against Alonso. This is also reflected in Caliban's plot to take back control of the island from Prospero, but there is more to this challenge than simply a land-grab: Caliban wants both what he sees as rightfully his, and revenge on his oppressor.

Caliban is a victim of Prospero's supernatural power; the magician keeps him in slavery and torments him if he disobeys: 'For this, be sure, tonight thou shalt have cramps, / Side-stitches [. . .] each pinch more stinging / Than bees that made 'em.' Ariel is also kept in servitude by the threat of Prospero's magic, and this magic orchestrates most of the action of the play. Even Prospero's own daughter is controlled by his machinations as well as by the power he has over her through his personal influence and the conventions of the time. The way he engineers the action has encouraged some critics to see Prospero as a representation of an artist creating his work, and in particular the way a writer controls the plots of his characters. Some scholars, pushing interpretation to its logical conclusion, would argue that Prospero is a representation of Shakespeare himself. So the celebratory masque that Prospero puts on for Ferdinand and Miranda, and the extravagant mirage banquet he conjures up for Alonso and his crew, are examples of sorcerer as 'playwright'.

Prospero's power is not seen as unequivocally good, despite the fact that he is the 'hero'. He is a deeply authoritarian father and master. It is worth noting that he lost his political power in part because he neglected his duties in favour of studying the books that gave him his magical power: 'The government I cast upon my brother / And to my state grew stranger, being transported / And rapt in secret studies.' In the end he has to renounce his 'charms' to return to his dukedom.

The Supernatural

CALIBAN
> Be not afeard; the isle is full of noises,
> Sounds and sweet airs that give delight and hurt not.
> Sometimes a thousand twangling instruments

Will hum about mine ears; and sometime voices,
That if I then had waked after long sleep,
Will make me sleep again; and then, in dreaming,
The clouds, methought, would open and show riches
Ready to drop upon me, that when I waked
I cried to dream again.

(ACT III, SCENE 2)

Caliban

The supernatural plays a significant role in *The Tempest*. Prospero's magic is central but the whole setting is enchanted – it's an island stuffed full of spirits and previously inhabited by Sycorax, a witch. Prospero's 'liberal arts' magic is contrasted with the 'mischiefs manifold and sorceries terrible' black magic practised by Sycorax but there doesn't seem to be a clear difference between the uses their supernatural power is put to as portrayed in the play. Prospero's threats to Ariel illustrate this, despite the fact that Prospero's magic comes from academic study, and the implication is that Sycorax's 'earthy' magic is more part of her nature. Shakespeare's audience were far more open to the possible existence of supernatural beings and forces than we are in our scientific and irreligious age. *The Tempest* was performed for King James, patron of Shakespeare's company, who had a particular interest in demonology and witchcraft (see page 237).

Colonisation

CALIBAN
   I must eat my dinner.
   This island's mine, by Sycorax my mother,

Which thou tak'st from me. When thou cam'st first
Thou strok'st me and made much of me; wouldst give me
Water with berries in't, and teach me how
To name the bigger light and how the less
That burn by day and night. And then I loved thee
And show'd thee all the qualities o'th'isle:
The fresh springs, brine pits, barren place and fertile.
Cursed be I that did so! All the charms
Of Sycorax –, toads, beetles, bats – light on you,
For I am all the subjects that you have,
Which first was mine own king, and here you sty me
In this hard rock, whiles you do keep from me
The rest o'th'island.

PROSPERO

Thou most lying slave,
Whom stripes may move, not kindness; I have used thee
(Filth as thou art) with human care and lodged thee
In mine own cell, till thou didst seek to violate
The honour of my child.

(ACT I, SCENE 2)

The theme of colonialism is a rich topic for discussion in *The Tempest*. Prospero did not set out to become a colonist, but has taken over control of the island and instituted his own rules on it. Gonzalo's utopian speech in Act II, Scene 1 is also a reflection on the idea of colonisers creating new societies with different rules. However, it's important to remember that the issues the play raises for a modern audience would not have been the same in Shakespeare's day when European exploration and the British Empire were only just in their infancy: his was an England with no gymkhanas, no treks and certainly no boomerangs. The predominant view of colonisation was that it benefitted the native populations to be 'civilised' and that they were not worthy of the same treatment as sophisticated

Europeans because of their more primitive natures. Prospero appears to follow this opinion in the exchange above, and when he describes Caliban as a 'born devil, on whose nature / Nurture can never stick', but Shakespeare undercuts this by making Caliban such an interesting and complex character. He speaks some of the most eloquent poetry in the play, regains his island in the end, and comes across more sympathetically than Stephano and Trinculo in their scenes together, and yet he is also an attempted rapist and murderer, whose mother is a witch. He's not exactly perfect son-in-law material.

KEY SCENE

The **masque scene** (Act IV, Scene 1) sees Prospero orchestrating a celebration of Ferdinand and Miranda's betrothal – 'some vanity of mine art'. In it various spirits of the island, under Ariel's direction, act out an encounter between three ancient Greek goddesses – Iris, Ceres and Juno – who offer their good wishes to the happy couple and put on a show of dancing nymphs. It is this masque that prompts Prospero to say the famous lines 'We are such stuff / As dreams are made on, and our little life / Is rounded with a sleep.'

Mask worn by ladies at the time of James I

A masque was a specific form of entertainment played out at court for the monarch, and in noble houses, which was very popular in Elizabethan and Jacobean times. Masques were essentially stylised short plays involving tableaux, dancing, music, mime and elaborate costumes, usually including classical gods or allegorical virtues. They were performed at celebrations such as weddings and feast days, often just before a banquet. Sir Philip Sidney and Ben Jonson both wrote masques for court. Masques were different from normal theatrical productions, not just in their style, but also because of their elaborate scenery and the fact that aristocratic women could perform in them.

KEY SYMBOL

Shakespeare uses **water** imagery throughout *The Tempest*, right from the opening scene of the 'wild waters' that give the play its title. Different forms of water including tears, dew, rain, frost and the 'filthy-mantled pool' Caliban wades through with his friends are mentioned, but the most important aspect is the sea. Prospero and Miranda are left to its mercy before the play starts and Prospero uses it to wreak his revenge by shipwrecking his enemies in the storm. As a direct product of his magic, the stormy sea is generally seen as a symbol of Prospero's power as well as of the vulnerability of ordinary humans in relation to nature and supernatural forces. Ariel's speech suggesting that Alonso has drowned is one of Shakespeare's most famous passages.

ARIEL
> Full fathom five thy father lies,
> Of his bones are coral made;
> Those are pearls that were his eyes:
> Nothing of him that doth fade
> But doth suffer a sea-change
> Into something rich and strange.
> Sea-nymphs hourly ring his knell.

> (ACT I, SCENE 2)

The word 'drown' recurs many times. Ferdinand and Alonso both believe the other to be drowned which leads Alonso to decide to 'seek him deeper than e'er plummet sounded / And with him there lie mudded', words which are echoed in Prospero's speech after he decides to renounce his magic to return to Milan: 'deeper than did ever plummet sound / I'll drown my book.'

The critical response to *The Tempest*

Like all plays, *The Tempest* disappeared from view during the English Civil War (1642–51) and republican Commonwealth (1649–60). It was rediscovered in 1667 when playwright and soon-to-be Poet Laureate John Dryden and the playwright William Davenant rewrote it as a more straightforward comedy with additional characters called *The Tempest: or, the Enchanted Island*. It wasn't until the nineteenth century that the original came back into vogue, although it was still seen predominantly as an opportunity for spectacle and musical entertainment. In more recent times the **post-colonialist** approach has been the most popular, investigating Prospero's role as coloniser and Caliban's and Ariel's different responses to servitude and subjugation. Caliban can be viewed contrastingly either as a rebel against oppression or as a character who is intrinsically conditioned to serve, as evidenced by his wish to make Stephano his new master. Ariel is cast as both a collaborator and a more canny operator in a colonised world. Religious and psychoanalytic interpretations have also seen Prospero as representing one part of a trinity – either as God (the island being the Garden of Eden) with Miranda as Daughter and Ariel as Spirit, or as Ego with Caliban as Id and Ariel as Superego. Feminist critics have also been interested in the play as Miranda is the sole female character and seems entirely in thrall to the patriarchal control embodied in Prospero.

Inspired by *The Tempest*

You might like to read, watch, look at, listen to and experience some of the following works of art that have been inspired by *The Tempest*. These other artists' responses illuminate or question specific aspects of the play that encourage a richer interpretation.

- ○ W. H. Auden's poem 'The Sea and the Mirror'
- ○ Peter Greenaway's film *Prospero's Books*
- ○ William Hogarth's painting *A Scene from the Tempest*
- ○ Pyotr Tchaikovsky's *The Tempest*, Symphonic Fantasia after Shakespeare, Op. 18

- ○ Fred M. Wilcox's film *Forbidden Planet*

- ○ Robert Browning's poem 'Caliban on Setebos'

- ○ Marianne Faithfull's song 'Full Fathom Five'

- ○ Marina Warner's novel *Indigo*

- ○ Aimé Césaire's play *A Tempest*

- ○ Ralph Vaughan Williams's choral composition 'Full Fathom Five' from *Three Shakespeare Songs*

- ○ Percy Bysshe Shelley's poem 'With a Guitar, to Jane'

THE HISTORIES

'Uneasy lies the head that wears a crown'
The history plays

The coat of arms of Richard III

Most of Shakespeare's plays are, strictly speaking, history plays: discussion of contemporary politics was banned onstage so the past was a safer place to be. It's also true to say that the history plays include aspects of both tragedy and comedy. However, the ten works dealing with English history are the ones usually referred to as the Histories: *King John, Richard II, Henry IV, Parts 1* and *2, Henry V, Henry VI, Parts 1, 2* and *3, Richard III* and *Henry VIII*. The major plays in this sequence are the two Wars of the Roses tetralogies which follow the consecutive reigns of Kings Richard II to Richard III (poor old Kings Edward IV and V don't get their own plays although they feature in *Richard III*). Confusingly, Shakespeare wrote about the later kings first (*Henry VI, Parts 2, 3, 1* and *Richard III*) so this is called the First Tetralogy. The Second Tetralogy (*Richard II, Henry IV, Parts 1, 2* and *Henry V*) is also, less cumbersomely, known as the Henriad. For how these rulers are related, and their connections to Elizabeth I and James I, see the family tree on page viii.

The Hundred Years War and The Wars of the Roses

The Hundred Years War (1337–1453) was a long-running series of conflicts between England and France over territory and claims to the French throne. The battles which take place in *Henry V* and *Henry VI*, including Agincourt and the interventions of Joan of Arc, are part of the Hundred Years War.

The Wars of the Roses (1455–85) were the result of competing claims to the throne from the descendants of Edward III. The descendants of his sons John of Gaunt, Duke of Lancaster, and Edmund of Langley, Duke of York, battled against each other for the Crown up until the Lancastrian Henry

VII unified the two houses by marrying Elizabeth of York, beginning the Tudor dynasty which ended with Elizabeth I. The symbol of the house of Lancaster was a red rose and the symbol of the house of York was a white rose, hence the wars' moniker. Henry VII amalgamated these into the Tudor rose.

Tudor rose

Shakespeare sets most of the action of the history plays in the lofty and elaborately mannered world of the court, but he often includes scenes with ordinary common people reflecting on the main action as a deliberate counterpoint. This is most pronounced in the *Henry IV* and *Henry V* plays where Falstaff's 'court' at the Boar's Head Tavern rubs up against the royal court through Falstaff's relationship with Prince Hal.

The action of these plays would have felt topical to an Elizabethan audience, who knew exactly how this history connected to their own lives. Shakespeare's treatment of the divine right of kings and the justification, and consequences, of rebellion are particularly interesting in the light of the way the Tudors, and then Stuarts, came to the throne. The plays also analyse the workings of political power and the contrast between a medieval feudal world and an emerging Machiavellian era with an acute eye. They were of course subject to censorship, and the players were patronised by the royal court, so there was a careful line to be trod with subject matter that still had the potential to be controversial. For example, *Henry VIII*, written with John Fletcher in 1613, judiciously ends with the celebration of the birth of Elizabeth, and doesn't mention anything about the execution of her mother, the declaration of her illegitimacy or the existence of her four subsequent stepmothers. A wise move considering how recent these events were for the audience and King James and how easily portraying them could have landed Shakespeare in hot water.

The plays' changing titles

The titles we use for Shakespeare's plays predominantly come from the First Folio. Many have slightly longer names there which we abbreviate, such as *The Lamentable Tragedy of Titus Andronicus*; *The Life of Timon of Athens* and *Cymbeline, King of Britain*. However, several have alternative titles recorded in different contemporary documents. For example, *Henry VIII* appears to have been called *All is True*. *Henry VI, Part 2* was first published under the snappy title *The First part of the Contention betwixt the two famous Houses of Yorke and Lancaster, with the death of the good Duke Humphrey: And the banishment and death of the Duke of Suffolke, and the Tragicall end of the*

proud Cardinall of Winchester, with the notable Rebellion of Jacke Cade: And the Duke of Yorkes first claime vnto the Crowne. *Henry VI, Part 3* was called *The True Tragedie of Richard Duke of Yorke, and the death of good King Henrie the Sixt, with the Whole Contention betweene the two Houses Lancaster and Yorke* and *Richard III* was first published as *The tragedy of King Richard the third. Containing, his treacherous plots against his brother Clarence: the pittiefull murther of his innocent nephewes: his tyrannicall usurpation: with the whole course of his detested life, and most deserved death*, which doesn't leave much room for suspense.

The Chronicles of England, Scotland and Ireland

One of Shakespeare's key sources was a history book written, in part, by Raphael Holinshed (1529–80), first published in 1577 and reissued in 1587, a couple of years before Shakespeare wrote his first history play, *Henry VI, Part 2*. Shakespeare used *The Chronicles of England, Scotland and Ireland* as the basis for all ten of his history plays, as well as for *Macbeth*, *King Lear* and *Cymbeline*. Holinshed usually gets the credit for the full book, which was actually neither his conception nor solely his work.

The printer and publisher Reyner Wolfe came up with the idea of creating the first continuous history of all known nations and he hired Holinshed to put

it together. When Wolfe died the project narrowed to focus on the British Isles. Holinshed wrote the part called 'The History of England'; William Harrison wrote 'The Description of England'. 'The Description of Ireland' was written by Richard Stanyhurst and Edmund Campion (more famous for later becoming a Catholic saint and martyr after he was hanged, drawn and quartered for sedition against Elizabeth). 'The History of Scotland', 'The Description of Scotland' and 'The History of Ireland' were translations of existing accounts. The Irish sections were censored due to the sensitivity of the Queen on this subject (see page 150).

Shakespeare worked Holinshed's material into his own gold: for example, he changed the description of the witches in *Macbeth* from fairies to those 'secret, black and midnight hags' we know so well, and he also made Banquo a hero where previously he was Macbeth's accomplice. This handy alteration paved the way for the scene where Banquo's descendants are seen to stretch down as Scottish kings through the ages to, it is assumed, the Scottish king the play was written for, James I.

The characters in the history tetralogies

You'll note that the same names and titles are used again and again in the plays so you might find it helpful to refer to the family tree on page viii to help you keep your Gloucesters and Yorks in order. Looking at the family tree, it's also clear to see just how possible a bid for the Crown was for many of the participants in these dramas. NB: the family tree should not be used for your history homework – it omits people who are not characters in the plays or part of the line of succession to Elizabeth and James, and uses the names Shakespeare gives his characters. It's also worth noting that in his *Henry IV* and *Henry VI* plays Shakespeare sometimes changes characters' ages and conflates different historical figures into one character, such as the Edmund Mortimers and the Earls of Somerset.

Falstaff

Sir John Fastaff is widely considered Shakespeare's greatest comic character. He appears in *Henry IV, Part 1*, *The Merry Wives of Windsor* and *Henry IV, Part 2*, and has an offstage role in *Henry V*. He is larger than life in every way, a drunken coward, a deceitful, yet charming and vital, personality. He first appears as Prince Harry's dearest companion in his irresponsible drinking and carousing days, an idyll that cannot last as the prince takes on greater state responsibilities.

Theatrical tradition from the eighteenth century, lacking any evidence, has it that Queen Elizabeth enjoyed Sir John so much in *Henry IV, Part 1* that she gave Shakespeare a fortnight to write a new play about him: *The Merry Wives of Windsor*. In this play Falstaff's pursuit of sex ends up with him being terrorised and pinched by children dressed as fairies in a wood. However, here his humiliation is carried out in a relatively friendly way and he is invited to the wedding feast that ends the play. *Henry IV, Part 2* does not end so well for him.

Despite Hal's indulgence of him, and his false boast to have killed Hotspur in combat in *Part 1*, *Part 2* sees the old rogue's fortunes decline. On the death of his father, the new king publicly renounces Falstaff as a bad influence. Their substitute father–son relationship has been replaced with Hal's new devotion to his kingdom, personified by the Lord Chief Justice. Hal essentially issues a restraining order keeping Sir John ten miles away from him at all times. Despite the farcical nature of Falstaff's character this scene is powerfully moving: Sir John's 'God save thee, my sweet boy!' is met by the new king's 'I know thee not, old man. Fall to thy prayers. / How ill white hairs becomes a fool and jester! [. . .] Presume not that I am the thing I was'. This climax to the play shows Hal choosing order over chaos as befits royalty, but the subversive attraction of Sir John's amoral, pleasure-seeking existence remains. In *Henry V*, we learn that Falstaff has died, no doubt of his own excesses but also of grief at the loss of his friendship: the Hostess says the 'king has killed his heart'.

Falstaff has many origins. He is a version of the Vice role familiar from morality plays (see page 45) and also of the Plautine stock character of the *miles gloriosus*, or boastful soldier (see page 163). Scholars believe that he was originally called Sir John Oldcastle after a real soldier, but that the Lord Chamberlain, who was related to Oldcastle, asked for the name to be changed. This is why the Epilogue to *Henry IV, Part 2* says: 'Falstaff shall die of a sweat, unless already a be killed with your hard opinions; for Oldcastle died a martyr, and this is not the man.'

Falstaff has captured the world's affection and imagination as a quintessentially English comic creation and inspired artists as wide-ranging as Orson Welles, Giuseppe Verdi, Edward Elgar, Ralph Vaughan Williams and Gus Van Sant.

Witty Words from Sir John

'The better part of valour is discretion, in the which better part I have sav'd my life.' *Henry IV, Part 1*

'If sack and sugar be a fault, God help the wicked.' *Henry IV, Part 1.* (Sack is sweet wine)

'Banish plump Jack, and banish all the world.' *Henry IV, Part 1*

'Can honour set to a leg? No. Or an arm? No. Or take away the grief of a wound? No. Honour hath no skill in surgery, then? No. What is honour? A word.' *Henry IV, Part 1*

'you may know by my size that I have a kind of alacrity in sinking' *The Merry Wives of Windsor*

'As good luck would have it . . .' *The Merry Wives of Windsor*

'I am not only witty in myself, but the cause that wit is in other men.' *Henry IV, Part 2*

'it was always yet the trick of our English nation, if they have a good thing, to make it too common.' *Henry IV, Part 2*

'I were better to be eaten to death with a rust than to be scoured to nothing with perpetual motion.' *Henry IV, Part 2*

'A good wit will make use of any thing; I will turn diseases to commodity.' *Henry IV, Part 2*

Richard II
Identity And The 'Hollow Crown'

Richard III

Richard II was probably written between 1595 and 1597, when Shakespeare was in his early thirties. As with most of his history plays, Raphael Holinshed's *Chronicles* provided Shakespeare's primary source material, although the play covers only the final tumultuous two years of the king's life. Richard II is often referred to as a poet king who loses his crown, largely due to his own errors, to the more pragmatic Bolingbroke. His beautiful introspective speeches are seen as prefiguring the amazing soliloquies of Hamlet. Bolingbroke goes on to become Henry IV and title role of the following two plays, *Henry IV, Part I* and *Henry IV, Part 2*. He is also the father of Henry V.

PLOT SUMMARY

Fittingly for a play about a two-sided conflict, *Richard II* begins (Act I) with a humdinger of an argument. King Richard's cousin, Henry Bolingbroke, Duke of Hereford, accuses Thomas Mowbray, Duke of Norfolk, of various crimes, including murdering the Duke of Gloucester, one of the king's uncles. This is a touch awkward for the king as Richard was in fact behind the murder. He prevents the two nobles from fighting a duel and banishes both, much to the sadness of Bolingbroke's father (and another uncle of

Richard's), John of Gaunt. Richard is not best pleased by how many commoners turn out to wish Bolingbroke well on his way into exile, and regards
them with disdain, but is cheered at least by the news that Gaunt is on his
deathbed.

Gaunt is heartbroken about the way that Richard is ruining his country
(Act II), and he also criticises the king to his face about his spendthrift ways,
his unfair taxes, his susceptibility to flatterers and his involvement in
Gloucester's death. Gaunt passes away soon after his advice is met with
hostility, and Richard seizes his lands. Already, abroad, Bolingbroke is plotting to return with his supporters and sort things out, and when Richard
leaves the country to put down a rebellion in Ireland, he lands in the north
and wins the support of many nobles.

Bolingbroke sweeps through the country gathering Richard's former
allies to his cause and executing his favourites (Act III). When Richard
returns from Ireland he initially believes his sacred status as king will
keep him safe but as the bad news floods in he turns to despair. Richard
and Bolingbroke meet at Flint Castle in Wales, and Bolingbroke claims
he is only after his inheritance but also insists that Richard come with
him to London. Once there, Richard agrees to adopt Bolingbroke as
his heir and abdicates, amid prophecies of civil war (Act IV). Richard
is taken to Pomfret Castle in Yorkshire and Bolingbroke immediately
faces an assassination plot from one of Richard's loyal nobles (Act V).
Stirring up passions by discussing the ongoing threat Richard poses, he
inspires one of his followers, Exton, to murder the ex-king. When Richard's body is brought to court, Bolingbroke is faced with conflicting emo-
tions and the realisation that he has been involved in something unholy.
How this will all work out for him is explored in the sequels, *Henry IV,
Parts 1* and *2*.

KEY THEMES

Identity and Kingship

RICHARD

> No lord of thine, thou haught insulting man;
> Nor no man's lord; I have no name, no title;
> No, not that name was given me at the font,
> But 'tis usurp'd. Alack the heavy day,
> That I have worn so many winters out,
> And know not now what name to call myself!
> O that I were a mockery king of snow,
> Standing before the sun of Bolingbroke,
> To melt myself away in water-drops!
> Good king, great king, and yet not greatly good,
> And if my word be sterling yet in England,
> Let it command a mirror hither straight,
> That it may show me what a face I have,
> Since it is bankrupt of his majesty.

(ACT IV, SCENE I)

This is part of the famous deposition scene, where Bolingbroke stage-manages Richard's abdication in his favour. Richard's speech makes it clear that his sense of self is completely bound up in his role as king. He has been monarch since he was ten years old and spends much of the play believing that despite Bolingbroke's rebellion this title could never be taken from him as it is his by divine right, decreed by God (see page 148). But he has recently come to the realisation that he is not invulnerable: 'For you have but mistook me all this while. / I live with bread like you, feel want, / Taste grief, need friends – subjected thus, / How can you say to me, I am a king?' This is a shock for a king who has shown great contempt for both his ordinary subjects and his nobles and family members. They have been alienated by his unpopular policies of taxation, keeping favourites and, of course, somewhat churlishly having his uncle murdered and his cousin's lands appropriated. However, Richard still believes he is ruler by God's will and cannot see the mistakes that have caused him to lose his crown, referring to himself as an innocent tragic Christlike figure and to those around him as Judases and Pilates. He also imagines his place in history and literature: 'For God's sake, let us sit upon the ground / And tell sad stories of the death of kings'; 'Tell thou the lamentable tale of me / And send the hearers weeping to their beds'. At the end of the play, Richard's sense of self seems completely unstable: 'Thus play I in one person many people, / And none contented. Sometimes am I king; / Then treasons make me wish myself a beggar, [. . .] and by and by / Think that I am unking'd by Bolingbroke, / And straight am nothing. But whate'er I be, / Nor I nor any man that but man is / With nothing shall be pleas'd, till he be eas'd / With being nothing.' But in death he becomes sure of himself again: 'Exton, thy fierce hand / Hath with the king's blood stain'd the king's own land.'

It is worth noting that names often shift in the play, just as loyalties and fortunes change. Several of the characters change name and title; the Duke of Aumerle is demoted to Rutland and most importantly Bolingbroke is referred to initially as Hereford and later insists on his title of Duke of Lancaster before finally becoming king.

Blood

DUCHESS OF GLOUCESTER
 Finds brotherhood in thee no sharper spur?
 Hath love in thy old blood no living fire?
 Edward's seven sons, whereof thyself art one,
 Were as seven vials of his sacred blood,
 Or seven fair branches springing from one root.
 Some of those seven are dried by nature's course,
 Some of those branches by the Destinies cut;
 But Thomas, my dear lord, my life, my Gloucester,

One vial full of Edward's sacred blood,
One flourishing branch of his most royal root,
Is crack'd, and all the precious liquor spilt,
Is hack'd down, and his summer leaves all faded,
By envy's hand and murder's bloody axe.
Ah, Gaunt, his blood was thine!

(ACT I, SCENE 2)

The theme of blood appears with different emphases in different parts of the play. One use in the speech above refers to the literal blood that has been spilled by Richard in murdering Gloucester. It is also used literally in prophecies of the civil war that Richard's own murder will unleash: 'But ere the crown he looks for live in peace, / Ten thousand bloody crowns of mothers' sons / Shall ill become the flower of England's face, / Change the complexion of her maid-pale peace / To scarlet indignation and bedew / Her pastures' grass with faithful English blood.'

Metaphorically in the Duchess's speech blood indicates the family bonds that come under such stress in the play. (The family tree on page viii will show you how closely related most of the main characters are.) Richard kills his uncle Gloucester and disrespects his uncles John of Gaunt and York, before being usurped by his cousin Bolingbroke. Family at this level of society means politics. Shakespeare emphasises the importance of family loyalties in the parallel scenes of sons being spared severe punishment by the king on account of their parents: Bolingbroke and Gaunt at the start of the play and Aumerle and his parents at the end. The father–son pairing of Northumberland and Harry Percy will become significant in the sequels to this play, *Henry IV, Parts 1* and *2*, and the absent, wayward son of Bolingbroke – 'Can no man tell me of my unthrifty son?' – will become important in these plays and central to the last play of the tetralogy as Henry V.

Hypocrisy

BOLINGBROKE

    Bring forth these men.
    Bushy and Greene, I will not vex your souls,
    Since presently your souls must part your bodies,
    With too much urging your pernicious lives,
    For 'twere no charity; yet, to wash your blood
    From off my hands, here in the view of men
    I will unfold some causes of your deaths.
    You have misled a prince, a royal king,
    A happy gentleman in blood and lineaments,
    By you unhappied and disfigured clean . . .

      (ACT III, SCENE I)

Another theme of *Richard II* is hypocrisy. In the speech above Bolingbroke has arrived back from exile with an army and is busy gathering nobles to his cause, and about to execute those who oppose him. He pretends to Richard's favourites, Bushy and Greene, that his intention is simply to free the king from their bad influence whereas it seems fairly obvious that he wants to take the crown. It is also hypocritical of Richard to object to Bolingbroke's attempt on the crown after his unfair usurpation of Bolingbroke's lands and his murder of his own uncle.

Richard II is a very poetic play, containing more poetry than any of Shakespeare's other dramas. It is full of high-flown language, extended metaphors, repeated symbols and formal verse, including many rhyming couplets. This decorous language draws attention to how words can be used to conceal true intentions and create false impressions. It is interesting that Richard uses words with more and more majesty as his political power wanes.

KEY SCENE

The **deposition scene** (Act IV, Scene 1) is the most charged moment in *Richard II*. It takes up the whole of Act IV and is full of tension and argument. It begins with Bolingbroke attempting to uncover who is really responsible for Gloucester's murder. This is interrupted by news that Richard has agreed to renounce the crown. The Bishop of Carlisle, who supports Richard's divine right to the throne, objects – 'My Lord of Herford here, whom you call king, / Is a foul traitor to proud Herford's king: / And if you crown him, let me prophesy – / The blood of English shall manure the ground' – and is promptly arrested for treason. Richard is then brought in and takes centre stage musing upon the treachery that has brought him to this position and his grief at losing his sacred status. Bolingbroke plainly asks him if he resigns the crown and Richard answers him with elaborate, ironic monologues before admitting 'With mine own tears I wash away my balm, / With mine own hands I give away my crown, / With mine own tongue deny my sacred state, / With mine own breath release all duteous oaths'. However, he baulks at reading the list of crimes he is asked to agree make him unfit for office. In a final theatrical flourish he calls for a looking glass and says: 'was this the face / That like the sun did make beholders wink? / Is this the face which fac'd so many follies, / That was at last out-fac'd by Bolingbroke? / A brittle glory shineth in this face; / As brittle as the glory is the face', before smashing the mirror. Although Bolingbroke then proceeds to set his coronation date the scene ends with Aumerle beginning to conspire against him in Richard's favour. Overall, this episode gives a vivid sense of the court in turmoil and the fragility of Bolingbroke's position. It also makes crystal clear the difference between the plain-speaking Bolingbroke and the eloquent, self-dramatising Richard.

KEY SYMBOLS

The central symbol of the play is the '**hollow crown**' which is a metonym for rule over the kingdom of England. There is wordplay around the idea of the crown meaning the role of king, an item of circular headgear and the top of a head. Gaunt tells Richard 'A thousand flatterers sit within thy crown', Northumberland wants to 'Redeem from broking pawn the blemish'd crown', and Richard sees it as a 'deep well' and as something he is married to, indicating the sacred bond he feels to his position. The power struggle between Richard and Bolingbroke is most vividly portrayed in the deposition scene where they both hold on to the physical crown: 'Here, cousin, seize the crown'.

The image of the **sun** is also repeated. First with reference to Richard, 'the blushing discontented sun', and then to Bolingbroke, 'O, that I were a mockery king of snow, / Standing before the sun of Bolingbroke'. Bolingbroke is also often associated with images of **height** – 'High stomach'd', 'How high a pitch his resolution soars!' – illustrating his ambition. This is physically enacted in the scene at Flint Castle (Act III, Scene 3) where Richard is forced to descend from the battlements to Bolingbroke, showing the shift in power between the two men.

The divine right of kings

Richard II is much concerned with whether the deposition of an anointed king can ever be justified. Richard II was the last English monarch to have inherited the throne in a direct line from William the Conqueror so Bolingbroke's usurpation is an extremely controversial act. In medieval times, when the play is set, and in Elizabethan times, when it was written, it was believed by many that God chose kings and queens to be His deputies on earth and removing them was blasphemous – only God could judge a bad king. The Bishop of Carlisle expounds on this in the play and Richard certainly believes it to be true: 'Not all the water in the rough rude sea / Can wash the balm off from an anointed king; / The breath of worldly men cannot depose / The deputy elected by the Lord'. The sanctity of Richard's position explains why at first the rebels say that they simply want to remove his bad advisers, and that Bolingbroke only wants his inheritance. Even in the deposition scene, Richard is made to apparently voluntarily accept Bolingbroke as his replacement, and is encouraged to read out reasons why he is unfit to hold office.

At various points different nobles discuss how bad Richard is at his job: 'The commons hath he pill'd with grievous taxes, / And quite lost their hearts: the nobles hath he fined / For ancient quarrels, and quite lost their hearts'; 'That England, that was wont to conquer others, / Hath made a shameful conquest of itself.' The garden scene (Act III, Scene 4) shows that the common people also feel he mismanages the kingdom, with his 'caterpillar' favourites. Bolingbroke is considered by many of the characters to have a personality more suited to kingship: he is less vain, more martial, more careful to curry favour with his subjects – 'Off goes his bonnet to an oyster-wench' – and more politically astute. However, he doesn't seem to have the spiritual connection to the role and to the country that Richard does: 'Feed not thy sovereign's foe, my gentle earth'. It is telling that where Richard's entrances are marked with flourishes (trumpet blasts signifying a royal arrival or departure) in the stage directions, Bolingbroke's are not, until the final scene, when Richard is dead.

Bolingbroke has a more pragmatic view of affairs and refers to human law rather than divine law in justifying himself. His father tells Richard 'Thy state of law is bondslave to the law', meaning that Richard is king thanks to the law of heredity that allowed him to inherit the throne from his grandfather (as his father died young). This same law allows Bolingbroke to pursue the inheritance that Richard stole from him, and casts the action in a different light: 'If that my cousin king be King in England / It must be granted I am Duke of Lancaster'.

Watch out for this theme in other plays: *Hamlet*, *Julius Caesar*, *Macbeth* and *Richard III* are all influenced by the idea of the divine right of kings as well.

The Earl of Essex and *Richard II* as incitement to rebellion

The dangerous politics of *Richard II* bled into real life in 1601 when Shakespeare's company was employed by supporters of the Earl of Essex to perform it, for a premium fee, the afternoon before they mounted a rebellion against Queen Elizabeth.

Born in 1565, the glamorous second Earl of Essex, Robert Devereux, had impeccable connections – his great-grandmother Mary Boleyn was the sister of Anne, the Queen's mother. He arrived at court in 1584 and due to a combination of deadly good looks and a silvery tongue on matters of courtly love, he soon became a firm favourite of Elizabeth's. But he was not a man afraid to speak his mind, and his increasing bad manners and hot temper made his position at times tenuous – Elizabeth is said to have boxed his ears

after a particularly bad episode, an action that so enraged him that he drew his sword on her. Amazingly he wasn't immediately thrown in the Tower, which must be an indication of how highly regarded he was in the Queen's eyes. Elizabeth was, however, displeased when he married Frances Walsingham without first seeking her permission. (Frances was herself no wallflower when it came to social connections – she was the daughter of Francis Walsingham, the Queen's spymaster, and the widow of the legendary poet Sir Philip Sidney.)

Essex was a poet himself and a keen patron of the arts, and he seems to have had a penchant for using literature as a kind of weapon. Before his fatal *Richard II*-themed rebellion he wrote a poem, 'Muses no more but mazes', as an attack on Sir Walter Raleigh, who was at that point supplanting him in the Queen's affections

He apparently commissioned the 1601 performance of *Richard II* in the hope that the subject matter would rouse Londoners to support his rebellion against the court. He was under house arrest at the time due to a serious faux pas committed in 1599. He had come back from Ireland, where the Queen had sent him to put down a revolt, without permission. On his return, throwing all proper respect to the wind, he had burst into her bedchamber before she was properly dressed, leading to his arrest and disgrace. Blaming Elizabeth's advisers for his loss of favour, his insurrection was apparently intended to remove them and restore him to her inner circle.

He and his followers' plans failed dramatically and they were executed for treason not long afterwards, Essex gaining the dubious honour of becoming the last person to be beheaded at the Tower of London.

Some critics think the deposition scene didn't appear in some quarto versions of the play because it was considered politically incendiary to perform the usurpation of a monarch in the current political climate. Like Richard, Elizabeth had no heir, relied on favourite advisers, was waging a war in Ireland and had imposed unpopular taxation on her people. In a conversation with William Lambarde, the Keeper of the Records of the Tower of London, she is supposed to have said of the play: 'I am Richard II, know ye not that?'

Henry V
Leadership, Patriotism And War
On The Vasty Fields Of France

'For yet a many of your horsemen peer / And gallop o'er the field.' ACT IV,
SCENE 7

If asked to pick an example of a heroic king from history, many people will
instantly imagine Henry V inspiring his troops at Agincourt in 1415. Shakespeare's play was a significant factor in creating this image of a man who
seems to epitomise everything a warrior leader should be. It is the final part
of his Second History Tetralogy, which explores the nature of kingship,
beginning with Richard II's loss of his crown to Henry's father, Henry IV.
As with the other history plays, Holinshed's *Chronicles* were Shakespeare's
primary sources, but there were also other biographies of this popular monarch in circulation. The play was written in 1599 and its patriotic spirit
reflects the feelings of a nation at war with Ireland, and still under threat of
Armada invasions from Spain.

PLOT SUMMARY

A character called the Chorus introduces the play and comments on the
action throughout. The first scene sees the Archbishop of Canterbury
describe how Henry V has turned into a splendid ruler, despite the wayward-
ness of his youthful days as Prince Harry (Act I). In order to divert attention

from a bill to reduce the clergy's wealth, Canterbury tells the king that, under English inheritance law, he is the rightful ruler of France. When the French ambassador delivers a scornful gift of tennis balls – of which more later – from the dauphin (the French crown prince) in response to Henry's claims to French territory, Henry is roused to anger and vows to invade.

Henry's old friends from the Boar's Head Tavern in Eastcheap prepare to join the army to sail to France (Act II). They are Pistol, Bardolph, Nym and a youngster known as the Boy. Henry's closest former carousing partner from his wild days, Falstaff, dies in bed, apparently heartbroken by the king's rejection of him in favour of a sober new life of responsibility. In Southampton, where ships are ready to sail to France, Henry discovers a plot on his life by another of his friends, the noble Lord Scroop, along with the Earl of Cambridge and Sir Thomas Grey. He has the traitors executed. In France, King Charles is nervous about Henry's attack but his son the dauphin is still scornful.

Henry begins his action in France by besieging the city of Harfleur (Act III), despite the fact that King Charles has offered him some dukedoms and his daughter Katherine's hand in marriage as a compromise. Pistol, Nym and the Boy are somewhat reluctant to get involved in the fighting until the Welsh captain Fluellen scolds them. Fluellen then discusses tactics with the English captain, Gower, the Scottish captain, Jamy, and the Irish captain, Macmorris. Henry's threats to the governor of Harfleur succeed in achieving the city's surrender and the king decides to rest there for the night before taking his sick and weary army to Calais.

At the French palace, Princess Katherine asks her maid to help her learn English and King Charles encourages his nobles to raise more troops to defend the country's honour. The French nobles enjoy ridiculing the English and are confident that their greater numbers will win the day. Back on the battlefield, Fluellen refuses Pistol's request for clemency for his friend Bardolph, who has been caught looting a church and is to be hanged. The king, despite their history of friendship back at the Boar's Head Tavern, agrees with this sentence and Bardolph is executed.

At Agincourt (Act IV), the night before the battle, Henry disguises himself and talks to his troops, discovering that some of them are concerned about his motives for waging war. He muses to himself on the responsibility of kingship and prays for success in the upcoming conflict.

When morning comes the French are still confident and Henry rallies his soldiers before battle commences. Pistol takes a captive, the Boy reveals that Nym has also been hanged for stealing and returns to guard the army's baggage with the other boys. The French nobles realise that they have been beaten but return to the fray, which leads Henry to order the execution of all French prisoners of war. He then discovers that the French have killed the boys guarding the camp. Victory is Henry's: ten thousand Frenchmen have died but only twenty-nine British soldiers.

After this triumph has been celebrated in England, Henry returns to France to negotiate peace (Act V). He allows King Charles to keep the throne so long as it passes to Henry on his death, instead of to the dauphin. He arranges to marry Princess Katherine to make sure his heirs inherit France. The Chorus ends the play on a downbeat note, telling the audience that Henry and Katherine's son, King Henry VI, will lose France and England will end up back at war.

KEY THEMES

Leadership

KING HENRY V
>   This day is called the feast of Crispian.
>   He that outlives this day and comes safe home,
>   Will stand a-tiptoe when the day is named
>   And rouse him at the name of Crispian.
>   He that shall see this day and live old age
>   Will yearly on the vigil feast his neighbours,
>   And say 'Tomorrow is Saint Crispian.'
>   Then will he strip his sleeve and show his scars,
>   And say 'These wounds I had on Crispin's day.'

Old men forget; yet all shall be forgot
But he'll remember, with advantages,
What feats he did that day. Then shall our names,
Familiar in his mouth as household words,
Harry the King, Bedford and Exeter,
Warwick and Talbot, Salisbury and Gloucester,
Be in their flowing cups freshly remembered.
This story shall the good man teach his son,
And Crispin Crispian shall ne'er go by,
From this day to the ending of the world,
But we in it shall be rememberèd,
We few, we happy few, we band of brothers.
For he today that sheds his blood with me
Shall be my brother; be he ne'er so vile,
This day shall gentle his condition.
And gentlemen in England now abed
Shall think themselves accursed they were not here,
And hold their manhoods cheap whiles any speaks
That fought with us upon Saint Crispin's day.

(ACT IV, SCENE 3)

This is Henry's famous St Crispin's Day speech, which he proclaims to his soldiers before the Battle of Agincourt. It is the model of a perfect inspirational speech and showcases Henry's leadership talents. He aims to excite his men with the promise of glory, the opportunity to prove their valour, the gratitude of their countrymen, and the special closeness they will achieve with their king, despite being common men, through fighting alongside him. This sense of comradeship with his troops is also shown in his visit to the camp in disguise as an ordinary soldier the night before Agincourt: 'I think the king is but a man [. . .] though his affections are higher mounted than ours, yet, when they stoop, they stoop with the like wing'.

Throughout the play Henry's eloquence proves a powerful weapon. He is an excellent motivational speaker but also shows a more subtle side: he is often seen publicly passing responsibility for the violence he brings to other people through grand speeches – at the start of the play he tells the Archbishop of Canterbury, who is advising him on his claim to France, to 'take heed how you impawn our person, / How you awake our sleeping sword of war' and, similarly, he tells the governor of Harfleur that his refusal to surrender will mean that 'you yourselves are cause, / If your pure maidens fall into the hand / Of hot and forcing violation'. He effectively wins Harfleur with this rhetoric.

The play shows a successful, admirable king but simultaneously seems to question whether this political and martial success can be achieved without some moral sacrifice. 'This star of England' is brutal in his dealings with old friends (Falstaff, Scroop and Bardolph), as well as with his enemies (he threatens rape and infanticide on the people of Harfleur and kills his prisoners of war). The responsibilities of power mean that personal relationships have to be sacrificed and ruthlessness embraced in the single-minded pursuit of victory. However, Henry is not Machiavellian in the sense of cynically looking to expand his power base at every opportunity, like Richard III. He is a pious man, who believes that God supports his claim to the French throne and that his military success is proof of this. He also regrets his father's actions in usurping Richard II, 'O, not today, think not upon the fault / My father made in compassing the crown', as he believes in the sanctity of kingship. Having come by the crown through inheritance himself, he is free from the taint of sin that his father had, while simultaneously displaying his father's superior gifts for politics. He feels his responsibility to his people and country deeply as is revealed in his soliloquy before Agincourt: 'Upon the King! "Let us our lives, our souls, / Our debts, our careful wives, / Our children and our sins lay on the King!" / We must bear all.'

Patriotism

FLUELLEN
> Captain Jamy is a marvellous falourous gentleman, that is certain, and of great expedition and knowledge in th' anchient wars, upon

my particular knowledge of his directions. By Cheshu, he will maintain his argument as well as any military man in the world, in the disciplines of the pristine wars of the Romans.

JAMY

I say guid day, Captain Fluellen.

FLUELLEN

God-den to your worship, good Captain James.

GOWER

How now, Captain Macmorris, have you quit the mines? Have the pioneers given o'er?

MACMORRIS

By Chrish, la, 'tish ill done; the work ish give over, the trompet sound the retreat. By my hand I swear, and my father's soul, the work ish ill done; it ish give over. I would have blowed up the town, so Chrish save me, la, in an hour. Oh, 'tish ill done, 'tish ill done; by my hand, 'tish ill done!

(ACT III, SCENE 2)

This scene involving the Welsh, Scottish, English and Irish captains gives the (historically false) impression that all the regions of the British Isles fought for Henry in a united front. Shakespeare enjoys making each character speak in a comic version of his accent but all of these men are seen as good soldiers. Fluellen, in particular, has an important role in the play as a contrast to the bombastic, immoral Pistol (whom he eventually punishes for mocking Wales by making him eat a leek) – 'There is much care and valour in this Welshman.' In contrast to the arrogant French nobles, who are all we ever see of the French forces, we get a broad and varied picture of the nation that Henry is so proud of, from the captains, to the Eastcheap ruffians, and from the tragic Duke of York and Earl of Suffolk, to the plain-spoken Williams. The foppish, disrespectful French are set up in opposition to this generally sturdy, plucky picture of the outnumbered 'English' forces: 'That island of England breeds very valiant creatures; their mastiffs are of unmatchable courage'; 'O England! model to thy inward greatness, / Like little body with a mighty heart'.

Henry's speeches often mention England and support this image of the country as courageous, as in his celebrated 'Once more unto the breach' speech discussed later. This message was important in Shakespeare's time as Elizabeth's rule was subject to serious threats from abroad. The play's power as an inspiring picture of English heroism continued into the twentieth century when Laurence Olivier's 1944 film of *Henry V* was subsidised by the British government as it was seen as a useful boost for morale in the final years of the Second World War.

War

WILLIAMS

> But if the cause be not good, the king himself hath a heavy reckoning to make when all those legs and arms and heads, chopped off in battle, shall join together at the latter day and cry all 'We died at such a place', some swearing, some crying for a surgeon, some upon their wives left poor behind them, some upon the debts they owe, some upon their children rawly left. I am afeard there are few die well that die in a battle.

(ACT IV, SCENE I)

This speech by the ordinary soldier Michael Williams, in discussion with the disguised king, gives a different picture of war to the one King Henry creates in his grand speeches about honour and glory, and in his assertion, while pretending to be a common soldier, that 'I could not die anywhere so contented as in the king's company, his cause being just and his quarrel honourable'. Williams is clear-eyed about the realities of battle and the consequences of each individual man's death for his family back at home. Here Shakespeare undercuts the magnificent vision of warfare as the ultimate heroic, masculine exercise which infuses the play, as he does later, with the execution of the boys guarding the baggage at Agincourt. It is made clear that the innocent and weak suffer in wartime and Henry's own speech threatening the women and children of Harfleur illustrates this.

The involvement of the Eastcheap characters like Pistol, Bardolph and Nym gives an unsavoury impression of the realities of war as well: these characters are cowards, braggarts and thieves who take advantage of what conflict offers them. The only survivor of this group, Pistol, returns to England, unrepentant, to make his money as a pimp and a pickpocket: he has not been transformed by his part in this noble enterprise.

Princess Katherine's role as peace settlement also shows that war is very much a male enterprise, and although Henry goes through the motions of wooing her, she makes it clear that the decision for her to marry him is down to 'de roi mon père'. She is one of only four minor female characters in the play (along with her mother, her maid and Pistol's wife, Nell) and is set apart from the main action, a fact that is accentuated by her inability to speak English.

KEY SCENE

The **night before Agincourt** (Act IV, Scene 1) is a key scene in *Henry V*. It shows the king disguising himself with a cloak in order to walk unnoticed among his troops. Here, he interacts with all the elements of his army. First he wishes his noble supporters an affectionate good night, then he's sworn at by Pistol before overhearing Fluellen and Gower chatting. He then meets Bates, Court and Williams who don't come across as raring for the fight in quite the way he might have hoped. They speak of their obligation to fight for the king whether his cause is just or not, and express their fear that while they may die in the battle the king may then decide to make peace and save himself. Williams and the disguised king quarrel over their differences of opinion on this subject and later, after the battle, Henry will reveal to Williams that he challenged the king before rewarding him for his plain-speaking. Despite Henry's speeches declaring that all his soldiers are his 'band of brothers' this scene shows the distance between the ordinary men and the monarch.

The scene ends with Henry's only soliloquy where he muses upon the empty ceremony that makes a king different from other men and how the responsibility he feels for his subjects' welfare weighs him down: 'What infinite heart's ease / Must kings neglect, that private men enjoy!'

KEY SYMBOL

The **tennis balls** which feature in Act I, Scene 2, symbolically represent the contrasts explored in the play: between France's glibness and England's seriousness, between Henry's old life and his new mission, between disrespect and honour, and between the luxuries of royalty and the practical hardships of war. The dauphin mocks Henry's territorial claims by sending him a box of tennis balls, suggesting that he better use his time in batting them about than attempting to invade France. In his message he refers to Henry's misspent youth, when he was only interested in enjoying himself. However, he has underestimated how seriously Henry has transformed himself since taking the throne. The message the king sends back to the dauphin is prescient and chilling:

> And tell the pleasant prince this mock of his
> Hath turned his balls to gun-stones, and his soul
> Shall stand sore chargèd for the wasteful vengeance
> That shall fly with them; for many a thousand widows
> Shall this his mock mock out of their dear husbands,
> Mock mothers from their sons, mock castles down,
> And some are yet ungotten and unborn
> That shall have cause to curse the Dauphin's scorn.

> (ACT I, SCENE 2)

Famous speeches explained

Henry V is famous for his oratory and there is no doubt that Shakespeare is the master of the monologue. He often gives his central characters beautiful, lengthy speeches to allow them to expound on their dilemmas. A monologue which gives the impression the character is speaking his thoughts aloud, letting the audience into his mind, but is apparently not heard by any of the other characters present, is called a soliloquy. A monologue, or part of a monologue, addressed to an absent character, abstract idea or imaginary person, such as Lady Macbeth's 'Come, thick night, and pall thee in the dunnest smoke of Hell', is called an apostrophe.

Henry V, Act III, Scene 1

Once more unto the breach, dear friends,
    once more,
Or close the wall up with our English dead.
In peace there's nothing so becomes a man
As modest stillness and humility;
But when the blast of war blows in our ears,
Then imitate the action of the tiger:
Stiffen the sinews, conjure up the blood,
Disguise fair nature with hard-favoured
    rage.
Then lend the eye a terrible aspect;
Let it pry through the portage of the head
Like the brass cannon; let the brow
    o'erwhelm it
As fearfully as doth a gallèd rock
O'erhang and jutty his confounded base,
Swilled with the wild and wasteful ocean.
Now set the teeth and stretch the nostril
    wide,
Hold hard the breath and bend up every
    spirit
To his full height. On, on, you noblest
    English,
Whose blood is fet from fathers of
    war-proof,

Let's ride into the break in the Harfleur city walls one more time, friends. Either that or we'll block the gap with our dead English soldiers. In peacetime it suits a man to be calm and humble, but when we hear the battle trumpet we should act like tigers, with taut muscles and stirred-up blood, and hide our better sides with ugly rage. Make your eyes look fierce, and make them stick out from your head like cannons from portholes; crease your forehead like a terrifying cliff overhanging its crumbling base in a wild, destructive sea.

Grit your teeth and flare your nostrils, take a deep breath and marshal all your resources.

Come on, you noblest Englishmen, who are descended from fathers who proved themselves in war. Fathers who, like lots of Alexander the Greats, have fought round here from morning to evening and only put their swords

Fathers that like so many Alexanders
Have in these parts from morn till even
    fought,
And sheathed their swords for lack of
    argument.
Dishonour not your mothers; now attest
That those whom you called fathers did
    beget you.
Be copy now to men of grosser blood
And teach them how to war. And you,
    good yeomen,
Whose limbs were made in England,
    show us here
The mettle of your pasture; let us swear
That you are worth your breeding – which
    I doubt not,
For there is none of you so mean and base
That hath not noble lustre in your eyes.
I see you stand like greyhounds in the slips,
Straining upon the start. The game's afoot.
Follow your spirit, and upon this charge
Cry 'God for Harry, England, and Saint
    George!'

away when there was no one left to
fight.

Don't let your mothers down. Prove that
you are your fathers' sons. Set a good
example for the commoners, and show
them how to fight.

And you, good farmers, who were born in
England, show us what you're made of,
so we agree that you're worth your
heritage – I'm sure you are – for none of
you here is so common that you don't
have a noble glint in your eyes.

I can see you standing like greyhounds in
their slip-collars at the start of a race,
raring to go. The game is on; follow
your instincts and when we make this
charge, yell 'God's on the side of Harry,
England and Saint George!'

THE ROMAN PLAYS

The Roman plays are a sub-category of Shakespeare's work that was not recognised in the First Folio, where they appeared as Tragedies, but is considered useful today by students and critics. These plays contain elements of both history and tragedy and, surprise surprise, tend to feature Romans. The three major Roman plays are *Julius Caesar*, *Antony and Cleopatra* and *Coriolanus*. *Titus Andronicus* is often added to this list, and also sometimes *Cymbeline*. Shakespeare used classical stories as source material or inspiration for many more of his plays, and for his poems *The Rape of Lucrece* and *Venus and Adonis*.

Rome exerted more of an influence on Elizabethan culture than ancient Greece, and translations of Roman writers' works were popular. The Roman past perhaps felt more closely connected with contemporary life in Shakespeare's day as the Eastern Roman Empire had only fallen in 1453 and, through Catholicism, the Pope's Roman influence in English affairs had been strong until 1531 when Henry VIII made himself Supreme Head of the Church of England. Medieval legend also had it that the first British king was Brutus, a relative of Aeneas, the founder of Rome.

Shakespeare's key classical influences were Plutarch, Seneca, Ovid, Plautus and Terence. He probably studied them at school. Despite Ben Jonson's snide comment that Shakespeare had 'small Latin and less Greek', an ordinary grammar-school education would have meant that Shakespeare could read Latin fluently. His creation of hundreds of Latinate neologisms illustrates his easy familiarity with the language.

Shakespeare's Roman influences

Plautus (*c*.254–184 BCE) wrote comedies influenced by Greek comic playwrights. He was popular in the early days of developing Roman drama and twenty of his plays survive. He often wrote about young men, in particular their relationships with their fathers, and his plays feature clever slaves, boastful soldiers and randy old men, and involve lots of puns and wordplay. His play *Menaechmi* provides the plot for *The Comedy of Errors* and his stock characters are believed to have influenced the creation of Falstaff.

Terence (*c*.190–159 BCE) was an ex-slave from Carthage who was also influenced by Greek comic playwrights. Six of his plays survive and he is considered a less lively and more moderate and sophisticated writer than Plautus, with a more epigrammatic style.

Ovid (43 BCE–17 CE) was a Roman poet who was extremely popular during the

Renaissance. He is a witty and elegant writer famed for his love poetry and for his accounts of Graeco-Roman mythology. His epic poem *Metamorphoses* provided the *Pyramus and Thisbe* play-within-a-play in *A Midsummer Night's Dream*, the story for *Venus and Adonis* and the horrible fate of Lavinia in *Titus Andronicus*. *The Rape of Lucrece* was based on Ovid's account in his poem *Fasti*, as well as on a version by the Roman historian Livy. Shakespeare's contemporary, Francis Meres, linked Shakespeare strongly with this urbane Latin poet, saying that 'the sweet witty soul of Ovid lives in mellifluous and honey-tongued Shakespeare'.

Seneca's (*c*.4 BCE– 65 CE) tragedies were one of the key influences on Elizabethan drama and inspired the genre of Revenge Tragedy (see page 208). They had only recently been translated when Shakespeare was working. Seneca also looked back to Greek predecessors like Euripides. His plays are violent, melodramatic, moralising and often involve ghosts and witches, and his style is very rhetorical. *Titus Andronicus* is Shakespeare's most Senecan play, but *Hamlet* also shows his influence. A philosopher as well as the Emperor Nero's tutor, Seneca was forced to commit suicide by his former pupil after being charged with treason.

Julius Caesar is the most popular of the Roman plays. The text we have from the First Folio appears to have come from the prompt-book version as it includes many stage directions. In it, the Roman general Caesar is murdered by his former friend Brutus and other conspirators, because they fear that he is growing too powerful and is going to turn the Roman Republic into a monarchy. Caesar is famously warned by a soothsayer to 'Beware the Ides of March' (15 March) but attends the Senate in spite of this and is stabbed there. His last words '*Et tu, Brute?*', expressing his sense of betrayal at seeing Brutus amid his murderers, are among the most iconic in all literature. Brutus makes a speech to the people explaining why Caesar had to go but this is undermined by Caesar's friend Mark Antony's amazing 'Friends, Romans, countrymen' oration, where he repeats 'Brutus is an honourable man' with intense irony until he inflames the crowd. Battle lines are drawn between Brutus and the conspirators and Antony and Octavius, Caesar's heir. The latter emerge victorious and the former commit suicide in their defeat.

Antony and Cleopatra is in some ways a sequel to *Julius Caesar* as it dramatises the subsequent power struggle between Antony and Octavius, who would go on to become the first and most famous Roman Emperor, Caesar Augustus (who, incidentally, is ruler of the Empire at the time of *Cymbeline*). You can find a full summary of *Antony and Cleopatra* on page 168.

Coriolanus is the least performed Roman play of the big three and the last tragedy Shakespeare wrote. It is set many years before the action of the other two plays, at the beginning of the Roman Republic. Coriolanus is a magnificent soldier but definitely not a people person. He is encouraged, after his military victories, to run for office but he and the Roman citizenry don't see eye to eye. Their rejection of him leads him to temporarily side with his former arch-enemy, Aufidius, leader of the Volscians, and plan to attack

Rome before his mother, Volumnia, manages to persuade him against it. Coriolanus is then murdered by the angry Volscians.

All these plays deal with themes of power, loyalty, courage, pride, fortune, honour, stoicism, the tension between public and private life, the conflict between the ruling class and the people, and the power of language, and they are full of omens, battles and suicides. They focus on male characters though Cleopatra and Volumnia are strong female roles. They generally express the Elizabethan perception of ancient Rome as a martial, ordered society, peopled with sophisticated politicians and bound by standards of behaviour and an emphasis on the importance of reputation. Despite being a pagan culture, Rome was much admired as a civilised society, which produced great literature, great rhetoricians and great soldiers, and many other contemporary writers were inspired by Roman stories. The golden age of Rome and that of Queen Elizabeth and King James were seen as having similarities, but the plays can also be seen to reflect anxiety around James's succession and the increased power of the monarchy.

The two minor plays which feature Romans, *Titus Andronicus* and *Cymbeline*, differ in tone from the three great tragedies discussed above. And they are often the subject of arguments about which of Shakespeare's plays is the worst.

Titus Andronicus is believed to be Shakespeare's first tragedy. It is set in the dying days of the Empire when the admirable values of the other Roman plays have somewhat fallen by the wayside. Civilised this play is not. The fictitious general Titus sets the horrible action in motion when he ignores his brother's reminder: 'Thou art a Roman, be not barbarous'. He makes an enemy of the captive Goth queen Tamora, who inconveniently ends up marrying his emperor, Saturninus. A bloody orgy of competitive revenge then ensues between the two, ending with Titus and his enemies dead and his son Lucius adopted as Emperor by the Roman people. This play is written in a very rhetorical style, and some commentators have referred to it as more of a poem than a piece of theatre, citing the example of Act II, Scene 4, where Titus's brother Marcus finds his niece mutilated and responds by giving a lengthy and metaphorical speech about how she appears: 'what stern ungentle hands / Have lopp'd and hew'd and made thy body bare / Of her two branches, those sweet ornaments, / Whose circling shadows kings have sought to sleep in . . .' Compared to Lear's response to Cordelia's body this seems a very formal and unnatural way to respond to the suffering of a young relative.

Cymbeline is the only non-tragic Roman play (although it was categorised as a tragedy in the First Folio). The Romans in *Cymbeline* are part of the subplot and are chiefly represented by their ambassador, the honourable Caius Lucius who later leads the Roman army against Cymbeline when he, under the influence of his evil queen, refuses to pay the necessary tribute due to Augustus. The romantic lead, Posthumus, changes back and forth between British and Roman clothes during the battles as he tries to punish himself by ending up on the losing side, before the Roman god Jupiter appears to sort things out for him. The end of the play sees reconciliations in the main family and marriage plots as well as in the political subplot. Cymbeline ends victorious over the Romans but agrees to resume paying the tribute, 'let / A Roman and a British ensign wave / Friendly together', binding Britain and Rome together in a happy relationship again.

A rough timeline of the classical plays

This list puts the settings of the plays which involve classical characters or models in a rough chronological order. The majority of the plays are based around legends rather than real historical events.

Greek Heroic Age (*c.*1600–1200 BCE)
A Midsummer Night's Dream
The Two Noble Kinsmen
Pericles
Troilus and Cressida

Greek Classical Era Early Roman Republic (*c.*500–300 BCE)
The Comedy of Errors
Coriolanus
Timon of Athens

Last Days of the Roman Republic
Julius Caesar (44 BCE)
Antony and Cleopatra (46–30 BCE)

Roman Empire
Cymbeline (*c.*9 CE–*c.*42 CE)
Titus Andronicus (fifth century CE)

Antony And Cleopatra
Sex And Reputation In Ancient Egypt

1900 illustration by Byam Shaw

Antony and Cleopatra was written around 1606–7 and the only surviving text we have of it comes from the First Folio, where it appears in the Tragedies section. However, many critics see it as more of a History play. One reason for this is that it covers so much ground: it has more scenes than any other Shakespeare play, it takes place in territories ranging from Alexandria to Rome as well as Sicily, Athens and Syria, and its time span is immense, covering the events of nearly a decade. Some believe it shouldn't qualify as a tragedy because the final vision of the play, despite the main characters' deaths, is triumphant rather than bleak, and the protagonists don't undergo the terrible soul-searching of Lear, Hamlet, Othello and Macbeth. Coleridge, however, ranked it alongside these great works, calling it 'by far the most powerful' of 'Shakespeare's historical plays' and commending its 'happy valiancy'. Along with *Julius Caesar* and *Coriolanus* it is now most commonly labelled a Roman play. It has also been referred to as a tragicomedy, as it has many scenes of irony and humour, and its ambiguity of message has meant that some classify it as a problem play. Its focus on beautiful poetry, perhaps at the expense of dramatic action, has even led some to say it fits best with Shakespeare's long poems. It is appropriate for a play that celebrates a woman of 'infinite variety' that the mixture of tones and sympathies makes it in some ways indefinable.

PLOT SUMMARY

The play begins with Antony in Alexandria with his lover, the Queen of Egypt, Cleopatra (Act I). From the beginning he is torn between his wish to stay with her living the high life and his more humdrum duties back at home. He is recalled to Rome by his co-ruler, Caesar (Octavius from *Julius Caesar*), who is put out that Antony is neglecting his political responsibilities because of his love affair.

Caesar and Antony rule the Roman Empire with Lepidus: together they are called the triumvirs. Their authority is being threatened by Sextus Pompey (Act II). Pompey is aware of the tensions between the three men, particularly between Caesar and Antony. Despite this, at a meeting at Lepidus's house they manage to resolve their differences and a marriage between Antony and Caesar's sister Octavia is arranged to bind them together. However, Antony's lieutenant Enobarbus is convinced Antony won't abandon his relationship with Cleopatra, because she is such an extraordinary woman. Indeed, Antony almost immediately decides to leave Octavia for Egypt, after a soothsayer tells him that he'll never be greater than Caesar in Rome. First, though, the triumvirs come to an arrangement with Pompey for him to back off and they celebrate with a banquet on his ship.

Cleopatra is unhappy about Antony's marriage but the accord between Caesar and Antony doesn't last long (Act III). Antony feels disrespected by Caesar and Caesar is angered by Antony giving Cleopatra various Roman territories. Caesar ousts Lepidus and decides to take on Antony in battle. Antony, possibly on Cleopatra's advice, decides to fight Caesar at sea at Actium instead of on land where his forces are strongest. When Cleopatra's ships flee during the battle Antony's follow, causing Antony deep shame and losing him support. Caesar refuses to negotiate with Antony but sends his representative to talk with Cleopatra. He also refuses Antony's barmy offer of a private duel. This foolish challenge leads Enobarbus to desert Antony (Act IV). But when Antony generously sends him his treasure to Caesar's camp, and he witnesses Antony's glorious victory at the next land battle, he recognises his own treachery and dies of grief. Antony's good luck doesn't hold, as at the next sea battle the Egyptian ships again let him down. He blames Cleopatra and decides to kill her. Wily Cleopatra hides herself in her monument (a mausoleum built with the intention of being her eventual tomb) and tells her servant to let Antony know she's killed herself. This news, and his great shame, inspires Antony to attempt suicide, but he only manages to injure himself. When he discovers his great love is in fact alive, he is taken to her, then dies in her arms.

After hearing of Antony's death Caesar sends his messengers, and then goes himself, to try to convince Cleopatra that they can negotiate a settlement (Act V). He really just wants to capture her alive to march her in triumph through the streets of Rome. Cleopatra is determined to thwart this plan and retain her honour and so she dresses in her full royal regalia and takes delivery of two asps in a basket of figs which she uses to kill herself. On discovering her body, Caesar states that she will be buried with Antony: they will have a great funeral, befitting of their places in history.

KEY THEMES

Conflict

PHILO

    Nay, but this dotage of our general's
    O'erflows the measure. Those his goodly eyes,
    That o'er the files and musters of the war
    Have glow'd like plated Mars, now bend, now turn
    The office and devotion of their view
    Upon a tawny front. His captain's heart,
    Which in the scuffles of great fights hath burst
    The buckles on his breast, reneges all temper
    And is become the bellows and the fan
    To cool a gipsy's lust.
    Flourish. Enter Antony, Cleopatra, her Ladies, the Train, with
    Eunuchs fanning her
    Look, where they come!

Take but good note, and you shall see in him
The triple pillar of the world transformed
Into a strumpet's fool. Behold and see.

(ACT I, SCENE I)

Antony and Cleopatra is, on one level, about the political conflict between
Caesar and Antony for control of the Roman Empire, but on a broader level
the play is full of thematic conflicts and oppositions. Through the action and
poetry of the play we see Egypt versus Rome, love versus war, youth versus
age, duty versus fun, male versus female, public versus private and reason
versus emotion. The Roman soldier Philo's speech above, which opens the
play, refers to several of these tensions. He bemoans the fact that Antony's
energy, which had previously been focused on military achievements, is now
directed solely at his sexual lust for Cleopatra. The great general's image has
changed from being one of the three most powerful people on earth (the
triumvirs) – 'the triple pillar of the world' – to the lovelorn suitor of an unworthy woman – 'a strumpet's fool'. The verse of the play reflects these antago-
nisms through Shakespeare's use of oxymoronic and paradoxical
constructions; for example, when Agrippa calls Cleopatra 'Rare Egyptian'
and 'Royal wench'. In Shakespeare's time the word 'Egyptian' was often used
synonymously and derogatively with 'gipsy' and so was at odds with the
complimentary word 'rare', meaning 'splendid'. Similarly, 'wench' was a
diminishing word for a woman, at odds with the adjective 'royal'. Much of
the play is taken up with contrasting the values of Rome – serious, diligent,
calculating, martial – with those of Egypt – sensuous, luxurious and emotional. Antony's love for Cleopatra sees him caught between these poles until
in the end he 'cannot hold this visible shape' any longer and is destroyed. For
Cleopatra, though, the oppositions she holds within her character – imperious leader versus playful mistress, vulnerable lover versus 'cunning past man's
thought' – seem to be the secret of her power, her seductive 'infinite variety'.
At the end of the play she triumphs in her defeat as she takes her own life:
'Give me my robe. Put on my crown. I have / Immortal longings in me.'

Public Image

ENOBARBUS
> I will tell you.
> The barge she sat in, like a burnished throne,
> Burned on the water; the poop was beaten gold;
> Purple the sails, and so perfumed that
> The winds were love-sick with them; the oars were silver,
> Which to the tune of flutes kept stroke, and made
> The water which they beat to follow faster,
> As amorous of their strokes. For her own person,
> It beggared all description: she did lie
> In her pavilion, cloth-of-gold of tissue,
> O'erpicturing that Venus where we see
> The fancy outwork nature. On each side her
> Stood pretty dimpled boys, like smiling cupids,
> With divers-coloured fans, whose wind did seem
> To glow the delicate cheeks which they did cool,
> And what they undid did.
> [. . .]

AGRIPPA
> Rare Egyptian!

(ACT II, SCENE 2)

Antony and Cleopatra are not often seen as private individuals. Both of their identities are bound up in their public images and the passage above shows Cleopatra's skill at giving an impression of majesty and opulence. It also becomes clear that the opposite of this display, being humiliatingly led through the streets of Rome in Caesar's triumph, is anathema to her, and she's willing to die to avoid that fate. The couple's position as world leaders means that even their intimate and adulterous love affair is a public spectacle and they, and others, describe themselves in consistently grandiose terms:

'The demi-Atlas of this earth', 'Noblest of men', 'The crown o' the earth', 'greatest soldier of the world', 'My queen', 'Egypt', 'a pair so famous'. The wide-ranging geography of the play, showing conflicts across the Roman Empire, and the high number of entrances and exits, particularly by messengers bearing news, enhances this impression of how their private life is significant because of their active role on the world's stage. The scene above gives an almost supernatural image of Cleopatra's splendour and the mythological references to the couple in the play add to this sense of them, and their passion, being somehow beyond ordinary humanity. Cleopatra's apotheosistic speech before her death – 'I am fire and air' – fits with this view, as does the sense at the end of the play that they will be together for eternity after death: 'husband, I come'.

Sex

CLEOPATRA

> That time? O times!
> I laughed him out of patience, and that night
> I laughed him into patience, and next morn,
> Ere the ninth hour, I drunk him to his bed,
> Then put my tires and mantles on him, whilst
> I wore his sword Philippan.

Enter a Messenger

> Oh, from Italy!
> Ram thou thy fruitful tidings in mine ears,
> That long time have been barren.

(ACT II, SCENE 5)

These lines and the wordplay of 'ram' and 'barren' make it clear that Antony and Cleopatra's relationship is very enjoyably sexual. Contrasted with that of, say, Romeo and Juliet it is a much more knowing and mature relationship between strong, confident adults. Cleopatra is unlike many of Shakespeare's other heroines in that, as a widow, she is not required to be a virgin in order to elicit the audience's sympathy: 'I take no pleasure / In aught a eunuch has'. However, the Roman characters are often disgusted with her overt sexuality and refer to her as a 'whore', and even Antony is not entirely comfortable with her sexual history: 'I found you as a morsel cold upon / Dead Caesar's trencher – nay, you were a fragment / Of Gnaeus Pompey's, besides what hotter hours, / Unregistered in vulgar fame, you have / Luxuriously picked out.' Using the metaphor of food, he describes her here as a scrap left behind on Julius Caesar's plate and also one of Gnaeus Pompey's leftovers (Gnaeus Pompey is the brother of the Pompey who features in the play). Her prominent lovers make clear that for Cleopatra sexual power is very closely bound up with political power and this links to the idea of sexual conquest mirroring the Romans' dedication to imperial conquest. One reading sees the play as the tragedy of Antony's fall from glory, because of his tragic flaw of being susceptible to lust for Cleopatra. Certainly this is how Caesar sees it: 'He hath given his empire / Up to a whore'. But it's worth noting that the whole final act is about Cleopatra's death rather than Antony's, and that the final vision of her does not feel tragic in the same way that Shakespeare's other great tragedies do. Cleopatra links her death with sexual longing in the words 'The stroke of death is as a lover's pinch, which hurts, and is desired'. This association of sex and death is not uncommon in this period when the word death was also used as a synonym for orgasm.

Honour

MENAS

> These three world-sharers, these competitors,
> Are in thy vessel. Let me cut the cable;
> And, when we are put off, fall to their throats.
> All then is thine.

POMPEY

> Ah, this thou shouldst have done
> And not have spoke on't. In me 'tis villany;

In thee't had been good service. Thou must know
'Tis not my profit that does lead mine honour;
Mine honour, it. Repent that e'er thy tongue
Hath so betrayed thine act. Being done unknown,
I should have found it afterwards well done.
But must condemn it now. Desist, and drink.

(ACT II, SCENE 7)

The play is much concerned with one particular aspect of public reputation that was of great concern in both Roman times and Shakespeare's day. It is hugely important to all the characters that they are perceived as honourable. In the scene above, Pompey admits that he would like to take the Machiavellian path to ruling the Roman Empire by murdering the triumvirs but that his sense of honour prevents him. Honour is especially crucial for the Roman characters, as Cleopatra recognises when Antony leaves her to return to his duties: 'your honour calls you hence'. It is Caesar's snubs to Antony's honour that lead him to finally turn against him: 'if I lose mine honour, / I lose myself'. And indeed, when Antony does lose his honour by fleeing at Actium, his sense of self deteriorates to the point where he can see no honourable way out except suicide. Suicide was not considered shameful in pre-Christian Roman times but rather as the only way to redeem one's reputation in defeat, hence Antony's line at his death: 'A Roman by a Roman valiantly vanquished.'

KEY SCENE

Antony's suicide scene (Act IV, Scene 14) sees tragedy finally catching up with the heroes of the play. The Egyptian ships have once again deserted Antony in battle and he has lost to Caesar. He is furious with Cleopatra and begins to feel his sense of identity ebbing away now he is not a successful soldier: 'here I am Antony, / Yet cannot hold this visible shape'. But when Cleopatra's servant comes to tell him that she has killed herself he is heartbroken and determines to commit suicide: 'I will o'ertake thee, Cleopatra, and / Weep for my pardon.' However, even his efforts for a glorious suicide come to nothing. He asks his slave Eros to kill him but Eros commits suicide himself to avoid hurting his beloved master, and Antony's own attempt with his sword is not immediately fatal. Dying, he discovers that Cleopatra has lied to him and is still alive and asks to be taken to her. In the next scene the lovers will be reconciled before Antony dies in his queen's arms. Antony's botched suicide here contrasts with Cleopatra's later triumphant death.

KEY SYMBOL

Antony's **sword** is a potent symbol of both his military prowess – 'I, that with my sword / Quartered the world' – and, as a phallic object, by metaphorical association, his sexual life. As a symbol of his virility it is clear how much Cleopatra has conquered him in the passage where she refers to them swapping clothes and her wearing his 'sword Philippan'. (This is the sword he used at the Battle of Philippi where he defeated Brutus. Interestingly, Antony refers to Octavius Caesar at the same battle keeping 'His sword e'en like a dancer' in a very unmasculine way.) At Actium Antony expresses his belief that his love for Cleopatra has undermined his military ability by referring to 'My sword, made weak by my affection'. He has sought to reinforce his sense of manliness in the private realm, just as he has been losing it in the political arena. The double meaning of 'sword' is also clear in Agrippa's comment about Octavius's uncle, Julius Caesar, when he notes that Cleopatra also seduced him: 'She made great Caesar lay his sword to bed.'

Mythological references

It's useful to know a bit of background about these three characters from Graeco-Roman legend to deepen your understanding of *Antony and Cleopatra*. Antony was closely associated with the famously strong hero and demigod Hercules (Herakles in the original Greek myth). Cleopatra refers to him as 'this Herculean Roman' and you'll notice the strange short scene in the soldiers' camp before Actium where odd music is heard and one of Antony's followers says: 'Tis the god Hercules, whom Antony loved, / Now leaves him.' A more oblique reference is made when Antony is raging against Cleopatra and says: 'The shirt of Nessus is upon me. Teach me / Alcides, thou mine ancestor, thy rage; / Let me lodge Lichas on the horns o' th'moon'. Alcides was another name for Hercules and this refers to the story of Hercules's death, when he was destroyed by a poisoned shirt from the centaur Nessus which his wife gave him, via their servant Lichas, thinking it was a love potion that would bind him to her.

Antony refers to Dido and Aeneas when he is imagining his romance with Cleopatra continuing in the afterlife and how their love will make them even more famous than the celebrated lovers: 'Dido and her Aeneas shall want troops, / And all the haunt be ours.' Their story is told in Virgil's *Aeneid* which was written for the Emperor Augustus (Octavius Caesar in the play). This tale has interesting resonances for *Antony and Cleopatra*. Aeneas escapes from the fall of Troy and is tasked with founding a new Troy (which will be Rome). On his way to Italy he stops at Carthage and has a romance with the queen Dido but leaves her in pursuit of his duty to lead his people to a new settlement. She then kills herself. Antony can be seen as the opposite of Aeneas as he neglects his political duty for love. Interestingly, despite what Antony says, Virgil states that Dido sticks with her original husband Sychaeus in the afterlife.

Plutarch

Shakespeare's principle source for his three great Roman plays was Sir Thomas North's 1579 translation of Plutarch's *Lives*. Plutarch (*c*.50–*c*.120 CE) was a Greek philosopher who wrote a series of biographical portraits of great Greeks and Romans, including Julius Caesar, Brutus, Antony (which includes a reference to Timon of Athens) and Coriolanus. Using various sources, he compared Greek figures to Roman figures with the aim of encouraging mutual respect and emulation of the noble characters he depicted. Via translations, his work was influential in the development of biographical writing from the sixteenth century.

Sir Thomas North (1535–*c*.1601) actually translated the *Lives* from the French translation of Jacques Amyot. The resulting work is celebrated as one of the first masterpieces of English prose. Shakespeare used some of North's lines almost verbatim in *Antony and Cleopatra*. In fact, the most famous speech in the play, a hymn to Cleopatra's flash barge, is fairly close to North's original in many places: 'her barge in the river of Cydnus, the poop whereof was of gold, the sails purple, and the oars of silver, which kept stroke in rowing after the sound of the music of flutes . . .' However, Shakespeare made various changes to his source material, including inventing the interesting character of Antony's lieutenant Enobarbus and compressing the time frame. He also compresses dates and locales in *Julius Caesar* and moves the place of assassination to the Capitol for dramatic effect.

Anachronisms in the Roman plays

- O When Cleopatra asks Charmian to join her for a game of billiards, she is asking the impossible. The action of the play takes place in the first century CE and billiards doesn't appear to have been invented much before the fourteenth century.

- O 'The clock hath stricken three': *Julius Caesar* is often said to be riddled with chronological glitches. Clocks, doublets, books with pages and nightcaps all appear, despite being very un-Roman.

- O 'Thou wast a soldier / Even to Cato's wish': *Coriolanus* is set in the fifth century BCE and Cato the Censor wasn't born until 234 BCE. The Greek doctor and writer Galen is also mentioned despite not being born until 129 CE.

- O 'I know thou art religious [. . .] With twenty popish tricks and ceremonies': This reference to the Pope in the late Roman Empire of *Titus Andronicus* is interesting. Rome fell in 376 CE and the title 'Pope' only became official in the eleventh century, although the Catholic Church recognises popes as having existed before this, stretching back to St Peter. This reference casts light on what 'Rome' meant to an Elizabethan audience: it was very much tied up with the Roman Catholic Church and the recent break from Rome made by Elizabeth's father.

It is amusing to note these anachronisms but important to realise that they are not necessarily 'bloopers'. Shakespeare's audience was less concerned with realism of detail of this kind and it can also be argued that the playwright was purposely closing down the distance between the events onstage and contemporary life to make the plays more relevant and thought-provoking.

Shakespeare's best insults

Ever called anyone a deboshed fish, an unnecessary letter, a base football player, a cockscomb or a canker-blossom? Next time you're lost for words in an argument, turn to the Bard to spice up your recriminations. He was a master at a fancy put-down as the quotations below reveal. Remember you can also always bite your thumb at your enemies, or people who cut you up at the traffic lights, *Romeo and Juliet*-style, as this was the Early Modern equivalent of giving someone the finger.

'Out, dunghill'

Lord Bigot to Hubert in *King John*

''Sblood, you starveling, you eel-skin, you dried neat's tongue, you bull's-pizzle, you stock-fish! O for breath to utter what is like thee! – you tailor's-yard, you sheath, you bow-case; you vile standing tuck!'

Falstaff to Prince Harry in *Henry IV, Part 1*

'You scullion! You rampallian! You fustilarian! I'll tickle your catastrophe!'

Falstaff to Mistress Quickly in *Henry IV, Part 2*

'Would thou wert clean enough to spit on'

Timon to Apemantus in *Timon of Athens*

'. . . your peevish chastity, which is not worth a breakfast in the cheapest country . . .'

Boult to Marina in *Pericles*

'Why no, you ruinous butt, you whoreson indistinguishable cur, no.'

Patroclus to Thersites, *Troilus and Cressida*

'Out of my door, you witch, you rag, you baggage, you polecat, you runnion! out, out! I'll conjure you, I'll fortune-tell you!'

Ford to 'the fat woman of Brentford' (Falstaff in drag) in *The Merry Wives of Windsor*

'A knave, a rascal, an eater of broken meats, a base, proud, shallow, beggarly, three-suited-hundred-pound, filthy, worsted-stocking knave; a lily-livered, action-taking knave, a whoreson, glass-gazing, super-serviceable, finical rogue; one-trunk-inheriting slave; one that wouldst be a bawd in way of good service and art nothing but the composition of a knave, beggar, coward, pandar and the son and heir of a mongrel bitch; one whom I will beat into clamorous whining, if thou deniest the least syllable of thy addition.'

Kent to Oswald in *King Lear*

Shakespeare's best speeches

Aside from being a useful and brain-power-enhancing exercise, making oneself intimately acquainted with Shakespeare's very best speeches has a plethora of other benefits too. OK, too much bursting into rousing oration at the drop of a hat might set your friends' teeth on edge, but a well-judged soliloquy at an appropriately stressful moment – a turbulent patch on an aeroplane trip, the twenty-seventh hour of your wife's labour, for example – can help to still the heart and remind us of universal truths about human nature. It's a great party trick too – and so much more artful than twerking.

Here are some tips on committing the speeches to memory, and on how to guarantee an unforgettable delivery:

○ Say it loudly, say it slowly. This is one occasion where speed is NOT of the essence.

○ Break it up – some actors use walking techniques: say two lines, then turn round and walk out the next two lines.

○ Write the speech out in your own handwriting to really familiarise yourself with the words.

○ Try to visualise some of the extraordinary imagery: Lady Macbeth's hoarse raven, Titania's jewels from the deep, Henry V's tiger will help the lines stick fast to your soul.

○ Note which words are alliterative, or opposites, or repetitions.

○ Finally, do a huge yawn to loosen up your lips and throat.

'Once more unto the breach, dear friends, once more . . .' Roared by King Henry in *Henry V*, ACT III, SCENE I. Feel free to pound yourself manfully on the chest during this one.

'The raven himself is hoarse / That croaks the fatal entrance of Duncan . . .' Delivered menacingly by Lady Macbeth in *Macbeth*, ACT I, SCENE 5.

'Time hath, my lord, a wallet at his back, / Wherein he puts alms for oblivion . . .' A philosophical Ulysses in *Troilus and Cressida*, ACT III, SCENE 3.

'This story shall the good man teach his son, / And Crispin Crispian shall ne'er go by, / From this day to the ending of the world, / But we in it shall be rememberèd . . .' Majestically rousing words from King Henry in *Henry V*, ACT IV, SCENE 3.

'To bait fish withal; if it will feed nothing else, it will feed my revenge . . .' An outraged Shylock demands revenge in *The Merchant of Venice*, ACT III, SCENE I.

'To be, or not to be, that is the question . . .' A suicidal Hamlet asks the ultimate question in *Hamlet*, ACT III, SCENE I. Some hand-wringing might not go amiss here.

'Grief fills the room up of my absent child . . .' A stricken Constance remembers her dead son in *King John*, ACT III, SCENE 4.

'Out of this wood do not desire to go . . .' A love-struck Titania in *A Midsummer Night's Dream*, ACT III, SCENE I.

'Friends, Romans, countrymen, lend me your ears . . .' Antony rabble-rouses in *Julius Caesar*, ACT III, SCENE 2.

'All the world's a stage, / And all the men and women merely players . . .' Melancholy Jaques philosophises in *As You Like It*, ACT II, SCENE 7.

'Why bastard? wherefore base? . . .' Edmund standing up for bastards in *King Lear*, ACT I, SCENE 2.

'If music be the food of love, play on . . .' A foppish Orsino in *Twelfth Night*, ACT I, SCENE I.

'But, soft! what light through yonder window breaks . . .' An infatuated Romeo in *Romeo and Juliet*, ACT II, SCENE 2. Much sighing and flinging around of arms might work a treat here.

'Well, 'tis no matter; honour pricks me on. Yea, but how if honour prick me off when I come on? . . .' The realist Falstaff in *Henry IV, Part I*, ACT V, SCENE I.

'Her father loved me; oft invited me; / Still question'd me the story of my life . . .' An unrepentant Othello in *Othello*, ACT I, SCENE 3.

'Gallop apace, you fiery-footed steeds, / Towards Phoebus' lodging . . .' Nervously expectant Juliet awaits her wedding night in *Romeo and Juliet*, ACT III, SCENE 2.

'Now my charms are all o'erthrown, / And what strength I have's mine own . . .' A conciliatory Prospero in *The Tempest*, Epilogue.

'What a piece of work is a man! how noble in reason! / how infinite in faculty! . . .' A mournful Hamlet in *Hamlet*, ACT II, SCENE 2.

'I have been studying how I may compare / This prison where I live unto the world . . .' Richard is full of regrets in *Richard II*, ACT 5, SCENE 5.

'Sir, spare your threats: / The bug which you would fright me with I seek . . .' A defiant Hermione in *The Winter's Tale*, ACT III, SCENE 2.

'Methinks I am a prophet new inspired . . .' A patriotic John of Gaunt in *Richard II*, ACT II, SCENE I.

THE TRAGEDIES

'For never was a story of more woe'
The Tragedies

Shakespeare's Tragedies are the big guns, with their potent mix of melodrama, angst, intensity of feeling and the power to genuinely shock audiences even today. Of the ten plays usually categorised as his Tragedies (*Titus Andronicus, Romeo and Juliet, Julius Caesar, Hamlet, Othello, Macbeth, King Lear, Antony and Cleopatra, Coriolanus* and *Timon of Athens*), *Hamlet, Othello, Macbeth* and *King Lear* are generally considered to be Shakespeare's true masterpieces, and among the greatest works of art of all time.

Shakespeare moved from mainly writing histories and comedies to the central tragedies in 1599, when he was in his mid-thirties, although he never stuck to just one genre at a time. The developing tradition of English tragic drama drew on both the classical examples of Greek and Roman playwrights, particularly Seneca (see page 163), and the medieval traditions of tragic poems, such as Chaucer's *Troilus and Criseyde*, and the mystery plays (see page 45). The first English tragic play in blank verse was Thomas Norton and Thomas Sackville's *Gorboduc* (1561) and this was followed by Thomas Kyd's influential *The Spanish Tragedy* (written sometime between 1582 and 1592). Christopher Marlowe is celebrated as the forerunner of Shakespearean tragedy and, between them, his masterful *Tamburlaine* and *Doctor Faustus* involve many of the elements that we appreciate in Shakespeare's work: magnificent poetry, an astonishingly vital central character, frustrated ambition, inner conflict, suffering and death.

The heart of this genre is the tragic hero – usually a man of significant qualities who collaborates in his own terrible downfall. The plight of the individual in conflict against those around him and his innermost self is key, leading to mental breakdown and, ultimately, greater self-knowledge through suffering. The sorrow provoked by the demise of these great men is usually somewhat assuaged by the final lines of the play which point to the political state in which they exerted their power being left in peace or renewed: no more fighting families in Verona, a good king in Scotland,

Venice safe from Iago, etc. Weighty themes recur, such as justice, identity, truth, family, fate, the natural order, both human frailty and strength, the conflict between medieval and Early Modern values, and the uncertain nature of human existence.

Aristotle

There is no direct evidence that Shakespeare read Aristotle's work but his theories on tragedy, and drama in general, were influential at the time he was writing and have often been discussed in criticism of his work over the ensuing centuries.

Aristotle (384–322 BCE) was educated at Plato's Academy and later, after acting as tutor to Alexander the Great, set up his own school called the Lyceum in Athens. He taught and wrote on many subjects, including logic, mathematics and psychology. Many of the concepts and terms which we still use to discuss literature come from Aristotle's theories

about Greek poetry, the *Poetics*. This work is believed to have been made up of a treatise on comedy and a treatise on tragedy but only his writings on tragedy survive. He divides tragedy into six separate elements: plot, character, thought, language, melody (songs featured in ancient Greek tragedy) and spectacle. Aristotle saw plot as the most important element and believed that good tragedies only follow one main plotline (unity of action). As his works were translated and interpreted throughout Europe in the Middle Ages and Renaissance this prescription was expanded to insist on the action taking place in just one day (unity of time) and just one place (unity of place). Like most of his contemporaries, Shakespeare was not particularly interested in following these rules – only *The Tempest* and *The Comedy of Errors* can be said to adhere to the unities.

According to Aristotle, plays should just include action that is probable and necessary for the plot of the story, so Shakespeare's love of subplots would not have pleased him either. Other famous terms that come from the *Poetics* are:

Catharsis – meaning 'purgation' – refers to the experience of strong emotion aroused while watching a play that benefits the audience by purging them of extreme feelings and leaving them in a calmer state. Aristotle believed that tragedies should inspire fear and pity. *King Lear* certainly inspires both of these but whether or not it leaves the audience feeling purged and calm is very much up for discussion.

Hamartia – meaning 'error' – refers to the crucial mistake a hero makes that causes the climax of the action. In later centuries hamartia was often interpreted to mean 'tragic flaw', a moral weakness inherent in the hero rather than just a mistake he makes. This led to the idea that you can neatly explain the tragic ends of Shakespeare's heroes through reference to one damaging character trait: e.g. Macbeth's flaw is ambition, Hamlet's is indecision, Lear's is pride, Romeo and Juliet's is recklessness and Othello's is credulity. However, a nuanced reading of the plays shows this is a simplistic approach. And in fact all of these 'flaws' could be recast as virtues in different circumstances: Macbeth's ambition doesn't have to lead to murder, Hamlet's thoughtfulness and wariness about committing murder are admirable, Lear's sense of his kingly dignity is perhaps appropriate and certainly doesn't deserve the suffering it causes, Romeo and Juliet's wholehearted leap into a love affair despite the enmity of their parents is delightfully romantic and Othello's trust of Iago wouldn't be a problem if Iago wasn't a psychopath.

Peripeteia – meaning 'reversal' – refers to the climax of a play where the fortunes or character of the hero change. Romeo's murder of Tybalt could be seen as a peripeteia.

Anagnorisis – meaning 'recognition' – refers to the moment in a play where the hero realises some crucial truth about his situation that has been previously hidden from him. Again, Shakespeare's plays don't necessarily include anagnorisis but Othello's horrifying discovery that Iago has been lying to him could be seen as one example.

Romeo And Juliet
Love, Passion And Violence In The Tale Of 'Star-Crossed Lovers'

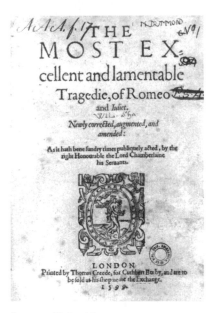

Romeo and Juliet title page, 1599

Romeo and Juliet is one of Shakespeare's early plays, probably written between 1591 and 1595, at the same time as he was composing some of his sonnets. It's a classic formula: boy meets girl and falls in love, but bitterly opposing families turn the romance to tragedy. It's a subject that had captured the imagination of storytellers for centuries – see Ovid's *Pyramus and Thisbe*, which features so memorably in *A Midsummer Night's Dream*, for example. A real pair of warring families in fourteenth-century Italy existed, called the Montecchi and the Capelletti, but whether they had children who fell in love is unclear, and we have no way of knowing if Shakespeare knew about them. It seems likely that his direct literary inspiration was a rather plodding narrative poem by Arthur Brooke called *The Tragicall Historye of Romeus and Iuliet*, written in 1562. Shakespeare transformed the story by compressing its time frame; Romeo and Juliet meet, flirt and get engaged over the course of one breathless evening: theirs is truly a whirlwind romance.

Even in the sixteenth century we can imagine that this formulaic love story was beginning to feel a little clichéd, but in Shakespeare's hands it becomes the greatest romance ever told. Why? Because Shakespeare's exquisite use of language breathes fresh, exhilarating life into tired platitudes, and exposes profound truths about the joy and fragility of human relationships, which resonate across a million Valentine's Day cards even today. It was one of his most performed plays when it was first aired, and remains so – in the last twenty years alone there have been several film adaptations, from Baz Luhrmann's modern reworking, which set the action in 'Verona Beach', Florida, to Julian Fellowes's version, which had a rather more traditional setting, but was nevertheless a radical departure from the original text.

PLOT SUMMARY

The play opens as yet another brawl between the Montagues and the Capulets echoes through the city of Verona (Act I). Prince Escales moves to break up the fight, threatening death to whomever next disturbs the streets. Young Romeo Montague is not present: he's been busy pining after Rosaline, his unrequited love *du jour*. His friends Benvolio and Mercutio tease him, and persuade him to gatecrash the Capulets' grand costume party: it'll take his mind off things. It certainly does. He meets Juliet Capulet, who has spent the day being persuaded to marry Paris, and the pair fall instantly and desperately in love – they kiss, not yet knowing their families are sworn enemies.

Each separately finds out the other's identity, and in the famous balcony scene (Act II), there's a revealing sense of Romeo's overblown artifice, and Juliet's more humble simplicity. Despite their differences, they swear their love for each other and decide to marry. Romeo leaves, promising to find Friar Laurence to preside over the ceremony. The Friar, believing their union could herald the end of the feud between the families, agrees, and Romeo asks Juliet's Nurse to arrange the rendezvous at Friar Laurence's cell (small house) that afternoon. The lovers meet, and the act ends with them rushing off to be wed.

Meanwhile, the Montagues and Capulets are still locked in bloody battle (Act III). Romeo, with one eye on his new position as bridge between the families, seeks to intervene, but his interference results in a fatal wound for his friend Mercutio delivered by Juliet's cousin Tybalt. Romeo's peacemaking policy is abandoned and he kills Tybalt. Prince Escales arrives to a scene of devastation, and, as Lady Capulet demands blood, he decides instead to banish Romeo. Juliet, on hearing of the day's events from her Nurse, reflects on that old chestnut appearance versus reality – how can her husband be a murderer, her 'Beautiful tyrant, fiend angelical'. For Romeo, the exile is as good as a death: 'there is no world without Verona walls'. He reacts badly, and when he hears how Juliet has taken the news, he tries to stab himself; the Nurse and Friar Laurence tell him to pull himself together.

Old Capulet decides to take fate into his own hands, and arranges for Juliet to be married to Paris on the following Thursday (Act IV). Juliet and Paris meet at Friar Laurence's – but she is already married to Romeo. Once alone with the Friar, she too threatens to kill herself. The Friar begins to conceive of a plan – he'll give her a potion that will make her appear dead, she'll be interred in the Capulet vault, and Romeo will whisk her off to Mantua when she wakes up. So Juliet pretends to acquiesce to the wedding to Paris, and Capulet brings the wedding forward by a day – Friar Laurence's already risky plan suddenly looks lethal. Juliet is terrified, but drinks the potion in good faith. On the morning of her wedding to Paris she's discovered, apparently dead, by her mother and the Nurse.

Romeo, meanwhile, ensconced in Mantua, is unaware of the turmoil back in Verona (Act V) until his man Balthasar arrives with the terrible news of Juliet's death. Friar Laurence has been unable to contact him to tell him of the plot, and Romeo plans to travel to the Capulet tomb and kill himself, with poison obtained from an apothecary.

The awful realisation that Romeo has not received his letter dawns on Friar Laurence. He decides to break into the Capulet tomb so he can be with Juliet when she wakes up. Paris goes to Juliet's vault to lay flowers, Romeo appears, attempts to break into the tomb, is confronted by Paris, and kills him, not knowing who he is. Romeo finds the 'dead' Juliet, drinks the poison and dies. Friar Laurence arrives too late; Juliet comes round from her slumber, sees her dead husband, and kills herself with Romeo's dagger. The

Capulets and Montagues, met with the sight of their two dead children, make up their quarrel and promise to build a pair of golden statues in their honour.

KEY THEMES

Passion and Violence

ROMEO

    He jests at scars that never felt a wound.

Enter JULIET *above*

    But, soft! what light through yonder window breaks?
    It is the east, and Juliet is the sun!
    Arise fair sun and kill the envious moon
    Who is already sick and pale with grief
    That thou her maid art far more fair than she.
    Be not her maid, since she is envious,
    Her vestal livery is but sick and green
    And none but fools do wear it. Cast it off.
    It is my lady, O, it is my love!
    O, that she knew she were!

      (ACT II, SCENE 2)

The balcony scene

This is one of the most famous scenes in world drama – the so-called **balcony scene** – though a balcony is never actually mentioned in the text. Romeo, hidden from Juliet's view, watches her appear at a window and is overwhelmed by the intensity of his feelings for her. The language is beautiful, poetic, lyrical, full of extraordinary imagery; it's hyperbolic, vaulting, even galactical. He compares Juliet to the sun, burning with power and light enough to kill 'the envious moon'. Teenagers are nothing if not grandiose. However, there's a real sense here of the strength of Romeo's longing for Juliet – it's this intensity that drives him to give up his family, friends, social standing and ultimately his life. There's a terrible foreshadowing of the death and destruction as well: in the same breath as praising Juliet, Romeo mentions the moon 'sick and pale with grief', 'sick and green'. It's yet another example of the genuis of Shakespeare, managing to pose an enquiry about the potential dangers of a passion as intense as Romeo's, even while demonstrating that passion so beautifully. Friar Laurence sums this up in Act II, Scene 6: 'These violent delights have violent ends / And in their triumph die, like fire and powder, / Which as they kiss consume.'

Conflict and contrast are also running motifs through the play. One of the key ways this is expressed in the following passage is in the now glittering and now granite-like imagery of light and dark, and night and day.

JULIET
> Come night, come, Romeo, come, thou day in night,
> For thou wilt lie upon the wings of night
> Whiter than new snow on a raven's back.
> Come gentle night, come loving, black-brow'd night,
> Give me my Romeo, and when I shall die,
> Take him and cut him out in little stars,
> And he will make the face of heaven so fine
> That all the world will be in love with night,
> And pay no worship to the garish sun.

> (ACT III, SCENE 2)

Here Juliet is anxiously awaiting news of Romeo, and looking forward to the first night they will spend together as a married couple. She is full of desire, and there's huge pathos in the fact that the news she's about to receive will set in motion a chain of events that will lead to their deaths. But before she hears that Romeo has killed Tybalt, in this stunningly beautiful and erotic soliloquy she compares him to a light that will break up the darkness of the night. The sun, which Romeo links with Juliet, here becomes 'garish'. Again, beneath the beauty there is the troubling sense of death and danger.

Fate

CHORUS

> Two households both alike in dignity
> (In fair Verona, where we lay our scene)
> From ancient grudge break to new mutiny,
> Where civil blood makes civil hands unclean.
> From forth the fatal loins of these two foes
> A pair of star-cross'd lovers take their life,
> Whose misadventur'd piteous overthrows
> Do with their death bury their parents' strife.
> The fearful passage of their death-mark'd love . . .

(PROLOGUE)

From the opening lines of the play, the idea of an individual's life being at the mercy of forces beyond our control is set forth, and we can see the many references to fate and fortune. Romeo and Juliet themselves have a sense of their love as 'death-marked': Juliet says 'a faint cold fear thrills through my veins', and even compares her wedding bed to a grave. And Romeo attempts to defy the stars. The inevitability of fate is a brilliant tool for ratcheting up the dramatic tension too; there's a feeling that the more the characters try to escape from the clutches of it the more they are entangled. The series of events that leads to Friar Laurence's plans going awry – the missed letter, the off-timing, the false awakenings and the mistakes of the lovers – has a horrible inevitability. In Elizabethan England this idea of fate would have felt entirely relevant, as many people believed in predestination and destiny.

Marriage and Society

LADY CAPULET
Marry, that marry is the very theme
I came to talk of. Tell me, daughter Juliet,
How stands your disposition to be married?
JULIET
It is an honour that I dream not of.

(ACT I, SCENE 3)

The idea of marrying for love rather than duty was a radical one in Shakespeare's time and Romeo and Juliet's union is an example of just how dangerous prizing individual happiness above familial expectation could be. By opposing society's idea of a good marriage, Juliet places herself in a terrifyingly vulnerable position. As always with Shakespeare there are no easy answers: Romeo and Juliet pay the ultimate price for pursuing their own marriage, but then so do the warring Montagues and Capulets; perhaps another way to read the play is as a warning to interfering parents.

KEY SCENE

While the balcony scene may be one of the most unforgettable in the history of romantic encounters, *Romeo and Juliet*'s **fight scene** (Act III, Scene 1) is in fact one of the play's most important turning points, and casts its shadow of hate and violence long over the rest of the play. Here, on a blistering, furiously hot day when there is a 'mad blood stirring', Mercutio and Benvolio joke about which of them is more up for a fight than the other. The language is playful, but as soon as Tybalt enters it becomes harsher and more brutal. Tybalt asks for a word, and Mercutio immediately responds with 'make it a word and a blow'. Romeo, fresh from his marriage, the happiest hour of his life, enters the highly charged, violent atmosphere as peacemaker. He has to tamp down his first instincts, which are to be full of fire himself, to react angrily to being called a villain, but he turns the other cheek, and completely wrong-foots Tybalt. There's a fleeting moment then where it looks as if the union of Romeo and Juliet will indeed end the terrible, lethal feud between the families, as Romeo says: 'And so, good Capulet, which name I tender / As dearly as my own, be satisfied.' But Mercutio's response puts a stop to all that. He winds Tybalt up even further and eventually they both draw and fight, and in the ensuing confusion Mercutio loses his life. Initially Tybalt flees, but when he returns to the scene Romeo is unable to hold back, and in revenge kills Tybalt, with dreadful and tragic consequences for himself and his new wife.

KEY SYMBOL

ROMEO
> Come hither, man. I see that thou art poor.
> Hold, there is forty ducats. Let me have
> A dram of poison, such soon-speeding gear
> As will disperse itself through all the veins,
> That the life-weary taker may fall dead,
> And that the trunk may be discharg'd of breath
> As violently as hasty powder fir'd
> Doth hurry from the fatal cannon's womb.

> (ACT V, SCENE I)

Poison plays a large part in propelling the action of the play forward and is also important metaphorically. It's a poison or potion that convinces Juliet there's a way out of their predicament, and immediately on hearing of Juliet's death Romeo wants to procure poison for himself. The final scene is the ultimate union of sex and death and full of heavily laden sexual imagery as Romeo drinks poison from Juliet's 'cup', and Juliet kills herself with Romeo's 'happy dagger'. Symbolically, poison is representative of the endless feud between the Montagues and Capulets, their 'civil blood' a venom that infects the entire society of fair Verona.

The critical response to *Romeo and Juliet*

Romeo and Juliet may be one of Shakespeare's best-loved plays, but it hasn't always gone down so well with audiences. Samuel Pepys wrote in 1662: 'it is a play of itself the worst that I ever heard in my life'. Perhaps it's the opacity of the moral message at the heart of the play that divides, but it's certainly made for some interesting and varied critical responses. The **feminist interpretation** has it that Verona's strict patriarchal society drives much of the action of the play, where Romeo's only course of action after the death of Mercutio is violence. In fact, Juliet upends Elizabethan ideas of **gender** – she is capable of manoeuvring, her language is often calm and full of clarity, particularly in the face of Romeo's at times exaggerated adulation. She's finally beaten by the male-dominated constructs around her, though, as her father is able to force her to marry Paris. **Freudian theories** highlight the intertwining of sex and death throughout the play, and **homoerotic interpretation** (or queer theory) has focused on the sexualised dialogue between Romeo and Mercutio.

Some other great doomed lovers

Pyramus and Thisbe
These two are the originals. They form part of Ovid's *Metamorphoses*, and their story has some startling parallels. They are next-door neighbours in the city of Babylon who fall in love but, because of their parents' feud, are banned from getting hitched. Sound familiar? The pair agree to meet in secret but on arriving first at their rendezvous spot by a mulberry bush, Thisbe is frightened by a lioness with bloody jaws from a recent kill. She runs off, leaving behind a veil.

Pyramus arrives and the lioness has the veil in her mouth, now also covered in blood, and believing his lover to be dead, kills himself. His blood spills and turns the white mulberry fruit red. Thisbe returns and finds the dead body of Pyramus, so kills herself with his sword. The gods were so moved by the lovers' plight that they commemorated their love by staining the fruit on a mulberry bush red for all eternity. Bottom undercuts this tragic tale somewhat in his portrayal of Pyramus in

A Midsummer Night's Dream: 'What dreadful dole is here! / Eyes, do you see? / How can it be? / O dainty duck! O dear!'

Tristan and Iseult

Next up is an unlucky pair from Celtic legend. Their tragic and adulterous love story has been immortalised on the stage and screen, most famously in Wagner's opera *Tristan und Isolde* (triggered by Wagner's own adulterous affair). Wagner revered Shakespeare, calling him 'the mightiest poet of all time', and his first work, composed as a thirteen-year-old, was a six-hour epic that attempted to combine *Hamlet*, *King Lear*, *Macbeth*, *Richard III* and *Romeo and Juliet*. Tristan and Iseult's tale was said to have also provided the inspiration for the story of Lancelot and Guinevere. The Cornish knight, Tristan, and the Irish princess, Iseult, fall in love when they unknowingly drink a love potion on a journey back from Ireland. Sadly their journey was for Tristan to bring Iseult to Cornwall to marry his beloved uncle King Mark. Iseult and Mark marry, but Tristan and Iseult can't keep away from each other and eventually Tristan is banned from Cornwall, moving to Brittany and marrying another woman named Iseult. After falling ill, Tristan sends for the original, believing she can cure him, and says that she should let him know her decision by the colour of the sails on the ship: if it returns with black sails she refuses his request; if it has white sails he will know she is on board. In a fit of jealousy, the new Iseult tells him the sails are black, whereupon he

dies of grief. In fact Iseult is aboard, but she too dies of grief when she hears what has happened.

Héloïse and Abélard

These twelfth-century lovers paid a hefty price for their illicit romance. Héloïse d'Argenteuil was a gifted Parisian scholar, and a ward of her uncle, Canon Fulbert. Peter Abélard was a renowned philosopher, one of the greatest thinkers of the twelfth century. Abélard persuaded Fulbert to allow him to move into their home in order to tutor Héloïse – inevitably they fall hopelessly in love. Even more inevitably, when Héloïse becomes pregnant their affair is discovered by a furious Fulbert. Abélard proposes marriage, and though Héloïse initially refuses, fearing for her lover's reputation, she eventually agrees. They are secretly married, but quickly realise Canon Fulbert plans to drive them apart. While Héloïse seeks refuge with nuns at Argenteuil, Fulbert and a gang of men set upon Abélard and castrate him. At this stage Héloïse and Abélard each take religious orders, she becoming a nun and he becoming a monk. They never see each other again, but exchange passionate intellectual letters for twenty years – theirs is a truly enduring love affair. There is a suggestion that in 1606 Shakespeare began work on a play entitled *Abelard and Elois, A Tragedie*, which in the end he abandoned in favour of *Antony and Cleopatra*.

Troilus and Cressida

Many years after *Romeo and Juliet* Shakespeare wrote another, far less romantic, play about doomed lovers, *Troilus and Cressida* (1602). Considered a problem play (see page 106) now, it mixes elements of tragedy, comedy and history together. Two centuries earlier that other great English literary giant, Geoffrey Chaucer, had also made this tale, based in part on Homer's *Iliad* and in part on later medieval embellishments to the Troilus story, the subject of his great epic poem *Troilus and Criseyde*.

Troilus is a Trojan prince, the brother of the famous Hector and Paris, and involved with them in defending his city from the besieging Greek army. He falls in love with Cressida, the daughter of a Trojan priest, and so her uncle Pandarus (from whom we get the word 'pander') arranges for them to be together. However, the morning after brings the couple a nasty shock when Cressida is involved in an exchange of prisoners with the Greeks and passed over to them to join her treacherous father who has defected to the Greek side. During a ceasefire the Greek commander Ulysses takes Troilus to see Cressida but, to his horror, he secretly witnesses her adjusting indecently rapidly to her new situation by beginning a relationship with the Greek soldier, Diomedes. Unaware he is watching, she says to herself: 'Troilus, farewell! one eye yet looks on thee / But with my heart the other eye doth see. / Ah, poor our sex! this fault in us I find, / The error of our eye directs our mind.' He leaves heartbroken. The love story intertwines with the trials and tribulations of the Trojan and Greek forces, including the Greek heroes Agamemnon, Achilles, Patroclus, Ulysses and Ajax, whose heroism is deflated and treated with cynicism throughout. The play ends with Troilus witnessing the ambush and killing of his brother, the noble Hector, and vowing revenge. It's not the most uplifting of Shakespeare's works, to be sure.

Hamlet
Doubt, Death And Family Relationships
In Medieval Denmark

'What would your gracious figure?' ACT III, SCENE 4

Hamlet is a very special play, not least because it has been one of Shakespeare's most popular works since his own time, and the source of his only Best Picture Oscar win (for Laurence Olivier's film version). According to hearsay it was also the occasion of his own greatest performances as an actor when he played the Ghost. Seen by many as a response to the insecurity brought about by the Reformation and the lack of an heir to the English throne, it also marked a step forward in the dramatist's portrayal of the inner workings of the human mind. It's true that not everyone's a fan – Voltaire was cutting, likening it to the 'fruit of the imagination of a drunken savage', and audiences and critics have been perplexed by many aspects of it for years – but its openness to interpretation, and the intensely complicated hero at its centre, whose concerns still feel frighteningly relevant, are two reasons why it has endured and been so widely recognised as a masterpiece.

PLOT SUMMARY

At the start of the play the ghost of the dead King Hamlet appears to the watchmen of Elsinore Castle in eastern Denmark, and to Horatio who is best friends with the king's son, (Prince) Hamlet (Act I). The king's brother, Claudius, has taken the throne and married his widow, Gertrude, and this, not surprisingly, is causing Hamlet great distress. The Ghost appears to Hamlet with some incendiary news: Claudius murdered him and Hamlet must avenge this crime. Meanwhile, Hamlet's girlfriend, Ophelia, is persuaded by her brother, Laertes, and father, the king's adviser, Polonius, that Hamlet isn't serious about her and she agrees to stop seeing him.

The Ghost has completely spooked Hamlet and he tells Horatio that he may pretend to be mad in order to buy him some time to work out what to do (Act II). Hamlet's behaviour disturbs Claudius and Gertrude who arrange for his university friends, Rosencrantz and Guildenstern, to spy on him. As if that's not enough to worry about they are also concerned with the threat of an invasion from Norway. After Ophelia reports an agitated interaction with the prince to her father, Polonius tells Claudius that Hamlet has gone mad because Ophelia has broken off their relationship. Meanwhile, Hamlet has rumbled Rosencrantz and Guildernstern: he knows they aren't just in Elsinore for a friendly visit. When a troupe of travelling players arrives to entertain the court Hamlet instructs the thespians to enact his father's murder to see how Claudius reacts.

Polonius and Claudius spy on yet another disturbing encounter between Hamlet and Ophelia, and Claudius becomes anxious enough about his nephew to decide to ship him off to England (Act III). But first the court gathers to watch the play. When the murder scene is acted out, Claudius runs off, convincing Hamlet of his guilt. When Hamlet goes to talk to his mother in her room, he passes Claudius praying, but doesn't take the opportunity to kill him. He tells his mother about the murder and viciously chastises her for marrying his uncle. Polonius has been hiding behind the tapestry on the wall of Gertrude's room to eavesdrop on their conversation and when Hamlet realises someone is there he stabs through the tapestry, thinking he's killing Claudius. Gertrude is horrified but even more horrified by what Hamlet has told her. The Ghost then appears again to Hamlet.

After her son leaves, Gertrude tells Claudius that Hamlet has gone completely mad and killed Polonius (Act IV). Claudius sends the prince off to England with Rosencrantz and Guildenstern, and, secretly, with instructions to the King of England to execute him. However, a pirate attack returns Hamlet to Denmark. Meanwhile, Polonius's death and her heartbreak over Hamlet have sent Ophelia insane, and Laertes has arrived back at the castle seeking revenge. Claudius plots with Laertes for him to kill Hamlet in a duel, using a poisoned sword and a poisoned cup of wine. Gertrude arrives while they are talking to tell them that Ophelia has drowned.

Hamlet returns to court via the graveyard where Ophelia is about to be buried (Act V). When her funeral procession arrives and he realises that Ophelia has died he ends up fighting with Laertes in her grave – yes, in her grave – over who loved her more. The next day Hamlet receives Laertes' challenge to a fencing contest. He also reveals to Horatio that he sent Rosencrantz and Guildenstern on to England to be executed in his stead. When the duel takes place Gertrude mistakenly drinks from the poisoned cup meant for Hamlet, and after being wounded by Laertes' poisoned sword, Hamlet manages to wound Laertes with it too. When Gertrude dies, Laertes tells Hamlet that Claudius is responsible and Hamlet kills the king with both the sword and the poison. Laertes grants Hamlet forgiveness before dying and then finally Hamlet himself dies, entreating his friend Horatio with his dying breath to tell the sad story of the play's events and bequeathing the throne of Denmark to Fortinbras, Prince of Norway, who arrives with impeccable timing at the very end.

KEY THEMES

Doubt

HAMLET

> To be, or not to be, that is the question:
> Whether 'tis nobler in the mind to suffer
> The slings and arrows of outrageous fortune,
> Or to take arms against a sea of troubles
> And by opposing end them? To die – to sleep,
> No more; and by a sleep to say we end

The heart-ache and the thousand natural shocks
That flesh is heir to: 'tis a consummation
Devoutly to be wish'd. To die, to sleep;
To sleep, perchance to dream – ay, there's the rub:
For in that sleep of death what dreams may come,
When we have shuffled off this mortal coil,
Must give us pause . . .

(ACT III, SCENE I)

No book on Shakespeare would be complete without reference to this, the most famous speech in all literature. In it Hamlet muses upon two of the key themes of the play: doubt and death. *Hamlet* has been said to be a play about delay, and this delay is caused by the prince's doubt. He is unsure whether the ghost who commands him to kill Claudius is 'a spirit of health or goblin damn'd'. Therefore he has to test Claudius with the *Mouse-trap* performance in order to be sure that he is guilty of murder. He is also unsure what the right course of action is, even if the Ghost is honest: should he commit a murder to avenge a murder? The play is full of different kinds of questions both in the dialogue and soliloquies and in the audience's minds after they have watched it: Is Hamlet ever really mad? Why is he so horrible to Ophelia? Does he know Polonius and Claudius are spying on him in the nunnery scene? Was he sleeping with Ophelia? Why does Claudius only leave during the play's enactment of the murder and not during the dumbshow? Is Gertrude betraying or protecting Hamlet when she talks to Claudius after the closet scene? Does Ophelia commit suicide? Ideas of doubt and distrust are also explored through Shakespeare's use of language. Claudius in particular works a bit like a modern spin doctor to present affairs in the light most favourable to himself. He metaphorically pours poison in the ears of those around him.

The most common interpretation of this speech is that Hamlet is considering committing suicide, whether he acknowledges this to himself openly or not. He is put off the idea predominantly by the thought of the afterlife and what it might hold. This is also a reason for his delay in murdering Claudius, an act that may damn him.

Death

HAMLET

Alas, poor Yorick! I knew him, Horatio, a fellow of infinite jest, of most excellent fancy. He hath borne me on his back a thousand times, and now – how abhorred in my imagination it is. My gorge rims at it. Here hung those lips that I have kissed I know not how oft. Where be your gibes now, your gambols, your songs, your flashes of merriment, that were wont to set the table on a roar? Not one now to mock your own grinning? Quite chop-fallen? Now get you to my lady's chamber and tell her, let her paint an inch thick, to this favour she must come. Make her laugh at that.

(ACT V, SCENE I)

In this speech, and others in this scene, Hamlet muses upon how death comes to everyone however lively, beautiful or important they are. Man is, after all, a 'quintessence of dust'. He shows his disgust for the physical deterioration that occurs after death, and this imagery of decay runs throughout the play and connects with the concept of something being 'rotten' in the state of Denmark because of the evil behaviour of King Claudius.

As with the 'To be, or not to be' speech, here Hamlet is also concerned with what happens after death. The Ghost is a visitor from the afterlife, 'Doom'd for a certain term to walk the night, / And for the day confin'd to fast in fires, / Till the foul crimes done in my days of nature / Are burnt and purg'd away.' This description fits with the Catholic idea of Purgatory, where sinners who aren't quite bad enough to go to hell suffer until they have paid off their debt of sin and can enter heaven. It is interesting that the Ghost appears to be a Catholic as Hamlet seems to be Protestant. The prince has attended university in Wittenberg which is the famous site of Luther's contribution to the Reformation. Protestants do not believe in Purgatory but simply in heaven and hell and so this explains Hamlet's doubt about the Ghost's true origins: 'The spirit that I have seen / May be the devil, and the devil hath power / T'assume a pleasing shape, yea, and perhaps, / Out of my weakness and my melancholy, / As he is very potent with such spirits, / Abuses me to damn me.' The play was written during the Protestant reign of Elizabeth I, who succeeded the Catholic Mary I, so there was a great deal of religious upheaval to contend with in Shakespeare's generation (see page 20).

Family

CLAUDIUS

  Though yet of Hamlet our dear brother's death
  The memory be green, and that it us befitted
  To bear our hearts in grief and our whole kingdom
  To be contracted in one brow of woe,
  Yet so far hath discretion fought with nature
  That we with wisest sorrow think on him
  Together with remembrance of ourselves.
  Therefore our sometime sister, now our queen,
  Th'imperial jointress to this warlike state,
  Have we, as 'twere with a defeated joy,
  With an auspicious and a dropping eye,
  With mirth in funeral and with dirge in marriage,
  In equal scale weighing delight and dole,
  Taken to wife . . .

  (ACT I, SCENE 2)

This is Claudius's first speech, given to his court. It freely admits that he has married his brother's widow swiftly after his death, but doesn't mention that he was responsible for this death. *Hamlet* is a soap opera of perverted family relationships: fratricide, incest, spying on your children, a daughter mourning a father and a brother mourning a sister, and sons avenging fathers (Hamlet, Laertes and possibly Fortinbras).

Hamlet repeatedly refers to his mother's remarriage as incest. In Elizabethan times marrying the wife of your dead brother was regarded this way. Infamously, this was the reason Queen Elizabeth's father, Henry VIII, used for divorcing his first wife, Catherine of Aragon, and marrying Anne Boleyn, Elizabeth's mother. Catherine had been betrothed to Henry's older brother, Arthur, but he died before they properly married. It has also been suggested that Laertes' attitude to his sister's love life has a whiff of the unhealthy about it, and, of course, Hamlet's feelings about his mother have been said to be anything but straightforwardly filial.

The families in the play are all broken in one way or another, and Hamlet's romantic love for Ophelia also fails. It is Hamlet's friendship with Horatio that gives the most positive image of human relationships: 'thou hast been / As one, in suff'ring all, that suffers nothing [. . .] / Give me that man / That is not passion's slave, and I will wear him / In my heart's core, ay, in my heart of heart, / As I do thee.'

KEY SCENES

For ease of reference some of the most important scenes in the play are often named rather than referred to by act and scene numbers.

The **nunnery scene** (Act III, Scene 1). This is where Ophelia, while Polonius and Claudius hide and watch, returns Hamlet's love letters to him to get the message across that they have truly broken up. Hamlet appears to take being dumped very badly and tells her 'Get thee to a nunnery', before launching into a generally misogynistic, and anti-make-up, tirade – 'God hath given you one face, and you make yourselves another. You jig, you amble, and you lisp'. Ophelia generously thinks he's having a nervous breakdown. It's worth noting that 'nunnery' was also

Elizabethan slang for a brothel. This scene includes the 'To be, or not to be' soliloquy.

The **Mouse-trap scene / play-within-a-play scene** (Act III, Scene 2). This is the scene where the touring theatre company, on Hamlet's instructions, enact the play *The Mouse-trap*, also called *The Murder of Gonzago*. They first act out the play's event in mime in a 'dumbshow', and then begin the main action, which involves a king being murdered by his brother pouring poison in his ear. This is the way the Ghost told Hamlet that Claudius murdered him and at this point Claudius appears deeply troubled and storms off.

The **prayer scene** (Act III, Scene 3). The following scene sees Claudius at prayer, wishing he could repent of his brother's murder, but unwilling to give up the throne or Gertrude. Hamlet sees him and is tempted to kill him there and then but doesn't want him to die in the state of grace that praying would confer on him. Instead he decides he'll kill him when he's engaged in an activity that 'has no relish of salvation in't'. This scene is interesting because through Claudius's soliloquy the audience is given full proof that he is guilty, but no character witnesses this.

The **closet scene** (Act III, Scene 4). This scene follows on from the prayer scene and sees Hamlet in his mother's 'closet', or bedroom, where he rages at her for marrying Claudius and seems to convince her that she's in the wrong. He also tells her that Claudius murdered her late husband. During their heated exchange he realises that someone is listening behind the 'arras', or tapestry, on the wall and leaps into action by stabbing them. It turns out to be Polonius and Hamlet is unrepentant, stating that 'Heaven hath pleased it so / To punish me with this, and this with me.' These words foreshadow how Polonius's death will lead to Hamlet's at the hands of his son Laertes. The focus of this scene is Hamlet's relationship with his mother and his obsession with her sex life with his uncle: 'to live / In the rank sweat of an enseamèd bed, / Stew'd in corruption, honeying and making love / Over the nasty sty'. It is often played in line with the famous Freudian interpretation of *Hamlet* which posits that Hamlet's central problem is his Oedipus complex. This interpretation sees Hamlet's rage against Claudius for seducing his mother as the product of repressed jealousy, as he himself would like to have a sexual relationship with her.

Ophelia's mad scene (Act IV, Scene 5). This scene shows Ophelia driven senseless by grief at the death of her father and Hamlet's brutal behaviour towards her. Laertes also returns in this scene, committed to avenging his father's death. Ophelia's songs appear bizarre and nonsensical to Claudius, Gertrude and her brother but on closer observation her words are all about sex and death: 'Young men will do't, if they come to't; / By cock, they are to blame. / Quoth she, before you tumbled me, / You promised me to wed.' She also uses the language of flowers to express herself: 'There's rosemary, that's for remembrance . . .' Interestingly she gives fennel and columbine to the king, which stand for flattery and faithlessness. She says to Gertrude 'There's rue for you; and here's some for me' and some commentators have also noted that rue was used to bring on abortions and so had a connection with illicit sex. Ophelia is associated with flowers throughout the play, being linked with violets, an emblem of innocence, three times, and Gertrude's famous speech in Act IV, Scene 7 describes her dying covered in flowers: 'with fantastic garlands did she come / Of crow-flowers, nettles, daisies, and long purples'.

The **gravediggers' scene** (Act V, Scene 1). This scene takes place in a graveyard and begins with the comic interlude provided by the two gravediggers who engage with Hamlet in wordplay before he discusses with Horatio the fact that death comes for us all in the end, however great we are: 'Imperious Caesar, dead and turn'd to clay, / Might stop a hole to keep the wind away.' It then descends into something far more unpleasant when the funeral procession arrives and Hamlet realises that Ophelia has died. He and Laertes fight in her grave after he tells Laertes to stop exaggerating his grief and says: 'I loved Ophelia: forty thousand brothers / Could not, with all their quantity of love, / Make up my sum.' Both the gravedigger and the priest imply that Ophelia committed suicide and shouldn't really be getting a Christian burial, unless 'she drowned herself in her own defence'. This scene has the often misquoted line 'Alas, poor Yorick! I knew him, Horatio' (feel free to scoff at anyone who says 'Alas, poor Yorick! I knew him well') as Hamlet stands by an open grave holding the skull of the former court jester who used to play with him as a child.

KEY SYMBOL

The enduring symbol of *Hamlet* is **Yorick's skull**. If you ever see an image of a young man holding a skull you know immediately that Hamlet is being referred to. It's even become a useful shorthand for Shakespeare himself as you'll see from the cover of this book. The skull is a fitting object to represent a play so much concerned with death. The imagery of disease and decay that runs throughout emphasises this: 'Something is rotten in the state of Denmark'; 'rank corruption, mining all within, / Infects unseen'; 'my wit's diseased'; 'is't not to be damn'd, / To let this canker of our nature come / In further evil?' Hamlet sees the whole country as being infected by Claudius's crimes and feels he needs to provide the 'remedy'.

Hamlet and Revenge Tragedy

Hamlet both belongs to and transcends the recognised tradition of Revenge Tragedy. Revenge Tragedies were popular from Elizabeth's reign through to Charles I's. They grew out of the Renaissance enthusiasm for classical models and harked back to the violent plays of the Roman playwright and philosopher Seneca which were first translated into English in 1559. Thomas Kyd's *The Spanish Tragedy* is regarded as the first great English Revenge play. In fact, many scholars believe that one of the sources for Shakespeare's *Hamlet* was a lost play of the same name written years before by Kyd.

Attitudes to revenge were complicated in Elizabethan times, and in many ways still are, as the idea of the personal vendetta has not disappeared. There was admiration for the pagan idea of repaying a wrong done to you directly, in line with the Old Testament 'eye for an eye' rule, but this conflicted with the Christian principle of turning the other cheek and leaving vengeance to God, and also with the idea that punishment for crimes should be the responsibility of the state, which was happy to engage in brutal capital punishment at this time.

Revenge Tragedies follow certain conventions: they often involve a ghost asking for vengeance, delay in the enactment of that revenge, disguises and faked insanity, elaborate bloody violence, a perverse sexual undercurrent and the death of the avenging hero. Shakespeare's twist on this formula makes the delay depend upon doubt about the veracity of the Ghost's account and the introspective musings of the hero. Laertes and Fortinbras are more typical active revenge heroes. Shakespeare's own *Titus Andronicus* (1593), Thomas Middleton's *The Revenger's Tragedy* (1605), John Webster's *The White Devil* (1612) and *The Duchess of Malfi* (1614) and John Ford's *'Tis Pity She's a Whore* (c.1630–33) are other significant examples of the genre. (John Webster appears as a literary in-joke in the film *Shakespeare in Love* as a bloodthirsty young boy torturing mice and a fan of *Titus Andronicus*.)

Famous speeches explained

Hamlet, Act I, Scene 2

O, that this too too sullied flesh would melt,
Thaw and resolve itself into a dew,
Or that the Everlasting had not fix'd
His canon 'gainst self-slaughter! O God! God!
How weary, stale, flat and unprofitable
Seem to me all the uses of this world!
Fie on't! ah fie! 'tis an unweeded garden

If only I could melt into dew.
If only God didn't forbid suicide.
Everything is pointless.
The world is like a shabby garden, gone to seed, where only disgusting things grow.
I can't believe it's come to this. My father has only been dead less than two months.

That grows to seed; things rank and gross
  in nature
Possess it merely. That it should come to
  this!
But two months dead – nay, not so much,
  not two –
So excellent a king, that was, to this
Hyperion to a satyr; so loving to my mother
That he might not beteem the winds of
  heaven
Visit her face too roughly! Heaven and
  earth,
Must I remember? Why, she would hang
  on him
As if increase of appetite had grown
By what it fed on; and yet, within a month
  –
Let me not think on't – Frailty, thy name
  is woman –
A little month, or ere those shoes were old
With which she follow'd my poor father's
  body,
Like Niobe, all tears – why she, even she –
O God, a beast, that wants discourse of
  reason
Would have mourn'd longer – married
  with my uncle,
My father's brother – but no more like my
  father
Than I to Hercules. Within a month,
Ere yet the salt of most unrighteous tears
Had left the flushing in her gallèd eyes,
She married – O, most wicked speed! To
  post
With such dexterity to incestuous sheets!
It is not, nor it cannot come to good.
But break, my heart; for I must hold my
  tongue.

He was an excellent king compared to
  my uncle Claudius. Like the Greek
  god of the sun compared to a satyr. He
  loved my mother so much he didn't
  even let the wind blow on her face too
  hard.

I wish I didn't have to remember all this.
  Mother was so keen on my father it
  seemed like the more she got of him the
  more she wanted. But still, within a
  month [she took up with my uncle]. . . I
  can't bear thinking about it . . . Women
  are weak.

Just a measly month, before the shoes she
  wore to my father's funeral were old
  – where she cried as much as the
  ancient Greek princess Niobe, who
  turned into a mountain spring after
  her children were murdered by the
  gods.

O God! Even an animal would have
  mourned longer. She married my uncle,
  my father's brother, even though he's
  less like my father than I am like the
  ancient Roman hero and strongman
  Hercules. She married him within a
  month. Before even the salt of her false
  tears had left her swollen eyes. How
  wickedly quickly she jumped into those
  incestuous sheets.

It can't turn out well. But my heart is
  going to have to break because I can't
  say anything about it.

Othello
Love, Jealousy And Betrayal
In *The Moor Of Venice*

'To my unfolding lend your
prosperous ear' ACT I, SCENE 3

Sandwiched neatly between those two other mighty masterpieces *Hamlet* and *King Lear*, *Othello* is one of Shakespeare's most devastating and, well . . . tragic of tragedies. It deals with all the biggest mysteries that still stir up our quintessence of dust even today: race, love, lust, betrayal, jealousy and the see-saw nature of solitude and connection.

PLOT SUMMARY

This is the story of Othello, a Moor and brilliant general who, as the play opens (Act I), has secretly married Desdemona, daughter of Venice's Senator Brabantio. Desdemona's dishonourable suitor Roderigo has been paying the extremely nasty Iago, Othello's third in command, to win him back Desdemona's favour. Iago is angry with Othello for passing him over for promotion in favour of the congenial Lieutenant Cassio. Roderigo and Iago plan to prevent Othello and Desdemona from eloping. Meanwhile the Duke of Venice is searching for Othello too, as his military muscle is needed to fend off the imminent invasion of Cyprus by the Turks. Brought before the Duke, Othello and Desdemona convince everyone that their love is genuine, and together they set out for Cyprus. Iago hastens to reassure Roderigo that all is not lost: he has a plan to split them up.

On Cyprus, the threat of the Turks has vanished with the entire fleet being fortuitously (for the Venetians at least) lost in a storm, and Othello is left rather twiddling his thumbs (Act II). We all know that idle hands are the devil's workshop, and here's where Iago really comes into his own as evil puppet master. He manages to convince Othello, via various machinations and manoeuvres, that Cassio and Desdemona are an item, the key evidence being a handkerchief of Desdemona's that Iago plants in Cassio's bedroom (Act III). His nerves suitably steeled and his heart suitably hardened, Othello arranges to kill Desdemona after Roderigo and Iago have killed Cassio (Act IV). Iago and Roderigo botch the job, but on hearing what he assumes to be Cassio's death cry, Othello smothers his wife with a pillow (Act V). In the final scenes Iago's wife Emilia, wise to the skulduggery of her horrible husband, reveals all, with the wounded-but-not-dead Cassio confirming that she's telling the truth. Othello, realising he's been entirely deceived, kills himself, and Iago is arrested.

KEY THEMES

Jealousy

IAGO

> O beware, my lord, of jealousy!
> It is the green-eyed monster, which doth mock
> The meat it feeds on. That cuckold lives in bliss,
> Who, certain of his fate, loves not his wronger,
> But O, what damned minutes tells he o'er
> Who dotes, yet doubts, suspects, yet strongly loves!

OTHELLO

> O misery!

>   (Act III, Scene 3)

Iago is essentially telling Othello here that the cuckolded man who knows his wife is unfaithful ('who, certain of his fate, loves not his wronger') is happier than the man who suspects his wife but is not sure, and thus is driven by his continuing affection to be tormented by 'the green-eyed monster, which doth mock / The meat it feeds on'. Being a cuckold was a big deal in Elizabethan times, having a profound effect not just on a man's state of mind, but his social standing too – it could lead to ostracism and financial ruin. Many male characters (and Cassio's lover Bianca) are affected by jealousy in *Othello*: Roderigo is jealous of Cassio and Othello, Iago is jealous of Cassio's career and also of Othello, and Othello becomes tormented by jealousy when he suspects Desdemona and Cassio are having an affair. Iago is the only one who, as well as being apparently motivated by jealousy, is savvy enough to use it as a means of manipulation. He is truly steeped in it. But what drives this rampant resentment? Why on earth has Iago got such terrible anger issues? Some wonder if the riddle of Iago's intent is part of the enduring fascination audiences and readers have with *Othello*, it's a mystery even our greatest minds can't seem to solve (see **critical responses** later).

Appearance and Deception

BRABANTIO
> Look to her, Moor, if thou hast eyes to see:
> She has deceived her father, and may thee.

(ACT I, SCENE 3)

Othello is also concerned with appearance and deception. In the quotation above Desdemona's father, Brabantio, warns Othello that Desdemona's independent nature in marrying him behind Brabantio's back may mean she goes on to betray Othello. In fact Desdemona is an honest and faithful person. However, obviously Iago is not the great and trusted friend Othello believes him to be, and the story he tells Othello is not the truth. The conversation he stages with Cassio, where Cassio apparently admits to sleeping with Desdemona, is fake: Cassio is actually talking about a different woman. The play is stuffed full of references to dreams and visions and trances, and the entire action hinges on Iago's ability to present his own versions of reality, and on the other characters' willingness to believe him.

Race and Otherness

IAGO
> Even now, now, very now, an old black ram
> Is tupping your white ewe! Arise, arise,

> (ACT I, SCENE I)

It's impossible to ignore the theme of race and otherness in *Othello*, although the term 'race' would not have been recognised by Elizabethans. Othello's race sets him apart from the other characters, and while he is respected for his military prowess, the play also portrays fear of miscegenation, demonstrating the terrible fallout of an interracial love affair. In the extract above Iago uses derogatory animal imagery to tell Brabantio that his daughter has run off with the Moor ('tupping' means 'mating with'). Even Othello himself cannot believe that Desdemona truly loves him, a Moor. And yet Shakespeare also challenges expectations: an Elizabethan audience would assume that the villain would be black, whereas in fact it's the white Iago who is the bad guy.

Isolation

DUKE
> Valiant Othello, we must straight employ you
> Against the general enemy Ottoman.

> (ACT I, SCENE 3)

Another key theme is the damaging nature of isolation. As the action moves from the teeming streets of Venice to the island of Cyprus, a place physically cut off from the world, the worst evils begin to emerge. Each character's downfall is hastened by isolation too: Othello, in trusting only Iago, becomes isolated, and Desdemona becomes so isolated from Othello that she is incapable of defending herself, and her fidelity. This isolation is also beautifully expressed in the many soliloquies in the play, like Othello's famous 'It is the cause, it is the cause, my soul', of Act V, as he's about to murder his wife.

KEY SCENE

The **temptation scene** (Act III, Scene 3) is central, both thematically and literally, and marks the moment that Othello turns from loving, protective husband to paranoid, jealous and bloodthirsty monster. Iago plants the seeds of doubt when he spots Cassio and Desdemona parting and utters in Othello's hearing, 'Ha, I like not that', quickly backtracking once he's piqued the Moor's curiosity. Still, even at this stage, Othello admits he'll do anything for Desdemona. It's when she leaves the room that Iago really ramps up the insinuation, and Othello falls for it hook, line and sinker. Even as Iago is beseeching him to beware the 'green-eyed monster', he is falling into the trap that Iago has laid. When Othello demands of Iago the 'ocular proof' of the terrible doubts beginning to eat at his soul, Iago is able to produce it – it's here that the lost handkerchief comes into play. In the following scene Desdemona's inability to locate the love token will truly condemn her, in Othello's eyes at least, to death. As Othello damns his 'lewd minx' of a wife, Iago is rising further in his estimation, and the scene ends with Iago's chillingly romantic words: 'I am your own for ever.' He has set in motion a complex string of deceptions that will end in the tragedy of the play.

KEY SYMBOL

Desdemona's handkerchief is a key symbol in Iago's manipulation. Its importance to Othello is explained in a very loaded speech to doomed Desdemona:

OTHELLO
                     That handkerchief
            Did an Egyptian to my mother give,
            She was a charmer and could almost read
            The thoughts of people. She told her, while
                she kept it,
            'Twould make her amiable and subdue my father
            Entirely to her love; but if she lost it
            Or made gift of it, my father's eye
            Should hold her loathèd and his spirits should hunt
            After new fancies. She, dying, gave it me
            And bid me, when my fate would have me wive,
            To give it her.

                (ACT III, SCENE 4)

Othello claims that fateful handkerchief was given to his mother by a 200-year-old Egyptian Sybil who told her that while she had possession of it, her husband would love her, but if she lost it her husband would look elsewhere ('my father's eye / Should hold her loathèd and his spirits should hunt / After new fancies').

In medieval and Renaissance times, handkerchiefs were a powerful symbol of women's romantic allegiances – we can all picture a lady loftily dropping her hankie while knights clamour to retrieve it. For Desdemona, the handkerchief is a symbol of Othello's love, and Iago manages to persuade Othello to see it as a symbol of Desdemona's infidelity. Its pattern, of red strawberries on a white background, is suggestive of bloodstains. Traditionally, red symbolises both death and love, and in *Othello* the two are inextricably and devastatingly linked.

Top ten Othellos

10. **Richard Burton** (1925–84). Richard Burton and his co-star John Neville swapped the roles of Othello and Iago on successive nights for their run at the Old Vic in 1955. According to critics Burton's star shone brightest in the role of villainous Iago.

9. **Anthony Hopkins** (b.1937) played Othello opposite Bob Hoskins's Iago in a BBC adaptation in 1981. Word has it that Hoskins stole the show.

8. The film **Orson Welles** (1915–85) made of *Othello* won the Palme d'Or when it premiered at Cannes in 1952, but was largely ignored in his native America.

7. **Chiwetel Ejiofor** (b.1977) gave an unadorned and classical performance in 2007 which put him 'into the front rank of modern Othellos' according to the *Guardian*.

6. In 1997 **Patrick Stewart** (b.1940) played a white Othello in an all-black cast, flipping the racial make-up of the play in an ingenious and radical interpretation which wowed the critics.

5. **Ira Aldridge** (1807–67), an American who emigrated to England as a child, became the first black man to play Othello, in 1826, stunning critics and, oddly, establishing him as the highest paid actor in Russia.

4. **William Marshall** (1924–2003), perhaps best known for his role in the unforgettably titled Blaxploitation vampire film *Blacula*, was also a prolific Othello, starring in no less than six productions. The *Sunday Times* called him 'the best Othello of our time'.

3. **Paul Robeson** (1898–1976), a civil rights activist, footballer, singer and all-round good guy, in 1943 Robeson also became the first black Othello Broadway had seen. Margaret Webster's staging ran for 296 performances, twice as long as any other of Shakespeare's plays on Broadway.

2. **Laurence Olivier** (1907–89) invented a special accent and a special walk, and went darker than many others had. His performance split the critics, some objecting to what they perceived as his high camp, others describing it as 'a perverse joy to behold'. Especially impressive is the fact that he performed while suffering a terrible case of stage fright. He was so terrified of being alone onstage that apparently Frank Finlay as Iago would stand offstage but constantly in Olivier's eyeline, just to settle his nerves.

1. **Edmund Kean** (1787–1833) (see page 284) was lauded as the greatest actor of his time, and Othello is perhaps Shakespeare's most challenging role. For Kean at least, it proved his undoing. He collapsed onstage in 1833 playing the Moor and died two months later. That's commitment, folks!

The critical response to *Othello*

Ever since *Othello*'s first performance the play has attracted the attention of critics eager to give their own spin on Will's words. Samuel Taylor Coleridge gave one of the most famous critical interpretations in the nineteenth century, addressing Iago's motivation, or lack of it:

> The remainder – Iago's soliloquy – the motive-hunting of a motiveless malignity – how awful it is! Yea, whilst he is still allowed to bear the divine image, it is too fiendish for his own steady view, – for the lonely gaze of a being next to devil, and only not quite devil, – and yet a character which Shakespeare has attempted and executed, without disgust and without scandal!

These days there are any number of specialist interpretations out there. A feminist reading might look at Desdemona and examine how she is trapped and suffocated by the entirely masculine world surrounding her. A Freudian critic might suggest that Iago had a bit of a thing for Othello. A post-colonial reading might cast Othello as the perfect symbol of the displaced 'Other' who attempts to assimilate into a white society but eventually collapses under the burden of his own history, and a Marxist interpretation would study the structures of class and power represented in the play.

Famous speeches explained

Othello, Act V, Scene 2

It is the cause, it is the cause, my soul! Let me not name it to you, you chaste stars, It is the cause. Yet I'll not shed her blood Nor scar that whiter skin of hers than snow And smooth as monumental alabaster:	I must do it, I must do it, my soul. Don't make me say why, pure stars, but I must do it. But I won't make her bleed, or scar her skin, which is whiter than snow and as smooth as marble. But she must die or she'll cheat on other men. I'll turn out the light and then kill her.

Yet she must die, else she'll betray more
    men.
Put out the light, and then put out the light!
If I quench thee, thou flaming minister,
I can again thy former light restore,
Should I repent me. But once put out thy
    light,
Thou cunning'st pattern of excelling nature,
I know not where is that Promethean heat
That can thy light relume: when I have
    pluck'd the rose
I cannot give it vital growth again.
It needs must wither. I'll smell thee on the
    tree.
O balmy breath, that dost almost persuade
Justice to break her sword! Once more,
    once more:
Be thus when thou art dead and I will kill
    thee
And love thee after. Once more, and
    that's the last.
[*He smells, then kisses her*]
So sweet was ne'er so fatal. I must weep,
But they are cruel tears. This sorrow's
    heavenly,
It strikes where it doth love. She wakes.

If I snuff you out, flaming candle, I
can relight you if I change my mind,
but once I snuff you out, Desdemona,
you clever model of a good person, I
don't know of any fire (the gift of the
Greek god Prometheus) that would be
able to revive you. Once I have picked
this rose, I can't make it grow again. It
will wither. Let me smell it while it is
still growing on the tree.

Her lovely breath almost persuades me
to renounce justice. One more kiss,
one more kiss. If you look like this
when you're dead then I will kill you
and then keep loving you after you're
dead. One more kiss, this is the last
one. [*He smells, then kisses her*] Such a
sweet kiss has never before been so
fatal. I'm crying, but they are cruel
tears. My sorrow is sanctioned by
God: I'm killing what I love. She's
waking up.

Shakespeare's most dastardly villains

1. **Richard III**, 'The slave of nature and the son of hell' (*Richard III*)
Crimes: Fratricide, Infanticide, Murder, Bribery, Treason, Slander, Regicide
Statement: '. . . since I cannot prove a lover

To entertain these fair well-spoken days,
I am determined to prove a villain,
And hate the idle pleasures of these days.
Plots have I laid, inductions dangerous,
By drunken prophecies, libels and dreams,
To set my brother Clarence and the king
In deadly hate, the one against the other:
And if King Edward be as true and just
As I am subtle, false, and treacherous,
This day should Clarence closely be
    mew'd up . . .'

2. **Iago**, 'O murderous coxcomb' (*Othello*)
Crimes: Murder, Conspiracy to Murder, Extortion
Statement: 'I'll pour this pestilence into his ear:
That she repeals him for her body's lust.
And by how much she strives to do him
    good

She shall undo her credit with the Moor –
So will I turn her virtue into pitch
And out of her own goodness make the net
That shall enmesh them all.'

3. **Aaron**, 'This ravenous tiger, this accursed devil '(*Titus Andronicus*)
Crimes: Conspiracy to Murder, Conspiracy to Rape, Forgery, Murder
Statement: 'Ah, why should wrath be mute and fury dumb?
I am no baby, I, that with base prayers
I should repent the evils I have done.
Ten thousand worse than ever yet I did
Would I perform, if I might have my will.
If one good deed in all my life I did
I do repent it from my very soul.'

4. **Claudius**, 'that incestuous, that adulterate beast' (*Hamlet*)
Crimes: Fratricide, Regicide, Incest, Treason, Attempted Murder
Statement: 'O, my offence is rank it smells to heaven;
It hath the primal eldest curse upon't –
A brother's murder. Pray can I not,
Though inclination be as sharp as will:
My stronger guilt defeats my strong intent,
And, like a man to double business
    bound,
I stand in pause where I shall first begin,
And both neglect.'

5. **The Macbeths**, 'this dead butcher and his fiend-like queen' (*Macbeth*)
Crimes: Treason, Murder, Regicide, Infanticide
Statement:
Macbeth: 'For mine own good,
All causes shall give way: I am in blood

Stepp'd in so far that, should I wade no
  more,
Returning were as tedious as go o'er.'
Lady Macbeth: 'Come, you Spirits
That tend on mortal thoughts, unsex me
  here,
And fill me, from the crown to the toe,
  top-full
Of direst cruelty!'

6. **Edmund**, 'the whoreson must be
  acknowledged' (*King Lear*)
Crimes: Sedition, Attempted Fratricide,
Murder, Accessory to Attempted Murder
Statement: '. . . an admirable evasion of
  whoremaster man, to lay his goatish
  disposition to the charge of a star. My
  father compounded with my mother
  under the dragon's tail and my nativity
  was under Ursa major, so that it follows
  I am rough and lecherous. Fut! I should
  have been that I am, had the maidenliest
  star in the firmament twinkled on my
  bastardising.'

7. **Shylock**, his 'desires / Are wolvish,
  bloody, starved and ravenous' (*The
  Merchant of Venice*)
Crimes: Attempted Murder
Statement: 'How like a fawning publican
  he looks!
I hate him for he is a Christian:
But more for that in low simplicity
He lends out money gratis and brings
  down
The rate of usance here with us in Venice.
If I can catch him once upon the hip,
I will feed fat the ancient grudge I bear
  him.'

8. **Angelo**, 'A man of stricture and firm
  abstinence' (*Measure for Measure*)
Crimes: Abuse of Office, Coercion,
Breach of Promise
Statement: 'The tempter or the tempted,
  who sins most, ha?
Not she; nor doth she tempt; but it is I
That, lying by the violet in the sun,
Do as the carrion does, not as the flower,
Corrupt with virtuous season. Can it be
That modesty may more betray our sense
Than woman's lightness? Having waste
  ground enough,
Shall we desire to raze the sanctuary
And pitch our evils there?'

9. **Cassius**, he of the 'lean and hungry
  look' (*Julius Caesar*)
Crimes: Sedition, Forgery
'Well, Brutus, thou art noble: yet, I see,
Thy honourable metal may be wrought
From that it is disposed. Therefore it is
  meet
That noble minds keep ever with their
  likes;
For who so firm that cannot be seduced?'

10. **Don John**, 'The Bastard' (*Much Ado
  About Nothing*)
Crimes: Slander
Statement: 'I had rather be a canker in a
  hedge than a rose in his grace, and it
  better fits my blood to be disdained of
  all than to fashion a carriage to rob love
  from any: in this, though I cannot be
  said to be a flattering honest man, it
  must not be denied but I am a plain-
  dealing villain.'

King Lear
Honesty And Justice In Ancient Britain

'Arms, arms, sword, fire, corrpution in the place!'
ACT III, SCENE 6

King Lear is based on the legend of the British King Leir who was said to have ruled around the eighth century BCE. It was first recorded by Geoffrey of Monmouth in around 1136. Shakespeare's most likely sources were Holinshed's *Chronicles,* John Higgins's contribution to *A Mirror for Magistrates*, and Edmund Spenser's *The Faerie Queene*. There was also an anonymous play called *King Leir* being performed in the 1590s as well as a couple of contemporary court cases involving fathers and daughters that may have inspired him. Shakespeare used the audience's expectations about the story to devastating dramatic effect, since the earlier versions have a happy ending. For many, *King Lear* is Shakespeare's bleakest and most moving masterpiece. Even George Bernard Shaw, who was not the Bard's greatest fan, said: 'No man will ever write a better tragedy than *Lear*.' It deals with issues of justice and honesty, power and responsibility, youth and age. As Goethe, writing in the nineteenth century, said: 'Every old man is a King Lear.'

PLOT SUMMARY

At the beginning of the play the elderly Lear summons his court in order to take the unusual step of abdicating and sharing out his kingdom among his three daughters (Act I). He asks each of them to speak about how much they love him. His oldest daughters, Goneril and Regan, both give effusive responses but his youngest, favourite, daughter, Cordelia, refuses to say more than that she loves him an appropriate amount. Lear is outraged and offended and immediately disinherits Cordelia. Despite this, one of her suitors, the King of France, still wishes to marry her and they leave England together. When his loyal nobleman Kent objects to Lear's treatment of Cordelia he also feels the royal wrath and is banished. In a subplot, another loyal noble, Gloucester, is deceived by his illegitimate son Edmund into turning against his legitimate son Edgar.

Lear discovers that Goneril and Regan are less affectionate and obedient in practice than their earlier effusions suggest and he is driven to leave Goneril's palace by her lack of hospitality (Act II). Visiting Gloucester's castle he meets both daughters again, and again he receives the same ill-mannered treatment from them. He is so distraught by their lack of respect that he starts to lose his mind and leaves to wander the nearby heathlands, accompanied by his Fool and Kent, who has returned to look after the king disguised as a servant called Caius.

Lear meets Edgar, disguised as a beggar called Poor Tom, during a mighty storm on the heath (Act III). Edmund betrays his father to Regan and her husband, Cornwall, by telling them that Gloucester is planning to help Lear. In response to this news, Cornwall gouges out Gloucester's eyes and is himself fatally wounded in a fight with a servant trying to protect Gloucester. Gloucester is sent out on to the heath where Poor Tom finds him and looks after him (Act IV), leading him to Dover, where Lear has also been taken, and saving him from committing suicide.

In Dover, Cordelia and her husband land with the French army, having heard of how her sisters have abused their father. She is reunited with her father by Kent. However, the French army is defeated by Edmund and the British, and Lear and Cordelia are both captured (Act V). Edgar manages to fatally wound Edmund in a duel while offstage Gloucester dies from the stress of his ordeal. Goneril and Regan have both fallen in love with

Edmund so Goneril poisons her sister and then kills herself when her
betrayal of her husband is discovered. Before dying, Edmund has a change
of heart and tells the survivors that he has given orders for Lear and Cordelia to be executed and if they hurry they may be able to save them. But his
confession comes too late, and the final scene sees Lear carrying in the body
of Cordelia. Lear dies of a broken heart.

Happy Endings

Shakespeare's sources for *King Lear* end
with Lear and Cordelia victorious over
Goneril and Regan, and Lear restored to
the throne. His radical decision to end
his version with the deaths of both Lear
and Cordelia has troubled audiences and
dramatists over the years. In 1681 the
playwright Nahum Tate rewrote the play
with a happy ending, preferred by
Samuel Johnson, that remained popular
for over 150 years. Tate's version omits the
Fool and sees Cordelia marry Edgar, as
well as Lear regaining his crown. In 1823
the actor Edmund Kean attempted to
restore the Shakespearean ending, telling
his wife 'The London audience have no
notion of what I can do till they see me
over the dead body of Cordelia', but
audiences weren't buying it. It took until
1838 and the production of William
Macready before the original version
replaced Tate's on the stage.

KEY THEMES

Justice

KING LEAR

> And my poor fool is hanged! No, no, no life!
> Why should a dog, a horse, a rat, have life
> And thou no breath at all? O thou'lt come no more,
> Never, never, never, never, never.
> Pray you, undo this button. Thank you, sir. O, o, o, o.
> Do you see this? Look on her: look, her lips,
> Look there, look there!
> *Dies*

(ACT V, SCENE 3)

This is the most heartbreaking speech in all Shakespeare's work. Lear has just entered carrying Cordelia's dead body, after she has been hanged on Edmund's orders. The disruption to the iambic pentameter, including the entirely trochaic line 'Never, never, never, never, never', the repetitions and the mid-line breaks vividly show Lear's incoherent, overwhelming grief. This speech comes at the end of the play when traditionally the villains would be receiving their just deserts and the heroes left triumphant. Certainly that's what Shakespeare's audience would have been expecting, particularly as Edgar has only just said 'The gods defend her'. However, although the deaths of the evil characters, Goneril, Regan and Edmund, have just taken place, and Edgar and Albany are in control, the true heroes of the play, Lear and Cordelia, both die – and Kent (arguably the most straightforwardly heroic character of all) is just about to announce his intention to follow Lear's fate: 'I have a journey, sir, shortly to go; / My master calls me, I must not say no.' This is not the usual poetic justice which allows many tragedies to finish with a feeling that order has been restored and justice, however harsh, has been done.

One might say that Lear has brought a certain amount of trouble on himself through his own unwise actions, but Cordelia is a blameless character. Can a universe that allows inconsequential beings like dogs, horses and rats to survive when such a good woman has been murdered be just? Albany's words 'All friends shall taste / The wages of their virtue, and all foes / The cup of their deserving' are undercut by the deaths of the 'good' characters. Despite Edgar's analysis that 'The gods are just, and of our pleasant vices / Make instruments to plague us: / The dark and vicious place where thee he got / Cost him his eyes', Lear and Gloucester's horrific experiences far outweigh their crimes. They remain 'More sinned against than sinning'. Shakespeare's message in *King Lear* seems pretty gloomy: the real world holds no guarantee of justice or fairness, and death comes to all of us, good or evil: 'As flies to wanton boys are we to the gods, / They kill us for their sport.'

Honesty and Deception

KING LEAR
So young and so untender?

CORDELIA
So young, my lord, and true.

KING LEAR
Well, let it be so. Thy truth, then, be thy dower,

(ACT I, SCENE I)

The theme of honesty and deception is explored from several different angles in the play. Lear's fatal mistake, which sets the tragedy in motion, is his refusal to accept Cordelia's candid statement: 'I love your majesty / According to my bond, no more nor less.' His response devalues her honesty by telling her that he is punishing her for offending him by withholding her 'dower' (dowry). He also rejects Kent's blunt honesty: 'What wouldst thou do, old man? / Think'st thou that duty shall have dread to speak, / When power to flattery bows? To plainness honour's bound, / When majesty stoops to folly.' Instead he chooses to believe Goneril and Regan's overstated affection for him which ultimately turns out to be a deeply false form of flattery. The sisters also show their dishonesty in their dealings with each other over Edmund. Edmund himself is even more malevolently deceitful in his plot to turn his father against Edgar. However, the good characters also engage in deceit in the play: both Kent and Edgar disguise themselves, as Caius and Poor Tom, in order to help their loved ones. Lear also comes to see his kingly robes as disguising his true nature as an animal: 'thou art the thing itself. Unaccommodated man is no more but such a poor bare, forked animal as thou art. Off, off, you lendings: come, unbutton here.' This theme of truth and lies is also reflected in the blinding of Gloucester – it is only after he loses his physical sight that he is able to perceive the truth about his sons. Similarly, it is only after Lear loses himself in the literal darkness of the storm and mental darkness of his madness that he finally comes to know his true self and the truth about his daughters: 'A man may see how this world goes with no eyes.'

Nature

CORDELIA

> Had you not been their father, these white flakes
> Did challenge pity of them. Was this a face
> To be opposed against the warring winds?
> To stand against the deep dread-bolted thunder,
> In the most terrible and nimble stroke
> Of quick, cross lightning? To watch, poor perdu,
> With this thin helm? Mine enemy's dog
> Though he had bit me should have stood that night
> Against my fire; and wast thou fain, poor father,
> To hovel thee with swine and rogues forlorn
> In short and musty straw? Alack, alack!
> 'Tis wonder that thy life and wits at once
> Had not concluded all.

(ACT IV, SCENE 7)

Nature and the natural order are also important themes in the play, and animal imagery is used frequently. By disrupting the accepted natural hierarchy in resigning his kingship, Lear has meddled with the proper order of the universe which sees subjects obey their king, children respect their parents and humans behave better than animals. He begins by justifying his demands for the retention of his retinue to keep up his royal image, despite his decision to 'shake all cares and business from our age', by stating that humans are superior creatures with more complex needs than animals – 'Allow not nature more than nature needs, / Man's life's as cheap as beast's' – but comes to the realisation that regardless of his kingship, he is just 'a poor bare, forked animal', and he ends the play almost beyond human language and howling in grief – 'Howl, howl, howl, howl!'

Gloucester makes the point that Goneril and Regan have treated their father worse than an animal by leaving him out in the storm: 'If wolves had at thy gate howled that stern time, / Thou shouldst have said, "Good porter, turn the key,"' and the two evil sisters are repeatedly referred to using negative animal terms such as 'vulture', 'kite', 'serpent', 'tigers' and 'cuckoo'. These bestial images add to the sense of wild lawlessness that permeates the play, where human hierarchies are overthrown and life is brought back to a primitive tooth-and-claw existence. It is this unregulated side of nature that Edmund worships: 'Thou, Nature, art my goddess; to thy law / My services are bound.' The storm on the heath exemplifies this view of the world as chaotic, untamed and dangerous.

KEY SCENE

The storm on the heath scene (Act III, Scene 2) is the image most often conjured up when people think of *King Lear* but the **blinding of Gloucester scene** (Act III, Scene 7) is also shockingly memorable. Regan and Cornwall discover that Gloucester has helped Lear escape to Dover to meet Cordelia and the French forces. To punish him, they tie him up in his own home, pull at his beard and then, finally, Cornwall gouges out his eyes – 'Out, vile jelly! Where is thy lustre now?' – before being mortally wounded by a servant defending the old man. Regan stabs this servant to death and tells Gloucester that it was Edmund who betrayed him before turning him out of the castle. This scene is important as it shows with chilling clarity just how nasty Lear's enemies are and presages the dark and violent ending of the play. Symbolically it also shows Gloucester being physically blinded at the point where he perceives the truth about his two sons. This mirrors Lear's discovery that Cordelia is his only loyal daughter.

KEY SYMBOL

The **storm** is a key symbol in *King Lear*. The most memorable image from the play is of Lear remonstrating with it on the heath.

KING LEAR
> Blow, winds, and crack your cheeks! Rage, blow!
> You cataracts and hurricanoes, spout
> Till you have drenched our steeples, drowned the cocks!
> You sulphurous and thought-executing fires,
> Vaunt-couriers of oak-cleaving thunderbolts,
> Singe my white head! And thou, all-shaking thunder,
> Strike flat the thick rotundity o'the world,
> Crack nature's moulds, an germans spill at once
> That make ingrateful man!

FOOL
> O, nuncle, court holy-water in a dry house is better than this
> rain-water out o' door. Good nuncle, in, and ask thy daughters'
> blessing. Here's a night pities neither wise man nor fool.

KING LEAR
> Rumble thy bellyful! Spit fire, spout rain!
> Nor rain, wind, thunder, fire, are my daughters;
> I tax not you, you elements, with unkindness.
> I never gave you kingdom, called you children;
> You owe me no subscription. Why then, let fall
> Your horrible pleasure. Here I stand your slave,
> A poor, infirm, weak and despised old man.
> But yet I call you servile ministers
> That have with two pernicious daughters join
> Your high-engendered battles 'gainst a head
> So old and white as this. O ho! 'tis foul.

> (ACT III, SCENE 2)

This speech comes as Lear has been overtaken by madness and run out of Gloucester's castle onto the nearby heath. The violent weather reflects the king's emotional upheaval and the rhythm and sounds of his words vividly whip up the image of a tempest. He addresses the storm directly and compares it with his daughters, acknowledging that he does not expect good treatment from nature – 'You owe me no subscription' – as, unlike his daughters, he hasn't given it his kingdom or raised it from childhood. His attribution of human motivations to the weather is a literary device called pathetic fallacy. It reflects Lear's woe, and his new powerless vulnerability – he is now just a 'poor, infirm, weak, and despised old man' instead of the 'majesty' and 'dear highness' of the first scene of the play. The storm also illustrates the chaotic political state of the country since his abdication. Lear comes out of the storm a wiser man. Shakespeare likes a good storm: he uses them in similar symbolic and transformative ways in *Julius Caesar*, *Macbeth*, *Pericles*, *Othello* and *The Tempest*.

Illegitimacy in Shakespeare's time

Illegitimacy and birthright were deeply emotive topics in Shakespeare's world, as Thersites' exclamation in *Troilus and Cressida* illustrates: 'I am a bastard begot, bastard instructed, bastard in mind, bastard in valour, in everything illegtimate'. Records show that the number of children born outside wedlock was rising, and changes were made to the Poor Laws to reflect this – illegitimate children were often the responsibility of the community, so there was a financial as well as moral implication. Unlawful or 'natural' children, i.e. those who were not the product of a marriage recognised by God and the law, were unable to enter churches and to inherit property. But, as so often, the rich had different rules: noble bastards seem to have been able to live freely within their social stratum. They weren't outcast until their actions made them so – like Don John in *Much Ado About Nothing* – although there was the suspicion that the sinful nature of their conception would impact on their characters and make them more likely to go off the rails, and they were often sent away for their education. As always, Shakespeare's approach is fluid and complex: *King Lear* raises interesting questions about the implications and consequences of the stigma of illegitimacy: is Edmund inherently evil because he is a bastard, or is he a bastard (in the modern sense of the word) because everyone treats him as one?

King Lear conundrum: Where does the fool go?

Lear's Fool has an important role as a commentator on the action of the play. This was a recognised ironic trope in Elizabethan drama – that the fool, or court jester, was actually one of the wisest characters and had licence to criticise the monarch with impunity so long as he was entertaining. The Fool would probably have spoken his lines from downstage near the audience in order to emphasise that his perspective is close to theirs. In *King Lear*, the Fool is present in the first three acts but disappears without explanation after this. One theory about this is that the same actor would have played both Cordelia and the Fool so they can't appear in the same scenes; another is that in the final scene when Lear says 'my poor fool is hanged' he is referring to the Fool rather than Cordelia and letting the audience know his fate.

King Lear and real kings

Shakespeare wrote many plays about kings and the responsibility of monarchy. Scholars believe he reflected concerns and hopes about the state in his own time through the prism of ancient and dead rulers. It was forbidden to write plays about contemporary events so any questioning of the current political situation had to be approached via the past.

King Lear was written between late 1605 and early 1606, so not long after James I had come to the throne in 1603. Its discussion of the way a ruler is responsible for his own succession reflected fears that were rife at the end of Elizabeth I's reign as she had no direct heirs. James was already the King of Scotland when he acceded to the English throne and there was also much tension about the idea of uniting the two countries. Lear's decision to abdicate and divide his kingdom between his daughters is seen as selfish and foolish, as is his wish to hold on to the trappings of his power despite his withdrawal from the responsibility of maintaining stability in his kingdom.

Shakespeare's genius for writing plays that resonate down the centuries has meant that *King Lear* has also interacted with the political realm long after its original performances. Perhaps Tate's decision to rewrite the play with a happy ending, where Lear regains his throne, was deemed more fitting for an audience that had in its memory the restoration of the monarchy in 1660? The play was in fact considered too powerful to perform during the mental illness of King George III when the populace were clearly not being encouraged to think about mad kings.

Elizabethan attitudes to insanity

Elizabethan medicine still relied on the ancient Greek and Roman theory put forward by Hippocrates, Aristotle and Galen of the four humours: that the health of a body relied on a perfect balance of blood, phlegm, yellow bile and black bile, and that physical suffering and disease occurred when there was a surplus or deficit of the humours. The humours were also aligned to one's personality and emotional balance: blood with the sanguine, black bile with melancholy, phlegm with sensitivity, yellow bile with ambition and a hot temper. Men were generally considered to be hotter and drier than their paler, cooler, female counterparts.

Madness was seen as an imbalance of the humours: too much black bile could make a person melancholic like Hamlet, too much yellow bile could drive a mania, a trait displayed by Macbeth for example. Interestingly, in Renaissance times there was a fine line between insanity and divine inspiration – so Lear's madness can be seen as a hardship he must endure before he can see with clarity the truth of the world around him.

Macbeth
Ambition, Madness And Witchcraft In 'The Scottish Play'

'All hail, Macbeth! hail to thee, thane of Glamis.' ACT I, SCENE 3

Macbeth is another eternally popular play – a bloodthirsty and psychologically acute take on the consequences of overarching ambition and the evil lengths men and women will go to in the pursuit of power, and Lady M is often held up as a terrifying female archetype by the more hysterical voices in modern media. Female politicians from Yvette Cooper to Hillary Clinton have been tarred with her brush. Of all of Shakespeare's plays, *Macbeth* is probably the one most rooted in its own historical context. It was composed a year after the Gunpowder Plot of 1605. King James had succeeded Queen Elizabeth in 1603 but he was by no means universally popular. Brought up a Protestant, he was nevertheless the son of the Catholic Mary, Queen of Scots (who, let's not forget, had been executed by Queen Elizabeth), and initially Catholics, Guy Fawkes among them, believed he would help their cause. When it transpired this would not be the case, the plotters planned to assassinate James during a state visit to the House of Lords. The plot was foiled, and the would-be king-killers were executed. As traitors they were hanged, drawn and quartered. *Macbeth* can almost be read as a cautionary tale for those who might think it's a good idea to attempt to overthrow the king. It hits the audience as a short sharp shock about the corrupting force of ambition.

PLOT SUMMARY

On a bloody, muddy battlefield, King Duncan of Scotland hears how, under the leadership of generals Macbeth and Banquo, his army has defeated twin invasions from Ireland and Norway (Act I). The Thane of Cawdor, however, has proved a traitor, and Duncan vows to give the title instead to Macbeth. Macbeth and Banquo, heading home in a storm over a barren heath after their travails, come across the three witches – the 'weyard sisters' – who tell him of their prophecies: that Macbeth shall first become Thane of Cawdor, and then king. They also promise that, while Banquo himself will not be king, his descendants will one day rule Scotland. The witches vanish, and Macbeth is deeply suspicious, until thanes Ross and Angus arrive to tell him he's been bestowed with the title of Cawdor. Now Macbeth begins to wonder, if the first part of the witches' prophecy is true, then why not the second: can he become the King of Scotland?

On the battlefield, King Duncan announces his son Malcom as his heir, and also tells Macbeth that he will travel to Macbeth's castle in Inverness for a great feast to celebrate their victory. Macbeth writes to his wife to tell her about the witches' prophecy, and then a messenger lets her know that old King Duncan will be coming to stay at the castle. She immediately sees the planets aligning for a wicked plan. Duncan must die in order that her husband can become king. Macbeth himself is more conflicted, but after a tongue-lashing, in which his masculinity is questioned, he acquiesces. The couple plan to murder Duncan after the feast, and to frame his chamberlains by smearing them with blood, and getting them so drunk that they cannot remember what they've been doing.

Macbeth has done 'the deed' (Act II). Macduff, the Thane of Fife, discovers the king's corpse and the alarm is raised. Duncan's sons, Malcolm and Donalbain, hear of their father's death and fear for their safety. They flee, which suggests they are responsible (Act III). Macbeth is now king and Banquo is beginning to have terrible suspicions about how the witches' prophecies have been realised. Banquo and Macbeth are publicly polite to one another, but in private each remembers the other part of the witches' vision, that Banquo's descendants will one day rule Scotland. Macbeth arranges for another great banquet, which he insists must be attended by Banquo. He plans to have Banquo and his son Fleance killed, reasoning that if he allows Banquo or any of his descendants to live, all of his actions will have been for Banquo's gain.

But Macbeth's plan fails. The hired killer appears in the middle of Macbeth's dinner to tell him Banquo was murdered but Fleance got away. The witches' prophecy remains unchanged if Fleance lives, and Macbeth's psychological torment deepens. He sees the ghost of Banquo – a manifestation of his guilt – and while his other guests are shaken by his panic attack, Lady Macbeth tries to rally him. He vows to visit the witches to discover his fate (Act IV). They show him a series of horrifying apparitions: a helmeted head tells him that he should beware Macduff, a bloodied child says he will not be harmed by anyone 'of woman born', and finally a child carrying a tree reveals he will be undefeated until Birnam Wood comes to Dunsinane Hill. Macbeth is satisfied his position is secure – after all, every single person in the world is born of woman, and woods surely cannot move. Finally, Macbeth is shown a procession of kings, each bearing a resemblance to Banquo. The witches vanish and Lennox appears to tell Macbeth that Macduff has fled to England. Seizing an opportunity, Macbeth sends murderers to kill Macduff's wife and children in his absence. In England, Ross tells Macduff of the terrible fate of his family, and Macduff swears to avenge their deaths. He joins with Malcolm, Duncan's son, who has raised an army in England – they know they must strike soon, that Macbeth is 'ripe for shaking'.

Back at Macbeth's castle at Dunsinane, Lady Macbeth is a shadow of her former iron-willed self (Act V). She's sleepwalking, suffering terrible visions, unable to wash imaginary blood from her hands – all a physical articulation of her inner turmoil. Meanwhile, Malcolm and Macduff's army of ten thousand men gather forces at Birnam Wood. They hatch a plan to camouflage themselves with branches and boughs – now Macbeth's conviction that woods cannot move is starting to look a little shaky. Macbeth receives word that Lady Macbeth is dead – the inference is that she has killed herself. Macbeth is in deep despair, but still clinging to the conviction that he is safe

because he will be killed by no man 'of woman born'. In the final confronta-
tion with Macduff it is revealed that Macduff was 'from his mother's womb
/ Untimely ripp'd' – in a process we now recognise as a Caesarean section.
The witches' prophecy has been realised. Finally, Macduff kills and decapi-
tates Macbeth. Malcolm is hailed King of Scotland.

KEY THEMES

Ambition

LADY MACBETH
>   The raven himself is hoarse,
>   That croaks the fatal entrance of Duncan
>   Under my battlements. Come, you Spirits
>   That tend on mortal thoughts, unsex me here,
>   And fill me, from the crown to the toe, top-full
>   Of direst cruelty! make thick my blood,
>   Stop up th'access and passage to remorse;
>   That no compunctious visitings of Nature
>   Shake my fell purpose, nor keep peace between
>   Th'effect and it. Come to my woman's breasts,
>   And take my milk for gall, you murth'ring ministers,
>   Wherever in your sightless substances
>   You wait on Nature's mischief! Come, thick Night,
>   And pall thee in the dunnest smoke of Hell,
>   That my keen knife see not the wound it makes,
>   Nor Heaven peep through the blanket of the dark,
>   To cry, 'Hold, hold!'

>   (ACT I, SCENE 5)

Just before this chilling soliloquy in which Lady Macbeth outlines exactly
how far she is prepared to go in the pursuit of power, Macbeth has been

wavering about what to do with the witches' prophecy. Lady Macbeth does not falter. She calls upon the spirits to 'unsex me here / And fill me from the crown to the toe top-full / Of direst cruelty'. She knows that usurping Duncan will involve violence and death, that his entrance to her castle is 'fatal', and that she needs to banish all thoughts of remorse, turn her mother's 'milk' into acidic 'gall'. Violence and ambition here are associated with masculinity, as later, when Macbeth again hesitates, she negates her own femininity with a particularly gruesome image: 'I have given suck, and know / How tender 'tis to love the babe that milks me: / I would, while it was smiling in my face, / Have plucked my nipple from his boneless gums, / And dashed the brains out, had I so sworn as you / Have done to this.' The corrupting nature of ambition is vividly portrayed: by putting personal ambition before the good of the country essential bonds are broken. The final time we see Lady Macbeth all this steel and resolve has gone – in the throes of madness she wipes at an imaginary spot of blood and is terrified of the dark which at the start she has willed heaven not to break.

Witchcraft and Superstition

Three witches of Belvoir, 17th-century woodcut

Thunder and lightning. Enter three Witches

FIRST WITCH

When shall we three meet again?
In thunder, lightning, or in rain?

SECOND WITCH

When the hurlyburly's done,
When the battle's lost and won.

THIRD WITCH

That will be ere the set of sun.

FIRST WITCH

Where the place?

SECOND WITCH

Upon the heath.

THIRD WITCH

There to meet with Macbeth.

FIRST WITCH

I come, Graymalkin!

SECOND WITCH

Paddock calls.

THIRD WITCH

Anon!

ALL

Fair is foul, and foul is fair:
Hover through the fog and filthy air.

(ACT I, SCENE I)

Aside from being a wonderfully atmospheric opening to the play – the dark
heath, a raging storm, the three 'weyard sisters' – this first scene explores
one of the key themes of *Macbeth*, of witchcraft and the upending of the
natural order of things.

Witchcraft was an important topic at the end of the sixteenth century
when scientific explanations for disasters such as crop failures, illnesses and

storms were unavailable. James I was particularly interested in it, even going so far as to publish his work *Daemonology* in 1597, in which he put forth arguments in favour of witch-hunting. It was a subject close to his heart because he was a firm believer in the idea of 'Divine Right', the idea that the king was a representative of God on earth (see page 148). Conversely, witches were the representatives of the devil on earth, with the power to disrupt and corrupt, just as the king's power was benevolent and healing.

The witches are emblems of darkness and conflict. That chiastic line 'Fair is foul' sums up brilliantly the sense of moral confusion that they herald, but it's there too in the sisters themselves. They are bearded women, with the power to make men infertile. Their speech takes the form of trochaic tetrameter – a quickfire metre rarely used by Shakespeare consisting of four trochees, one stressed syllable followed by one unstressed syllable, making a sound a little like: DAdoom, DAdoom, DAdoom, DAdoom . . . It becomes incantatory, a chant to invoke evil and darkness and to mess with Macbeth's mind. As an aside, it's worth asking whether the witches control Macbeth's fate or if they are simply fate's mouthpiece. Certainly when Macbeth attempts to change his fate he calls on them, but in the play we never witness the witches committing acts of evil – Macbeth takes care of that all by himself.

The pervading atmosphere of the supernatural that is established by the witches in the opening lines feeds into the other visions and hallucinations that crop up throughout the action. For example, there is the floating dagger just as Macbeth is about to commit his first murder: 'Is this a dagger, which I see before me, / The handle toward my hand? Come, let me clutch thee – / I have thee not, and yet I see thee still.' The dagger comes to represent Macbeth's conscience, and materialises at this moment of extreme conflict. He hasn't yet killed Duncan, but already his mind is rolling and coursing with guilt. Similarly the appearance of Banquo's ghost points to Macbeth's overwhelming sense of fear and anxiety, virtually forcing him to admit to his guilt in the presence of Ross, Lennox and the other lords. It's part of Shakespeare's genius to show that Macbeth and his wife are haunted and psychologically complex, instead of depicting them as straightforwardly evil. We are left asking why it is they turn to evil – is it witchcraft, ambition, jealousy, arrogance or madness?

KEY SCENE

Until **the banquet scene** (Act III, Scene 4), the Macbeths' evil plans have just about been holding together, but now the fragile facade they have constructed for themselves begins to crumble, in full view of their dinner guests. The supper has been arranged as a means to secure Macbeth's kingship, and though it ends spectacularly badly, it does begin promisingly. The Macbeths are relaxed and welcoming, the perfect hosts. But then Macbeth discovers that his scheme to kill Banquo and his son has gone awry: though Banquo is dead, brutally killed by the two murderers, his son Fleance has escaped. This poses an enormous threat to Macbeth not just in the immediate present – Fleance can reveal Macbeth and his Lady's murderous intentions – but also because it enables the prophecy of the witches, that Banquo's descendants will ultimately prevent his success. The appearance of Banquo's ghost at the dinner completely unhinges Macbeth, and he is finally unable to hide or suppress the turmoil of his soul. At first the apparition prompts him to accuse the other lords of playing a trick on him, but soon he finds himself berating a ghost that no one else can see: 'Thou canst not say, I did it: never shake / Thy gory locks at me.' Lady Macbeth tries to placate the gathering, who are clearly disturbed, by explaining Macbeth has suffered from 'fits' since he was a young man, but eventually, as Macbeth's agitation heightens, she ends the party, and tells her husband he needs to sleep. This is the last moment where we see Lady M as a pillar of steel and strength: in our next encounter she is struggling with the ravings of her own mind in the sleepwalking scene.

KEY SYMBOL

The pages of *Macbeth* are among the most **blood**stained in all of world literature. From the opening scenes of battle and war, to the further bloody business of a baby Macduff being 'untimely ripp'd' from his mother's womb, rivers of the stuff run through it – in fact it's hard to find a scene in which blood is *not* used as an emblem of the violence and murderous nature of power. King Duncan's first words are 'What bloody man is that?', and for Macbeth and his wife bloodstains come to literally and figuratively represent the guilt that haunts them because of the acts of tremendous evil they have carried out. Again, it's Macbeth who falls prey to the madness first; in the immediate aftermath of Duncan's murder he looks at his blood-stained hands and asks: 'Will all great Neptune's ocean wash this blood / Clean from my hand?' Lady Macbeth, in contrast, states: 'My hands are of your colour, but I shame / To wear a heart so white': she too is bloodstained, but she's ashamed of his cowardice. By the time we meet her in Act V her confusion is externalised in madness, sleepwalking and visions, and she is obsessed with the blood she believes she can see on her hand: 'Out, damned spot! Out, I say!', but has the clarity of thought, even within the madness, to realise that ultimately nothing will cleanse her: 'All the perfumes of Arabia will not sweeten this little hand. Oh! Oh! Oh!'

James I of England and VI of Scotland

James had ruled Scotland for more than thirty years when Elizabeth died without issue and he took the throne of England. A scholar himself, he was a committed patron of the arts and he published books on witchcraft, the divine right of kings, and Scottish poetry. Henry IV of France called him 'the wisest fool in Christendom'. By the end of his reign he was mostly held in deep affection by his subjects, though history has looked on him a little less kindly – his court was profligate and often in debt, and he dismissed Parliament when they couldn't find a way to bail him out financially. His tendency to indulge his favourites and his blurred relationships with them didn't help either. Despite a marriage to Queen Anne that produced eight children, he was famous at court for having an eye for young men, too. An early and passionate relationship with the Duke of Lennox ended badly when Scottish nobles banished the duke to France. His relationship with Robert Carr turned sour and Carr and his wife were imprisoned in the Tower of London for seven years. He made commoner George Villiers a knight, and later the Duke of Buckingham, referring to him often as his wife. James died inelegantly of gout and an attack of dysentery at Buckingham's side in 1625.

'The Scottish play'

From telling someone to 'Break a leg' before they go onstage and giving a director flowers stolen from a graveyard on closing night, we all know that theatre folk are uncommonly superstitious, but perhaps the most infamous superstitions surround *Macbeth*. If you want to upset your thespian friends all you have to do is mention the word 'Macbeth' in a theatre. The only remedy for the bad luck this brings is for you to run immediately outside, curse, spit, turn round in three circles and then plead to be let back in. Or you can quote from *Hamlet*: 'Angels and ministers of grace defend us!'

There are many theories suggesting the origins of this superstition. There is a school of thought that dictates that Shakespeare lifted the witches' incantations verbatim: that they were actual spells, and, moreover, the witches he plagiarised weren't best pleased, placing a curse on the play and those who performed it. There are many examples of the curse at work, from a seventeenth-century Dutch production in which the actor playing Macbeth pulled a real dagger on Duncan and murdered him in front of his audience to a 1948 production in which Lady Macbeth sleepwalked her way off a fifteen-foot-high stage. Another more prosaic reason for the play's cursed reputation is that it does involve a lot of sword-fighting and daggers, as well as moody low lighting and fog, so there is indeed more potential for injury and mishap. Perhaps the most plausible explanation is that, due to its popularity, it was often put on by theatres which were running out of money and needed a show-stopper – these companies often went bankrupt soon after so it gained a shady reputation.

Class in Shakespeare's time

In Elizabethan times social mobility was just emerging. Social class was not something one could easily change, in the way we think we can today. Kings, nobles, churchmen, merchants and peasants were considered by many to be part of the Great Chain of Being, which assumed that everything in the world had its natural and right place, decreed by God, as expressed by Ulysses in *Troilus and Cressida*: 'O, when degree is shaked / Which is the ladder to all high designs, / Then enterprise is sick!' Animals, plants and minerals came further down the chain. It was feared that upsetting the natural order in which everything was held in perfect equilibrium would result in chaos, disorder and death – thus Macbeth's vaulting ambition leads to madness and carnage. And Caesar's assassination at the hands of the Roman conspirators in *Julius Caesar* leads to pandemonium in heaven as well as on earth. However, Shakespeare did live to see the middle and merchant class start to gain power and he himself was able to transform himself from provincial son of a glove-maker to a coat-of-arms-wielding 'gentleman' (see page 15).

Famous speeches explained

Macbeth, Act II, Scene 1

Is this a dagger, which I see before me,
The handle toward my hand? Come, let
me clutch thee: –
I have thee not, and yet I see thee still.
Art thou not, fatal vision, sensible
To feeling, as to sight? or art thou but
A dagger of the mind, a false creation,
Proceeding from the heat-oppressèd
brain?
I see thee yet, in form as palpable
As this which now I draw.
Thou marshall'st me the way that I was
going;
And such an instrument I was to use. –
Mine eyes are made the fools o' the other
senses,
Or else worth all the rest: I see thee still;
And on thy blade, and dudgeon, gouts of
blood,

Is that a dagger I can see in front of me?
With its handle pointing at my hand?
Come on, dagger, let me grab you. I
can't touch you but I can still see you.
You're a dangerous vision – are you
untouchable even though you're visible?
Or are you just an imaginary dagger; a
hallucination from a stressed-out mind?

I can still see you, looking as real as my
own dagger, which I've got out here.
You're encouraging me towards
Duncan's room, and I was planning to
use a dagger to kill him. My eyes are
either idiots compared to my other
senses, or they are better than them.

I can still see you, and now I can see blobs
of blood on your blade and hilt, which
weren't there before. You must be

Which was not so before. There's no such
    thing.
It is the bloody business which informs
Thus to mine eyes. – Now o'er the one
    half-world
Nature seems dead, and wicked dreams
    abuse
The curtain'd sleep: Witchcraft celebrates
Pale Hecate's off'rings, and wither'd
    Murther,
Alarum'd by his sentinel, the wolf,
Whose howl's his watch, thus with his
    stealthy pace,
With Tarquin's ravishing strides, towards
    his design
Moves like a ghost. – Thou sure and
    firm-set earth,
Hear not my steps, which way they walk,
    for fear
Thy very stones prate of my where-about,
And take the present horror from the time,
Which now suits with it. – Whiles I threat,
    he lives:
Words to the heat of deeds too cold breath
    gives.

A bell rings

I go, and it is done: the bell invites me.
Hear it not, Duncan; for it is a knell
That summons thee to Heaven or to Hell.

imaginary; it's the murder I was
planning that's making me imagine you.

Now half the world is asleep, making
everything seem dead. Horrible dreams
are interrupting people's sleep, witches
are celebrating the rites of Hecate, the
goddess of sorcery, and Murder,
announced by the howling of his pal
the wolf, is stealthily making his way,
like the evil rapist Roman king
Tarquin, or a ghost, towards carrying
out his plans.

Steady earth, please don't listen to my
footsteps, in case your stones tell on me
and prevent the horrible event that the
time is right for.

While I'm planning, Duncan's still alive.
Talking doesn't accomplish anything.

A bell rings.

I'm going now and I'm going to do it. The
bell is encouraging me. I hope you don't
hear it, Duncan, because it's a funeral
bell for you, which will lead to you
ending up in heaven or hell.

THE POEMS

'Who will believe my verse in years to come?' Shakespeare's sonnets

SONNETS
by William Shakespeare

London: J. M. DENT & SONS LTD.
New York: E. P. DUTTON & CO. INC.

Celebrated for centuries as the ultimate declarations of romantic love (and appropriated shamelessly for almost as long by the peddlers of greetings cards), Shakespeare's sonnets have also, virtually since their publication in 1609, caused great controversy. Like almost every debate surrounding Shakespeare's work, there are more questions than answers: Did Shakespeare authorise the publication of the 154 sonnets? And was it his or another hand that arranged them in the sequence we recognise today? Is the 'speaker' of the poems Shakepeare himself, and does that mean they can be read as autobiographical in a way that the other poems and plays cannot? Who is the 'Fair Youth' being addressed in the first 126 poems, and who is the 'Dark Lady' that features in the rest of the sequence? Are the speaker's feelings towards the 'Fair Youth' homosexual in nature? And what on earth does that strange dedication actually mean? Finally, do any of these questions actually matter when we look at the poems, the vast majority of which are brilliantly clever little jewels of rhetoric, philosophy and form?

Here is what we *do* know, or at least what we can surmise from the material available. The sequence follows a loose narrative arc – with three dramatis personae: the male 'Fair Youth' who features in the bulk of the sonnets, the 'Speaker' who is a poet, older and not as wealthy as the fair youth, and a 'Dark Lady' who stalks the last poems in the arrangement. Expanding on an idea explored in *Venus and Adonis*, the first seventeen poems are known as the **procreation poems**, and in general their theme is an exhortation to reproduction – a call for the young man to settle down, get married and have children. Then there's a shift in tone that suggests that in fact the young man doesn't necessarily need to get married, that the poet's art might in fact act as an agent of preservation, a literary descendant. Then a love triangle emerges, in which the poet, in thrall to the young man, is devastated by his affair with the poet's mistress, but manages to forgive him. The last of the Fair Youth sonnets, number 126, is two lines shorter than usual, and ends with a set of double, blank parentheses. Isn't it amazing that the world's greatest ever poet might suggest a terrible emptiness or sadness by using absolutely no words at all? The 'Dark Lady' section that completes the sequence is full of tortured self-loathing and longing. Here is sexual attraction characterised by a sort of malice – you don't have to look too far into the plays to see where this idea might end up taking root. *Much Ado*'s Beatrice and Benedick anyone?

The **sonnet form** was first popularised by the Italian Renaissance poet **Petrarch** who wrote a starry-eyed sequence in the fourteenth century addressed to an idealised and unattainable woman called Laura. That he penned 366 songs to a lady he only met once is an indication of the lamentable lovesickness from which this poor man was suffering. The traditional Petrarchan sonnet has **fourteen lines**, divided into the **octave** and the **sestet**, of eight and six lines respectively. The octave usually follows a rhyming sequence of ABBAABBA, or ABBACDDC, and the sestet's rhyme scheme is usually CDCDCD, or CDECDE. There will often be some opposition or tension between the octave and the sestet: sometimes the octave poses a problem or dilemma that the sestet might attempt to answer.

A **Shakespearean sonnet** is written in iambic pentameter (see page 49) and comprised of **four parts**. The first three are made of four lines each, called **quatrains**, which rhyme ABAB, CDCD, EFEF, with the final two lines being a **rhyming couplet** with the rhyme scheme GG. Often the quatrains establish and develop a sequence of ideas which is then transformed by the time we get to the rhyming couplet. The transformation is usually heralded by a **volta**, or turn in the argument, which the couplet affirms. They are like mini philosophical debates, expert lessons in the art of rhetoric and persuasion and Shakespeare is a genius at manipulating expectations of the form to spectacular effect.

The riddle of the dedication

TO.THE.ONLIE.BEGETTER.OF.
THESE.INSVING.SONNETS.
Mr. W. H. ALL.HAPPINESSE.
AND.THAT.ETERNITIE.
PROMISED.

BY.

OVR.EVER-LIVING.POET.

WISHETH.

THE.WELL-WISHING.
ADVENTVRER.IN.
SETTING.
FORTH.

T. T.

One of the great puzzles of Shakespeare's sonnets is the dedication, which has vexed and divided scholars over the years, on occasion leading to some marvellous academic spats. The first thing to note is that for a dedication of a collection of poetry whose power has lasted over four hundred years, the syntax here is clumsy, awkward and repetitive, even without the Roman practice of inserting full stops between each word (though some cryptographers have run with this idea of classical imagery and suggested the layout makes it look a little bit like an ancient urn). There are strange line spaces, after 'promised', 'by', 'poet' and 'wisheth', and there appear to be too many subjects vying for our attention. It's unclear if the 'onlie begetter' means the person who created the sonnets – 'our ever-living poet' – or the elusive Mr W. H. to whom they seem to be dedicated.

It's been suggested that there are two serious contenders for the identity of Mr W. H. – if we assume he is the fair youth being addressed in the following verses – and they are William Herbert, Earl of Pembroke, or Henry Wriothesley, Earl of Southampton (see page 262), both of whom had been Shakespeare's patron in the past. But since the sonnets seem to refer to the fair youth as a wealthy man it seems odd that social conventions would be ignored by referring to him so informally as 'Mr'. Another suggestion is that this is a printer's error and Shakespeare's initials were accidentally transposed. The theory that appeals to romantic conspiracy theorists is that Mr W. H. is Anne Hathaway's brother: that Anne gave the sonnets to her brother William who took them to London and gave them in turn to Thomas Thorpe, the publisher – the T. T. of the dedication. For those wondering why Shakespeare's wife would want a series of love poetry in which her husband addresses a fair youth and a dark mistress, well, one suggestion is that Anne viewed herself as both of those characters: two sides – one light, one dark – of a marriage that had lasted over thirty years.

More realistically, though, the 'eternitie promised' probably refers to the recurring theme of art as bestower of immortality, and it's also possible to read the dedication as a half-hearted apology from the publisher Thomas Thorpe for putting the sonnets in the public domain without the author's permission:

> In setting forth, the well-wishing adventurer, T [homas] T [horpe], wisheth to the onlie begetter of these ensuing sonnets, Mr W. H., all happiness and that eternity promised by our ever-living Poet.

Though that still doesn't sound *completely* convincing. The argument continues . . .

Sonnet 1

From fairest creatures we desire increase,
That thereby beauty's rose might never die,
But as the riper should by time decease,
His tender heir might bear his memory:
But thou, contracted to thine own bright eyes,
Feed'st thy light's flame with self-substantial fuel,
Making a famine where abundance lies,
Thyself thy foe, to thy sweet self too cruel.
Thou that art now the world's fresh ornament,
And only herald to the gaudy spring,
Within thine own bud buriest thy content,
And, tender churl, mak'st waste in niggarding.
    Pity the world, or else this glutton be,
    To eat the world's due, by the grave and thee.

This is the opening sonnet, and the first of the so-called 'procreation' poems. It introduces many of the themes that are explored in the rest of the sequence: love, beauty, the passing of time, nature and selfishness, and sets the tone for what's to come. The first quatrain lays out the argument: the beautiful people among us must reproduce, 'increase', in order that beauty will continue to exist. The passing of time is inevitable, but in a person's offspring beauty can live on forever: 'His tender heir might bear his memory'. In the second quatrain the tone shifts from admiration and appreciation to something a bit darker as the speaker chides his subject on his dangerous self-obsession and narcissism, 'to thy sweet self too cruel'. There's a clever contrasting of 'famine' and 'feed'st', foreshadowing the final couplet's ideas of gluttony and eating. And the bud of the third quatrain recalls the rose of the opening lines, with a possibly racy nod to masturbation.

    It's interesting to note that in this poem about beauty and the passing of time, Shakespeare uses the language of finance and commercialism, which will recur again and again throughout the sequence, so we see 'increase', 'contracted' and 'niggarding' (which means hoarding), reinforcing the sense of waste. There's a distinction between the temporary nature of transient physical wealth and more permanent spiritual riches. By refusing to marry and have children the youth is depriving the whole world of his beauty, and by the final lines the world knows what it is due.

Sonnet 18

Shall I compare thee to a summer's day?
Thou art more lovely and more temperate:
Rough winds do shake the darling buds of May,
And summer's lease hath all too short a date:
Sometime too hot the eye of heaven shines,
And often is his gold complexion dimmed;
And every fair from fair sometime declines,
By chance, or nature's changing course, untrimmed:
But thy eternal summer shall not fade,
Nor lose possession of that fair thou ow'st;
Nor shall death brag thou wander'st in his shade
When in eternal lines to time thou grow'st:
    So long as men can breathe or eyes can see,
    So long lives this, and this gives life to thee.

Sonnet 18 is one of Shakespeare's most famous love sonnets, following the classic ABAB CDCD EFEF GG pattern. But if we look a little closer we can see he's enhancing the classic sonnet with his own style to say something new about love, longing and art.

After the procreation sonnets this is the first to suggest that there might be another way to preserve the young man's beauty aside from having children: through the eternal stayng power of art. The poem kicks off with brilliant use of pathetic fallacy – comparing his lover favourably to summer, with the acknowledgement that summer can be brutal, 'Rough winds do shake the darling buds of May', that the sun or the 'eye of heaven' can burn too brightly, whereas the young man is 'more lovely and more temperate'. Nature and the passing of time will eventually destroy every 'fair' person, but the youth's 'eternal summer shall not fade' when the artist is there to bear witness in these very lines we're reading four hundred years later, 'When in eternal lines to time thou growest'. This is pretty mind-boggling when you think about it: Shakepeare is doing something quite new and experimental here in exploring the relationship not just between the artist and his subject, but also between the artist and his audience. And look at how the iambic pentameter stresses the 'I' of the opening line, while the 'thou' of line two is unstressed – perhaps this hints at the real subject of the poem? Far from being a hymn to his lover, maybe another way to look at Sonnet 18 is as a celebration of the triumph of the poet and his dominance over the passing of time.

Renaissance sexuality

On paper, sex and sexuality in Elizabethan times were strictly policed and monitored. The Church was full of condemnation for carnal desire, and even sponsored the so-called 'Bawdy Courts' – ecclesiastical courts that could impose jail sentences and public humiliation for sexual transgressions. Sodomy was strictly forbidden and prostitution was illegal. In practice, though, it was a different story. Throughout Elizabeth's and James's reigns there were only six charges of sodomy ever brought to legal scrutiny, and brothels flourished – in fact

Shakespeare's co-author of *Pericles*, George Wilkins, owned a brothel.

Sexual preference was not an either or choice, in the way that it's viewed today. Male homosexual love was common in Elizabethan times. Indeed, King James was famously sexually in thrall to some of his male favourites. In a society that placed the value of men leagues above that of women, why wouldn't men be attracted to their equals in perfection: other men?

Sonnet 29

When in disgrace with fortune and men's eyes
I all alone beweep my outcast state,
And trouble deaf heav'n with my bootless cries,
And look upon myself, and curse my fate,
Wishing me like to one more rich in hope,
Featured like him, like him with friends possessed,
Desiring this man's art and that man's scope,
With what I most enjoy contented least;
Yet in these thoughts myself almost despising,
Haply I think on thee, and then my state,
Like to the lark at break of day arising,
From sullen earth, sings hymns at heaven's gate;
    For thy sweet love remember'd such wealth brings
    That then I scorn to change my state with kings

Here the speaker is miserable, outcast, paranoid, and jealous of those around him. The 'Fortune' of the opening line has a double meaning, of luck, of course, but it could also mean the poet is broke. There's some wonderfully emphatic alliteration at 'I all alone', along with the repetition of 'and', and a shifting of rhythm from iambic to trochaic at 'trouble deaf heaven' – all accumulating in the first quatrain to suggest how out of step and alienated the poet is.

The second quatrain moves the tone on from gloomy self-reflection to a sort of envious observation of the people around him. Again there's double meaning of 'rich in hope' – either the poet is wishing he was more hopeful, or he's voicing the age-old lament that he wishes he had more cash. A volta at the 'Yet' of line 9 marks a sudden dramatic shift on the poet's emotional roller coaster – on remembering 'thee' the speaker is transformed, his spirits soaring like 'lark at break of day arising' and by the final couplet he acknowledges that he wouldn't swap places with a king. There's some stunning imagery here, and the enjambment – where the lark phrase carries on over the line break without pause – makes the lines soar. A bit like a lark . . .

Sonnet 130

My mistress' eyes are nothing like the sun;
Coral is far more red than her lips' red;
If snow be white, why then her breasts are dun;
If hairs be wires, black wires grow on her head;
I have seen roses damasked, red and white,
But no such roses see I in her cheeks;
And in some perfumes is there more delight
Than in the breath that from my mistress reeks.
I love to hear her speak, yet well I know
That music hath a far more pleasing sound;
I grant I never saw a goddess go;
My mistress when she walks treads on the ground:
    And yet, by heaven, I think my love as rare
    As any she belied with false compare.

Here, with humour that manages to echo across four centuries, Shakespeare tells a brilliant extended joke to undercut and lampoon the traditional Petrarchan love sonnet. Petrarch was not a man shy of grand passions, he was so in love with his cat that after its death he had the moggy embalmed and placed in a glass case above a doorway into his library. In his *Canzoniere*, Laura's smile is remembered as a flashing of angelic rays, her hair golden, her teeth like pearls, her cheeks like red and white flowers. It's not hard to imagine that even in Shakespeare's time this overblown style might have been mocked. But the speaker's lover's eyes are nothing like the sun, in comparison to perfume her breath 'reeks', and music sounds better than her voice. There's a clever extension, from the first two lines telling us what she's *not* like, to the next two lines telling us what she *is* like, and it's not flattering – her breasts are dun-coloured, a sort of muddy grey, her hair is not silky and golden, instead it's rough and coarse. It's a pretty audacious approach to a love poem. Nevertheless it's full of poetic devices to take the breath away:

the elegant alliteration of line 11, 'grant I never saw a goddess go', means the line takes on a kind of rhythmic swaying, for example. And in fact the mistress stalks this poem – she's present in every line, unlike, say, the subject of Sonnet 18. The rhyming couplet acts as the punchline for the joke, the poet swearing that his love is just as extraordinary ('rare') as any of the objects of other sonnets who are flattered by false comparisons. It's an attack on idealised notions of women and femininity – his love is a real woman, not some perfect pedestal-posing princess. In that, we think it's more an expression of true love than any highfalutin hyperbole.

Sonnet 146

Poor soul, the centre of my sinful earth,
[. . .] these rebel powers that thee array,
Why dost thou pine within and suffer dearth,
Painting thy outward walls so costly gay?
Why so large cost, having so short a lease,
Dost thou upon thy fading mansion spend?
Shall worms, inheritors of this excess,
Eat up thy charge? Is this thy body's end?
Then soul, live thou upon thy servant's loss,
And let that pine to aggravate thy store;
Buy terms divine in selling hours of dross,
Within be fed, without be rich no more:
    So shalt thou feed on death, that feeds on men,
    And death once dead, there's no more dying then.

This sonnet stands out for a number of reasons: first there is the missing text at the beginning of line 2 which was originally reprinted as 'my sinful earth these rebels powers', repeating the end of line 1. But the consensus now is that our beloved Bard wouldn't have broken the rhythm with some lazy repetition; in fact it's most likely to have been a printer's error – the printing process was staggeringly arduous and mind-numbingly repetitive, with each letter being set by hand: it's no surprise that mistakes were often made.

Another distinguishing feature of Sonnet 146 is that, rather than addressing the Fair Youth or the Dark Lady, the speaker turns the spotlight on himself, or rather his soul. He interrogates it, asking why his soul allows itself to starve, to 'pine within and suffer dearth', even while appearances are being lavished with attention – 'Painting thy outward walls so costly gay'. The first two quatrains are composed of a series of questions, and the last quatrain offers up a way to salvage the soul's situation: telling it to rise above 'thy servant's loss'. In the context of the sequence, this 'loss' might refer to frustrated passion – it sits among the Dark Lady sonnets with their recurring refrain of the dangers of desire – so the body's starvation might just provide the soul's nourishment. The final couplet suggests a sense of victory – in the end the soul can overcome death. It's worth noting again that the poet returns to one of his favourite metaphors of financial entrapment: 'short a lease', 'inheritors of this excess', 'selling' – there's a reference to money or finance in virtually every line.

Other masters of the sonnet form

Shakespeare isn't the only poet to have nailed the sonnet form, and with the tools of deciphering the sonnets safely at your disposal, here is a list of poems to look at next:

'I Abide and Abide and Better Abide' by Sir Thomas Wyatt

Sonnet sequence 'Astrophel and Stella' by Sir Philip Sidney

'Happy ye leaves! whenas those lily hands' by Edmund Spenser

'Batter my heart, three-person'd God' by John Donne

'To the Nightingale' by John Milton

'Ozymandias' by Percy Bysshe Shelley

'Bright Star' by John Keats

'Now Sleeps the Crimson Petal' by Alfred, Lord Tennyson

'The Cross of the Snow' by Henry Wadsworth Longfellow

'Design' by Robert Frost

'To Speak of Woe That is in Marriage' by Robert Lowell

'Sonnet' by Elizabeth Bishop

Shakespeare's Other Poems

The sonnets are Shakespeare's most famous non-dramatic works but he also wrote four other poems you should know about. During the early 1590s and 1600s the theatres were shut down several times to try to limit the spread of bubonic plague. All public gatherings apart from church were banned in an effort to halt transmission of this terrifying disease. The closure of the theatres meant that playwrights had to turn elsewhere for work and pay. Shakespeare used this time to write the long poems discussed below.

Venus and Adonis (1593): Dedicated to the Earl of Southampton, this lively poem is based on the Roman poet Ovid's version of the myth of the same name. It describes the efforts of the Roman goddess of love, Venus, to seduce a handsome young man, Adonis. Sadly for Venus, Adonis is only interested in hunting boar, a hobby which leads to his death and Venus' curse that from this point on love will hurt: 'Sorrow on love hereafter shall attend'. It was the first work by Shakespeare to be formally published and proved extremely popular, reprinting many times. One reason for its success could be that it is rather saucy: 'I'll be a park, and thou shalt be my deer; / Feed where thou wilt, on mountain or in dale: / Graze on my lips; and if those hills be dry, / Stray lower, where the pleasant fountains lie . . .'; 'She sinketh down, still hanging by his neck, / He on her belly falls, she on her back. / Now is she in the very lists of love / Her champion mounted for the hot encounter . . .' It is written in iambic pentameter stanzas of six lines, in the bouncy rhyming pattern of ABABCC.

The Rape of Lucrece (1594). This poem was also dedicated to the Earl of Southampton and can be seen as a counterpoint to its predecessor's treatment of lust. It is similar in style, involving many rhetorical flourishes and elaborate literary effects. Ovid is again the principal source but this poem has a far more serious tone. It describes the rape of the Roman noblewoman, Lucrece, by the son of the king, Tarquin, and Lucrece's subsequent honourable suicide after her call for her husband and his friends to avenge her. Its key themes are desire and honour: 'Such hazard now must doting Tarquin make, / Pawning his honour to obtain his lust; / And for himself himself he must forsake: / Then where is truth, if there be no self-trust?' It is written in rhyme royal, a poetic form first used by Chaucer, using seven-line stanzas of iambic pentameter, rhyming ABABBCC.

Henry Wriothesley, third Earl of Southampton

The two dedications to the Earl of Southampton that precede *Venus and Adonis* and *The Rape of Lucrece* are the only direct addresses that we have from Shakespeare. These dedications were conventional but they still give us some information about the playwright as a person. The first, in *Venus and Adonis*, is very formal and distant, 'I know not how I shall offend in dedicating my unpolished lines to your lordship', and the second is much more intimate, 'The love I dedicate to your lordship is without end . . .', so it seems likely that *Venus* had met with favour with the twenty-year-old Earl. As a patron of Shakespeare, Southampton is also one of the candidates scholars consider for the mysterious dedicatee of the Sonnets, 'Mr W.H.', and also the 'Fair Youth' that they describe.

The man behind these dedications was a great enthusiast and supporter of the arts, patronising other writers such as Thomas Nashe and John Florio. His good looks and easy charm were legendary, and he became part of the entourage of the captivating Earl of Essex. However, Wriothesley annoyed Queen Elizabeth by marrying without her permission and fighting with one of her attendants, before ending up sentenced to death for his part in Essex's rebellion (see page 150). Happily for him, his sentence was commuted and the new king had him released. He entertained James's queen with a performance of *Love's Labour's Lost* at his house the same year. This wasn't to be his last spell in prison and he didn't exactly mend his ways with regards to fighting and intriguing but he continued to be active at court. He became interested in colonisation and was a member of both the Virginia and East India Companies, before dying of fever in 1624 at the age of fifty-one in the Netherlands, while commanding English troops against the Spanish.

N.B: Wriothesley was pronounced 'Rizeley'. Hilary Mantel refers to this in her nicknaming of the Earl's grandfather as 'Call-me-Risley' in her Booker-winning novel, *Wolf Hall*.

The Phoenix and Turtle (1601): This allegorical poem calls together a gathering of different birds to mourn the death of, and celebrate the ideal spiritual love of, the mythical bird, the phoenix (a symbol of rarity and immortality), and the turtle dove (a symbol of fidelity): 'Beauty, truth, and rarity. / Grace in all simplicity, / Here enclos'd in cinders lie'. It was originally untitled and part of a collection called *Love's Martyr* which comprised a long poem about the birds' love by Robert Chester and then other shorter poems on the subject by Shakespeare, John Marston, George Chapman and Ben Jonson. Various theories have been put forward as to what the poem might symbolise. It is dedicated to Sir John Salusbury so some believe it is a celebration of his marriage, others that it represents Elizabeth I's union with her people (the phoenix was one of Elizabeth's symbols) or even with the Earl of Essex, or that it is about the impending Jacobean succession. Another school of thought sees it as subversively referring to Catholic martyrs. It takes the shape of thirteen quatrains (four-line stanzas), rhyming ABAB, followed by five triplets (stanzas of three rhyming lines), in solemn trochaic tetrameter.

A Lover's Complaint (1609): This poem was part of the original publication of Shakespeare's *Sonnets* in 1609. In it, the narrator sees an old shepherd meet a woman weeping and throwing love tokens into a river. She tells him of her betrayal by a persuasive lothario – 'For, lo, his passion, but an art of craft, / Even there resolved my reason into tears; / There my white stole of chastity I daffd, / Shook off my sober guards and civil fears' – but ends up admitting that she'd probably fall for him again. The Complaint was a recognised poetic form which sometimes followed collections of sonnets. Like *The Rape of Lucrece*, this poem is written in rhyme royal. It is not the most highly rated of Shakespeare's works and over the years there have been various discussions about whether or not he really is its author.

The (Pirated) Passionate Pilgrime (*c*.1599)

THE
PASSIONATE
PILGRIME.
By W. Shakespeare.

AT LONDON
Printed for W. Iaggard, and are
to be sold by W. Leake, at the Grey-
hound in Paules Churchyard.
1 5 9 9.

After the brilliant success of *Venus and Adonis* and *The Rape of Lucrece*, there was great appetite for more poetry from Shakespeare. Around 1599, the naughty publisher William Jaggard decided to fulfil this by publishing a collection of twenty poems under Shakespeare's name. However, only five are now considered to be by Shakespeare: two of the at-the-time-unpublished Sonnets (138 and 144) and three purposefully bad poems from *Love's Labour's Lost*. The most famous poem in the collection is actually Marlowe's 'The Passionate Shepherd to his Love'. In a later edition Jaggard also added poems by Thomas Heywood, who complained about it and recorded that Shakespeare was also 'most offended' to have his name used in this way. Jaggard then removed Shakespeare's name from the title page of later editions.

THE EPILOGUE

Further fascinating facts for the Shakespeare fan

After reading the previous chapters we hope you feel your basic knowledge of Shakespeare has been enhanced and you are well equipped to venture into the world of his plays and poems without trepidation. In this last section we'll introduce you to some more specialist information about our great poet to enhance your Shakespertise even further.

The great gift of the first folio

First Folio, title page, 1623

When a playwright today writes a play it is usually published simultaneously with the first performance of the work. Changes made during rehearsal can be taken in up until the play goes to print and the final text has been approved by the author and copy-edited and proofread by the publisher. Things were very different in Shakespeare's day. His first draft (colourfully named his **foul papers**) was likely written out neatly (into what was called a **fair copy**) by him or a secretary, and then annotated with stage directions to become the **prompt copy** used by the theatre company. Individual actors only took their parts copied from the prompt copy to learn, so full scripts were rare. Plays were also not necessarily available for the reading public, and those that were wouldn't always have been approved by the author, or the copyright holder (usually the theatre company).

None of Shakespeare's manuscripts survive and he did not oversee the publication of any of the printed editions of his plays. About half of them were published in his lifetime in quarto format and then, seven years after his death, two of his friends and fellow actors, John Heminges and Henry

Condell, published thirty-six of his plays together in folio format. This 1623 publication became known as the **First Folio**.

Quartos and folios

Folio is a term used to describe a book printed in a certain size. Folios were made by printing on sheets of paper folded in half once to produce two leaves and four pages and then sets of pages like this were sewn together. The First Folio has 454 leaves and is roughly 22cm wide and 32cm tall (which makes it a bit smaller than a standard folio of around 38cm tall). Folios were a posh, expensive format and drama was generally considered too downmarket to be published like this, though Ben Jonson changed all that when, in 1616, he published a collection of his plays in folio.

Quartos were made by folding the paper sheets four times, to give four leaves and eight pages per sheet. They were a smaller, cheaper and more popular format. They were stitched together but unbound and people who bought them would sometimes have them sewn into bindings of their choice. Twenty-one of Shakespeare's plays appeared in quarto, in print runs of around eight hundred copies, eighteen of these before the publication of the First Folio. The first was *Titus Andronicus* in 1594. From the 1598 publication of *Love's Labour's Lost* onwards Shakespeare was clearly well known

enough to have his name included on the title pages. The abbreviations Q1, Q2, etc., refer to the edition of the relevant quarto. Some of the quartos appear to have been made from Shakespeare's foul papers and scholars have also theorised that others come from actors' memories (**memorial reconstruction**).

Bad quartos are quarto editions that are considered inferior to other quarto versions and the First Folio. They are usually much shorter and contain many errors, e.g. Q1 of *Romeo and Juliet* (1597), which is half the length of Q2, and Q1 of *Henry V* (1600), which is half the length of the First Folio version. Q1 of *Hamlet* is also referred to as a bad quarto and appears to have been put together by the actor playing Marcellus as he remembers his lines best.

For comparison, modern hardback books are usually printed in octavo format of eight leaves and sixteen pages: you'll notice that the books on your shelf all have a total page number (including any blanks at the end and preliminary material) divisible by sixteen, because of the way the paper has been folded.

Heminges and Condell stated in the preface that their project was a noble one: 'without ambition either of self-profit, or fame: only to keep the memory of so worthy a Friend & Fellow alive, as was our Shakespeare'. They wanted to supplant the various quarto editions that had appeared without Shakespeare's, or the King's Men's, supervision before 1623.

The First Folio saw the first ever publication of eighteen of Shakespeare's plays. It is a chilling thought, but without it we would not have *The Tempest*, *The Two Gentlemen of Verona*, *Measure for Measure*, *The Comedy of Errors*, *As You Like It*, *The Taming of the Shrew*, *All's Well that Ends Well*, *Twelfth Night*, *The Winter's Tale*, *King John*, *Henry VI, Part 1*, *Henry VIII*, *Coriolanus*, *Timon of Athens*, *Julius Caesar*, *Macbeth*, *Antony and Cleopatra* and *Cymbeline*. It did not include *Pericles*, *The Two Noble Kinsmen* or the other plays Shakespeare co-wrote, or *Cardenio* or *Love's Labour's Won* (if indeed these latter two plays ever existed, see page 277).

The First Folio versions of some of the plays that also survive in quarto have significant differences. Hamlet's famous line 'To be, or not to be, that is the question' comes from the Folio version. Q2 reads 'To be, or not to be, I there's the point'. The texts of *Hamlet* and *King Lear* in the different formats differ very significantly and have caused lively literary debate for decades. There are three different editions of *Hamlet*: Q1 (bad) from 1603, Q2 from 1604 and the Folio. Q2 is double the length of Q1 and would take four hours to perform if acted in full, and the Folio version is not much shorter. Modern editions usually print a mixture of Q2 and the Folio, but recent scholarship has postulated that the different versions could be for different purposes – the shorter versions refined in performance or developed from a longer first draft. Possibly the longer versions were intended for reading, once printed.

Publishing in Shakespeare's time

Condell and Heminge's preface to the First Folio includes an exhortation to the reader that many authors, editors and publishers today would second: 'From the most able, to him that can but spell : . . . the fate of all Bookes depends upon your capacities: and not of your heads alone, but of your purses.'

The market for bookselling in the early seventeenth century was limited as literacy was low and printing was a new and expensive craft. The printing industry worked differently from today as copyright did not remain with the author. Playwrights would sell their copyrights to theatre companies, who would submit them to the Master of the Revels for approval to perform them and make any censor-demanded cuts, and then possibly go on to sell them to printers. Printers would claim their right to print these plays by registering them in the Stationers' Register. Works were often published anonymously and printers also sometimes printed material for which they didn't hold the rights.

The plays in the First Folio were collected together by Condell and Heminges from the versions in use by the King's Men and the collection was printed and sold by Edward Blount and William and Isaac Jaggard. Textual analysis has established that the type was set by five different compositors (known by the letters A to E, with E being an apprentice who didn't do such a great job of his sections). Hundreds of corrections were made during the book's printing so earlier copies are different from ones that came off the press later in the process. The prices of the folios ranged from 15 shillings for those sold unbound to £1 for a bound version. Nowadays you're looking at shelling out a few million for one of the 228 known to have survived from the probable 750-copy print run; in 2001 one sold for $6,166,000 in New York.

Beyond F1: later folios

The Second Folio appeared in 1632, incorporating many corrections and a new poem from John Milton. In 1663–4 the Third Folio came out, and its second impression included *Pericles* and six plays now not generally considered to be by Shakespeare (see page 271). This is the version you want to find in your attic if you can't have a First, as it's very rare, probably because of the Great Fire of London in 1666 destroying many of the copies not yet sold by the publishers. 1685 saw the final Fourth Folio, reprinting the Third with corrections and, as with every new printing, new errors.

Modern editions of the plays

Modern editions of Shakespeare have traditionally been based on the First Folio with some emendations from quarto versions included or referred to in annotations. The editors usually modernise spelling and punctuation and regulate verse layout (in the original, prose and verse were sometimes compressed or expanded to fit page lengths). They also heroically attempt to correct typographical errors and resolve cruxes. (A crux is a point in a play where the text is corrupted and it is difficult to establish the true meaning or version.) They generally divide all the plays into the conventional five acts, absent in the First Folio. Different editions have different line numbers, as well as different annotations, depending on the editor. For plays with significant differences between quarto and folio versions editors have usually published conflations, but recently there has been a move to publish different versions together in one volume, emphasising the integrity of both.

The collaborative plays and the apocrypha

The Romantic idea of Shakespeare is of a lone genius, scribbling away with his quills in his garret, far from family and home. However, recent scholarship has led the way in painting a different picture of how Renaissance playwriting worked. There is evidence to show that in many, many instances playwrights worked together as co-authors, collaborators and editors of one another's plays. Shakespeare was no exception. In fact, it seems that the practice of drama in Shakespeare's time was more like that of modern television or film writing, with many contributors to a script being the norm, rather than the single voice of a novelist. The best playwrights working in London at this time were part of a small world of colleagues who appear to have happily taken both major and minor roles in originating and revising the plays they were involved with.

For a long time the **Shakespeare canon** was generally considered to consist of the thirty-six plays published in the First Folio plus the co-authored *Pericles* and *The Two Noble Kinsmen*, along with the poems *Venus and Adonis*, *The Rape of Lucrece*, *A Lover's Complaint*, *The Phoenix and Turtle* and the 154 sonnets. Other works that were at one time attributed to Shakespeare on title pages or by hearsay, or appear to have his hand in them somewhere as a contributor or reviser, were designated part of the **apocrypha**. In fact, the line between these two categories is blurred and recent scholarship has seen formerly apocryphal plays moved into the canon by some publishers: e.g. the Arden Shakespeare includes *Double Falsehood* (thought to be the missing *Cardenio*, co-written with John Fletcher), the RSC Shakespeare includes a scene from the play *Sir Thomas More*, and the Oxford Shakespeare includes *Sir Thomas More* and also *Edward III*. Computer stylometric analysis has allowed scholars to judge more clearly which individual parts of works are likely to have come from which playwrights, and although it is impossible to definitively establish authorship, a number of scholars agree that Shakespeare collaborated with others on (sometimes with a very minimal input), or had some hand in revising, the plays listed below. However, there is no overall consensus on these issues and before you start throwing your knowledge of that little-known Shakespeare play *Mucedorus* around at cocktail parties you should be aware that some of the propositions below are controversial, or do not adhere to the current majority view. Research and analysis continues.

Play	Possible Collaborators
Henry VI, 1, 2 and *3*	Several other unidentified dramatists, particularly Thomas Nashe
Titus Andronicus	George Peele
Measure for Measure	Revised by Thomas Middleton
Timon of Athens	Thomas Middleton
Macbeth	Thomas Middleton (the Hecate scene and two songs from his play *The Witch*)
Pericles	George Wilkins
Henry VIII	John Fletcher
The Two Noble Kinsmen	John Fletcher

Play	Possible Collaborators
Arden of Faversham	Thomas Kyd, with only one scene possibly by Shakespeare
Sir Thomas More	Originally by Anthony Munday and Henry Chettle, revised by Thomas Heywood, Thomas Dekker and Shakespeare. Contains what is believed to be three pages of additions to the manuscript in Shakespeare's own handwriting (referred to as Hand D): the only example of this beyond his six extant signatures
The Spanish Tragedy	Written by Thomas Kyd, with Shakespeare possibly providing some later additions
Locrine	Unknown, possibly written by George Peele or Robert Greene, with an epilogue possibly by Shakespeare. Included in the 1663 Third Folio along with other plays no longer thought to be by Shakespeare: *The London Prodigal, A Yorkshire Tragedy, Thomas Lord Cromwell, The Puritan* and *Sir John Oldcastle*. These remained part of the canon until Alexander Pope removed them from his 1725 edition
Edward III	Written by Thomas Kyd. According to some theories, excluded from the First Folio due to anti-Scottish content leading to a prohibition against its performance
Mucedorus	Unknown, with a later additional scene possibly by Shakespeare
Double Falsehood	1727 play by Lewis Theobald believed to be an adaptation of Shakespeare and Fletcher's lost *Cardenio*

How stylometry helped us to learn more about Shakespeare

Scholars have various methods for establishing the authorship and chronology of literary works. They look at external factors, such as printing and professional records and contemporary references to performances, but they also look closely at the texts themselves. On an obvious level, they look for references to events and to recently published source material that might help prove that a writer was writing at a certain time or had a certain background. However, it is also possible to look closely at an author's style and compare this to that of disputed works.

Everyone has their own particular writing style: a preference for certain words or turns of phrase, grammatical and spelling mistakes they consistently make, a preference for long or short words and simple or elaborate sentences, writers they prefer to quote from, ways they contract common words, types of imagery they use and habits of metrical rhythm. All of these can be analysed using sophisticated computer programs and, although it's not a perfect science, such studies have led to breakthroughs in the attribution of work to Shakespeare.

For example, the only surviving quarto of *The Two Noble Kinsmen* has a title page attributing the play to John Fletcher and William Shakespeare and was entered in the Stationers' Register in 1634. Despite this, because it is considered a relatively weak play and did not appear in the First Folio, the extent of Shakespeare's hand in it was doubted for some time. However, close textual analysis has supported his authorship of Act I, Act II (Scene 1) and Act V. In establishing chronology, scholars note that a masque by Francis Beaumont from 1613 and a play by Jonson from 1614 have connections with elements of the play, leading to the view that it was first performed around this time, putting it right at the end of Shakespeare's writing career.

The difficulty of dating Shakespeare's plays

Unhelpfully, the First Folio does not list the plays in order of composition so scholars have had to work very hard to try to put together a chronology, and there still isn't agreement over the exact dates or order of Shakespeare's works. The documentary evidence from the time does not often clearly establish when a play was first composed or performed as they generally weren't published straight after performance. This means that the records of the Stationers' Register (where, between 1562 and 1911, publishers and printers had to register their rights to print a work) are helpful but not definitive in establishing dates of origination. Academics have had to fall back on external evidence, such as references to seeing certain plays in private documents. For example, the surviving diary of a student called John Manningham records his attendance at a feast at Middle Temple on 2 February 1602 where they 'had a play called Twelfth Night, or What You Will' which has helped date this play's composition to 1601.

Scholars also look at internal evidence within the plays, such as references to specific contemporary events or books or analysis of the development of Shakespeare's literary style. For example, *Henry V* contains lines referring to 'the General of our gracious Empress . . . from Ireland coming, / Bringing rebellion broached on his sword', which seems to refer to the anticipated triumphant return of the Earl of Essex (see page 150) from his military campaign in Ireland. Essex left England in March 1599 and returned defeated in September so the play must have been written between these two dates.

The *RSC Complete Works* gives the following chronology:

The Taming of the Shrew	1589–92
The Second Part of Henry the Sixth	1591
The Third Part of Henry the Sixth	1591

The Two Gentlemen of Verona	1591–2
The Lamentable Tragedy of Titus Andronicus	1591–2 (perhaps revised 1594)
The First Part of Henry the Sixth	1592
King Richard the Third	1592/1594
Venus and Adonis	1593
The Rape of Lucrece	1593–4
Sonnets and *A Lover's Complaint*	1593–1608
The Comedy of Errors	1594
Love's Labour's Lost	1595
Love's Labour's Won (a lost play, unless the original title for another comedy)	1595–7
A Midsummer Night's Dream	1595–6
The Tragedy of Romeo and Juliet	1595–6
King Richard the Second	1595–6
The Life and Death of King John	1595–7 (possibly earlier)
The Merchant of Venice	1596–7
The First Part of Henry the Fourth	1596–7
The Second Part of Henry the Fourth	1597–8
Much Ado About Nothing	1598
The Life of Henry the Fifth	1599
As You Like It	1599
The Tragedy of Julius Caesar	1599
The Tragedy of Hamlet, Prince of Denmark	1600–1 (perhaps revising an earlier version)
The Merry Wives of Windsor	1600–1 (perhaps revising version of 1597–9)

The Phoenix and Turtle	1601
Twelfth Night, or What You Will	1601
The Tragedy of Troilus and Cressida	1601–2
The Tragedy of Othello, the Moor of Venice	1604
Measure for Measure	1604
All's Well that Ends Well	1605
The Life of Timon of Athens	1605
The Tragedy of King Lear	1605–6
The Tragedy of Macbeth	1606
The Tragedy of Antony and Cleopatra	1606–7
The Tragedy of Coriolanus	1608
Pericles, Prince of Tyre	1608
The Tragedy of Cymbeline	1610
The Winter's Tale	1611
The Tempest	1611
Cardenio (lost)	1612–13
Henry VIII	1613
The Two Noble Kinsmen	1613–14

The lost plays

There are two plays the mention of which is guaranteed to get ardent Shakespeare fans all a-froth: *Cardenio* and *Love's Labour's Won*. Never seen your local amateur dramatics troupe perform them? That's because these are the two famous lost plays of Shakespeare. They are among the most sought-after as-yet-undiscovered works of literature in the world. They are mentioned in historical documents but no text for them has ever been conclusively discovered. They remain shrouded in mystery.

Cardenio is thought to be by Shakespeare and John Fletcher, based on an episode from Cervantes' *Don Quixote*. It is believed to involve two contrasting sets of lovers, mix-ups, betrayals, interrupted scenes of violence and disguise: all ingredients we know and love from Shakespeare's other plays. The eighteenth-century Shakespeare specialist Lewis Theobald claimed that he had in his possession three original manuscripts of a lost Shakespeare play on which he based his work *Double Falsehood or the Distrest Lovers*, but these were never seen by anyone else. At the time, this was dismissed as a hoax, most scathingly by Alexander Pope, who added insult to injury by making Theobald the King of the Dunces in his 1728 satire *The Dunciad*. History has been a little kinder, though, with most experts agreeing that *Double Falsehood* appears to be an adaptation of Shakespeare and Fletcher's work.

Love's Labour's Won is mentioned in a 1598 essay on poetry called *Palladis Tamia* by Francis Meres. Later, in the mid-twentieth century, the wonderfully named Solomon Pottesman, an antiquarian bookseller in London, discovered a packing slip dated from 1603 which listed: 'marchant of vennis, taming of a shrew, . . . loves labor lost, loves labor won'. No text exists, but theories abound: is it the lost sequel to *Love's Labour's Lost*? Or just a different title for *The Taming of the Shrew*? Or *Much Ado About Nothing*, or even *Troilus and Cressida*? In all probability we'll never know, but do keep your eyes peeled next time you're rooting around in granny's attic.

Tips for watching Shakespeare's plays

The hushed anticipation, the dimmed lights, the expensive interval drinks: a trip to the theatre should be a pleasure for all the senses, but the truth is that going to watch Shakespeare can be daunting. Some people are put off by the apparently impenetrable language, the incomprehensible jokes that some show-off always guffaws at loudly, the sheer number of characters and their complicated relationships, and that's before we've even got to the cross-dressing. Luckily, we have a few tips on how to get the most out of your theatrical experience.

1. **Do some homework**. It will be much easier to orientate yourself if you've read up on what the play is about. Shakespeare's plays aren't so much about twists or surprises, particularly as they are so famous, so don't worry about plot spoilers.

2. **Have a look at the programme** before the play begins. Apart from spotting all the actors you've seen in *Casualty*, this will probably also give you some information about the play and the director's interpretation of it. That way if you suddenly find yourself watching *A Midsummer Night's Dream* set in 1970s America or *Coriolanus* set in Soviet Russia you'll have some sense of why the director has made the decision to use these modernised settings.

3. **Don't fixate on trying to understand every word**. It's much easier to follow Shakespeare's verse if you let it wash over you and watch the actors carefully. It's amazing how clear what is being communicated can be in the performance onstage, when on the page it can seem confusing and opaque.

4. **Identify the central conflict of the play**. This means you'll be able to anticipate what may be about to happen and what its implications could be. For example, it's clearly signposted that Richard III is going to go up against everyone to get the crown right at the start of the play so you can sit back and marvel at the inventive ways he does this once you have that clear in your mind.

5. **Enjoy Shakespeare's characters**. He really is very good at them. You can revel in Henry V's heroism, or Iago's evil, delight in Rosalind's wit, sigh and remind yourself of your first love with Juliet and it won't matter at all that they are living in a different world or time. It's also worth looking out for a clear-eyed character who acts as the audience's guide by telling the truth about proceedings – fools are particularly useful on this front.

6. **Consider the context**. It is more rewarding to watch the plays if you know a bit about the background to the plots and how they relate to the time Shakespeare was writing. But remember, one of the great things about the Bard is that he speaks to all ages. It is just as fascinating to interpret what you see in the light of today's events and concerns. *Othello* has a very different impact for an audience that has

witnessed the oppression of black people, *The Merchant of Venice* cannot avoid being judged differently in a post-Holocaust age and *Antony and Cleopatra* will affect an audience influenced by feminism differently from its original spectators.

7. **Be aware of the general themes and motifs** that Shakespeare likes to return to. Look out for what the play might seem to say about the responsibility or transfer of political power, the importance of order, the difficulty of attaining justice, the difference between appearance and reality, the tensions between different mindsets or generations, and the enlightening possibilities of madness and the liberating power of disguise.

Recurring themes to keep an eye out for

If you're a fan of soap operas or even big blockbusting movies, you'll have noticed that, whether you're in Weatherfield or Los Angeles, certain plot elements are likely to recur: if someone gets hit on the head they will end up with amnesia, if a teenager has sex they will get pregnant, brothers- and sisters-in-law are always getting it on, whomever a character thinks is their father probably isn't, weddings all end in fisticuffs, and so on . . . Shakespeare is of course an artist of the highest order, but it is true that he had some favourite themes, motifs and events that crop up again and again in all the plays. Knowing what to look out for thematically can help your enjoyment of a performance so feel free to use this ready reckoner below to cross-reference to your heart's content.

Theme	Plays
Appearance versus reality	*King Lear, A Midsummer Night's Dream, Twelfth Night, Henry IV, Henry V, Julius Caesar, Macbeth, Othello, Measure for Measure, Much Ado About Nothing, Timon of Athens*

Theme	Plays
Power, ambition and corruption	*Macbeth, Richard II, Othello, Richard III, Hamlet, Julius Caesar, Measure for Measure, Antony and Cleopatra, King John, Coriolanus, Henry IV, Henry V, The Henry VI plays, Henry VIII, The Tempest*
Jealousy	*Othello, Troilus and Cressida, Much Ado About Nothing, Henry V, The Taming of the Shrew, The Merry Wives of Windsor, The Winter's Tale*
Fate and destiny	*Henry V, Julius Caesar, Macbeth, Romeo and Juliet, Hamlet, Titus Andronicus, Pericles, Richard III, King Lear, Richard II, Henry IV, The Henry VI plays*
Revenge and violence	*Hamlet, Othello, Pericles, Timon of Athens, The Two Noble Kinsmen, Coriolanus, The Merchant of Venice, Macbeth, Titus Andronicus, King Lear*
Order and disorder	*Macbeth, As You Like It, Henry V, Richard II, Henry IV, A Midsummer Night's Dream, Twelfth Night, Troilus and Cressida, Julius Caesar, Antony and Cleopatra*
Disguise	*The Two Gentlemen of Verona, The Merchant of Venice, As You Like It, Twelfth Night, Henry IV, Henry V, Cymbeline, The Merry Wives of Windsor, All's Well that Ends Well, Love's Labour's Lost, Measure for Measure*
Doubles and twins	*Much Ado About Nothing, The Merchant of Venice, The Merry Wives of Windsor, Hamlet, Twelfth Night, The Comedy of Errors, Henry IV*
Fake deaths	*Romeo and Juliet, Henry IV, Pericles, The Winter's Tale, King John, Cymbeline, Measure for Measure, Much Ado About Nothing*
Bastards	*King Lear, As You Like It, Troilus and Cressida, King John, Henry V, Henry VIII, Much Ado About Nothing*
Ghosts	*Hamlet, Macbeth, Julius Caesar, Cymbeline, Richard III, The Winter's Tale*

Theme	Plays
Fools and clowns	*As You Like It, King Lear, Twelfth Night, A Midsummer Night's Dream, The Tempest, All's Well that Ends Well, The Two Gentlemen of Verona, The Merchant of Venice, The Taming of the Shrew, Macbeth, Henry IV*
Magic	*Macbeth, The Tempest, The Winter's Tale, A Midsummer Night's Dream*
Parents and children	*Romeo and Juliet, The Tempest, King Lear, Hamlet, Pericles, Much Ado About Nothing, The Comedy of Errors, Cymbeline, The Merchant of Venice, The Winter's Tale, Henry IV, Richard II, Coriolanus, Titus Andronicus, The Henry VI plays, Othello, The Taming of the Shrew*
Madness	*The Two Noble Kinsmen, Hamlet, King Lear, Macbeth*

Great Shakespearean actors

Richard Burbage (*c.*1568–1619)

Richard Burbage was one of the most popular actors of the sixteenth century and the most famous actor to appear at the Globe in his day. He was born into a theatrical family and his father was an actor and theatre manager before him. As well as acting, Burbage was also a shareholder in the Globe and Blackfriars theatres and a painter. He worked for Shakespeare's company, the Lord Chamberlain's Men (later the King's Men), and took the starring role in many of his plays. He was the first Richard III, Romeo, Henry V, Hamlet, Macbeth, Othello and King Lear that anyone ever saw. His performances and theatrical presence are widely praised in contemporary accounts, despite the fact that he was apparently a bit on the short and tubby side. Shakespeare was fond enough of Burbage to leave him money in his will to buy a mourning ring to remember him by. Burbage continued acting right up until his death and is buried in St Leonard's, Shoreditch.

David Garrick (1717–79)

After being taught by Samuel Johnson at school, David Garrick began his working life in London as a wine merchant in the family business, but was soon seduced by the stage. He was both a playwright and an actor but became a sensation as the latter after his revolutionary performance of Richard III in 1741. The prime minister, William Pitt, referred to him as the greatest English actor ever and Alexander Pope said of him: 'that young man never had his equal as an actor, and he will never have a rival'. From 1747 Garrick ran the Drury Lane Theatre. He had a particular interest in Shakespeare, restoring many of the texts which had been adapted from their original versions and popularising his work. However, he did also make his own changes to the plays whenever he fancied it, including allowing Cordelia to live in *King Lear* and adding deathbed scenes between Romeo and Juliet. In 1769 he promoted the ill-fated Shakespeare Jubilee celebrations in Stratford-upon-Avon, which were a washout thanks to heavy rain but still contributed to the rise in popularity of Shakespeare's work. In 1775 he built a temple to Shakespeare in the grounds of his Hampton home and this can still be visited on Sundays today. Garrick retired in 1776 and sold his share in Drury Lane to Richard Brinsley Sheridan. He died in 1779 and is buried in Poets' Corner at Westminster Abbey, underneath Shakespeare's statue.

Sarah Siddons (1755–1831)

Sarah Siddons was born into a famous Welsh travelling acting troupe led by her parents, Roger and Sarah Kemble. The eldest of twelve children, she soon gained a reputation as a great actress, and after performing as Rosalind in *As You Like It* in 1775, David Garrick asked her to audition for him. It was a disaster, and she went back on tour until she was called up by Garrick's replacement at Drury Lane, Richard Brinsley Sheridan. She was an instant success, and cemented her reputation as a great tragedian, in particular in the role of Lady Macbeth. In her farewell performance of June 1812, the audience refused to allow the play to carry on past the famous sleepwalking scene, which she had performed to perfection. During her lifetime she was immortalised in portraits by Sir Thomas Gainsborough, Sir Joshua Reynolds and Sir Thomas Lawrence. She even had a Metropolitan Railway locomotive named after her, the No. 12 'Sarah Siddons', preserved today and used in heritage events. And since 1952 the Sarah Siddons Award has been given in America to actresses for Distinguished Achievement. Recipients include Deborah Kerr, Lauren Bacall, Bette Davis, Lynn Redgrave, Liza Minnelli, Faye Dunaway and Kathleen Turner.

Edmund Kean (c.1787–1833)

Edmund Kean grew up in unstable circumstances, and his life was never simple. The illegitimate child of performers, he was brought up by his father's brother's mistress, a member of the Drury Lane Theatre troupe. He became an actor at fifteen for a company in Sheerness and then moved to companies in Belfast, Tunbridge Wells and Gloucester before making his sensational debut at Drury Lane in 1814 as Shylock in *The Merchant of Venice*, by which time he had become a volatile alcoholic. (He later named his horse Shylock and sometimes slept in his stable with him.) His style of acting was considered fresh and authentic and he became famous for his portrayals of Shakespeare's great villains: Richard III, Iago and Macbeth. Byron gave him a sword in commendation of his performance as Othello and another admirer gave him a lion, who Kean liked to leave in his Clarges Street drawing room to surprise guests. His elephantine ego, destructive drinking and scandalous private life led to a decline in his reputation. In 1833 he collapsed onstage playing Othello opposite his son Charles as Iago. At the words 'Villain, be sure', in Act III, Scene 3, he broke down, and cried, 'O God, I am dying. Speak to them, Charles.' He died a few weeks later.

Sir Henry Irving (1838–1905)

Henry Irving was born John Henry Brodribb and worked as a clerk before an inheritance in 1856 allowed him to buy the leading role in an amateur production of *Romeo and Juliet* at the Royal Soho Theatre and devote himself to the dramatic arts. He joined a company in Sunderland and learned his craft over the following years. He became a star at the Lyceum Theatre in 1871 and took over managing that theatre in 1878. In the same year he employed the legendary Ellen Terry as his leading lady and their performances in roles such as Hamlet and Ophelia and Shylock and Portia made them hugely popular. In 1895 Irving was the first actor to be knighted. Despite financial difficulties blighting his later years, Irving was still much admired at the time of his death in 1905. He is buried in Westminster Abbey next to David Garrick.

Dame Ellen Terry (1847–1928)

Ellen Terry came from a theatrical family and played her first Shakespeare role at the age of nine (as the doomed Mamillius) in Charles Kean's production of *The Winter's Tale*. Her acting career was interrupted by various ill-fated relationships, including her marriage to the painter G. F. Watts. She first appeared opposite her great collaborator, Sir Henry Irving, in a staging of *The Taming of the Shrew* in 1867. From 1878 to 1902 she acted as his leading lady in many Shakespeare productions and she continued to act well into her late 70s. She is also celebrated for her correspondence with George Bernard Shaw, who called her 'irresistible Ellen'.

Laurence Olivier, Baron Olivier (1907–1989)

The son of a clergyman, Laurence Olivier gave his first Shakespeare performance aged nine in a school production of *Julius Caesar*. Ellen Terry wrote of his debut in her diary: 'The small boy who played Brutus is already a great actor.' He attended the Central School of Speech and Drama and made his professional debut as Lennox in *Macbeth* in 1924. His reputation increased with a 1935 performance of *Romeo and Juliet* where he alternated the roles of Romeo and Mercutio with John Gielgud. This led to a season of Shakespeare at the Old Vic. It was at this theatre that he played Hamlet to Vivien Leigh's Ophelia. They eventually married in 1940 after divorcing their previous spouses and performed numerous Shakespearean roles together before their own divorce in 1960. Between 1944 and 1955 Olivier directed and starred in films of *Henry V*, *Hamlet* (which won Best Actor and Best Picture Oscars) and *Richard III*. In 1963 he co-founded the National Theatre and in 1965 acted the title role in the Oscar-nominated film of *Othello* based on that theatre's production. In 1970 he became the first actor to be granted a peerage. His last Shakespeare performance was a television version of *King Lear* in 1983, six years before his death. He was only the third actor to be buried in Westminster Abbey, after David Garrick and Henry Irving. All three of them rest at the foot of the statue of Shakespeare.

Dame Judi Dench (b.1934)

Judi Dench originally trained as a set designer but went on to study at the Central School of Speech and Drama. In 1957 she made her debut as Ophelia for the Old Vic Company and she joined the Royal Shakespeare Company in 1961. Her 1976 performance as Lady Macbeth opposite Ian McKellen in Trevor Nunn's production was particularly highly praised (especially impressive as the show was put on with such a small budget that Dench wore a dyed tea towel on her head as part of her costume). She made her debut as a director in 1988 with a staging of *Much Ado About Nothing* for Kenneth Branagh's Renaissance Theatre Company. In 1999 she won a Best Supporting Actress Oscar for her portrayal of Elizabeth I in the popular film *Shakespeare in Love*. Her most recent Shakespeare performance was as Titania in Peter Hall's 2010 production of *A Midsummer Night's Dream*, a role she first played at school in the 1940s. She is a patron of the Shakespeare Schools Festival, which encourages UK schools to collaborate on Shakespeare productions every year.

Sir Ian McKellen (b.1939)

Ian McKellen began his theatrical career while at Bolton School, in a performance as Malvolio in *Twelfth Night* aged thirteen. He continued to act at Cambridge University and, after working in regional repertory theatres and the West End, joined Laurence Olivier's National Theatre Company at the Old Vic in 1965. In the following decades he frequently worked for the Royal Shakespeare Company and the National Theatre, gaining particular acclaim for his performances in Trevor Nunn's productions of *Macbeth* and *Othello*. In a *Daily Telegraph* Shakespeare survey in 2008, he was voted the public's favourite Shakespearean actor.

Sir Kenneth Branagh (b.1960)

Inspired to pursue an acting career by his admiration for Laurence Olivier, John Gielgud and Alec Guinness, Kenneth Branagh trained at RADA and gained great accolades for his portrayal of Henry V for the Royal Shakespeare Company in 1984. He co-founded the Renaissance Theatre Company in 1987 which made its name with several critically acclaimed Shakespeare productions. He is particularly well known for his film adaptations of *Henry V* (for which he was nominated for Best Actor and Best Director Oscars at the grand old age of twenty-nine), *Much Ado About Nothing*, *Hamlet*, *Love's Labour's Lost* and *As You Like It*. He was named the 'living person who has contributed most to the enduring popularity and appeal of Shakespeare' in the *Daily Telegraph*'s Shakespeare survey.

'The course of true love never did run smooth' Shakespeare's words of wisdom

Like a sort of secular Gideon's Bible giving solace in dark hours in lonely hotel rooms, one of the many amazing things about Shakespeare is that his plays can still offer up pearls of sagacity to even the most wearied and troubled traveller through life.

For those Afraid of the Future

'Men at some time are masters of their fates
The fault, dear Brutus, is not in our stars
But in ourselves, that we are underlings.'

Julius Caesar

For the Angry

'Your betters have endured me say my mind
And if you cannot, best you stop your ears.
My tongue will tell the anger of my heart,
Or else my heart concealing it will break . . .'

The Taming of the Shrew

For the Anxious

'Our doubts are traitors
And make us lose the good we oft might win
By fearing to attempt.'

Measure for Measure

For those with Children

'How sharper than a serpent's tooth it is
To have a thankless child!'

King Lear

'A thousand times, goodnight!'

Romeo and Juliet

'Those that do teach young babes
Do it with gentle means and easy tasks.'

Othello

'Woe to the land that's governed by a child!'

Richard III

For those Dealing with Grief

'Everyone can master a grief but he that has it.'

Much Ado About Nothing

'Ne'er pull your hat upon your brows.
Give sorrow words. The grief that does not speak
Whispers the o'erfraught heart and bids it break.'

Macbeth

For those in Love

'I love thee so, that, maugre all thy pride,
Nor wit nor reason can my passion hide.'

Twelfth Night

'Love is a smoke made with the fumes of sighs;
Being purged, a fire sparkling in lovers' eyes;

Being vexed, a sea nourished with lovers' tears;
What is it else? A madness most discreet,
A choking gall, and a preserving sweet.'

   Romeo and Juliet

'Love is a spirit all compact of fire.'

   Venus and Adonis

For the Broken-Hearted

'A wretched soul, bruised with adversity
We bid be quiet when we hear it cry,
But were we burdened with like weight of pain,
As much or more we should ourselves complain.'

   The Comedy of Errors

'These violent delights have violent ends
And in their triumph die, like fire and powder
Which, as they kiss, consume.'

   Romeo and Juliet

'Men have died from time to time, and worms have eaten them,
but not for love.'

   As You Like It

For those Worried about their Careers

'Some are born great, some achieve greatness, and some have
greatness thrust upon 'em. Thy Fates open their hands. Let thy
blood and spirit embrace them. And, to inure thyself to what thou
art like to be, cast thy humble slough and appear fresh.'

   Twelfth Night

'Neither a borrower nor a lender be,
For loan oft loses both itself and friend,
And borrowing dulls the edge of husbandry.'

> *Hamlet*

For the Lazy

'I rather would entreat thy company
To see the wonders of the world abroad,
Than, living dully sluggardised at home,
Wear out thy youth with shapeless idleness.'

> *The Two Gentlemen of Verona*

'Wisely and slow; they stumble that run fast.'

> *Romeo and Juliet*

For the Tired

'Methought I heard a voice cry "Sleep no more!
Macbeth does murder sleep," the innocent sleep,
Sleep that knits up the ravell'd sleave of care,
The death of each day's life, sore labour's bath,
Balm of hurt minds, great nature's second course,
Chief nourisher in life's feast.'

> *Macbeth*

For those Contemplating Marriage

'For what is wedlock forced but a hell,
An age of discord and continual strife?
Whereas the contrary bringeth bliss,
And is a pattern of celestial peace.'

> *Henry VI, Part 1*

'Thou art sad; get thee a wife, get thee a wife!'
   Much Ado About Nothing

'Fools are as like husbands as pilchards are to herrings, the husband's the bigger.'
   Twelfth Night

'Men are April when they woo, December when they wed: maids are May when they are maids, but the sky changes when they are wives.'
   As You Like It

For those Coping with Failure

'All that glisters is not gold —
Often have you heard that told.
Many a man his life hath sold
But my outside to behold.
Gilded tombs do worms enfold.'
   The Merchant of Venice

For those Dealing with Criticism

'Great lords, wise men ne'er sit and wail their loss,
But cheerly seek how to redress their harms.'
   Henry VI, Part 3

For those Worried about Going to the Dentist

'For there was never yet philosopher
That could endure the toothache patiently.'
   Much Ado About Nothing

For Drinkers

'I will ask him for my place again; he shall tell me I am a drunkard! Had I as many mouths as Hydra, such an answer would stop them all. To be now a sensible man, by and by a fool, and presently a beast! O strange! Every inordinate cup is unblessed and the ingredient is a devil.'

Othello

'Lechery, sir, it provokes, and unprovokes; it provokes the desire, but it takes away the performance: therefore, much drink may be said to be an equivocator with lechery: it makes him, and it mars him; it sets him on, and it takes him off; it persuades him, and disheartens him; makes him stand to, and not stand to; in conclusion, equivocates him in a sleep, and, giving him the lie, leaves him.'

Macbeth

For the Jealous

'How many fond fools serve mad jealousy?'

The Comedy of Errors

'As, I confess, it is my nature's plague
To spy into abuses, and oft my jealousy
Shapes faults that are not.'

Othello

For those Facing Death

'Cowards die many times before their deaths;
The valiant never taste of death but once.
Of all the wonders that I yet have heard,
It seems to me most strange that men should fear;
Seeing that death, a necessary end,
Will come when it will come.'

> *Julius Caesar.*(This is the passage that Nelson Mandela underlined as a source of inspiration in the 'Robben Island Bible' copy of Shakespeare's works that was smuggled into his prison.)

'The stroke of death is as a lover's pinch,
Which hurts, and is desired.'

> *Antony and Cleopatra*

'To die – to sleep,
No more; and by a sleep to say we end
The heart-ache and the thousand natural shocks
That flesh is heir to: 'tis a consummation
Devoutly to be wish'd.'

> *Hamlet*

'After life's fitful fever, he sleeps well;
Treason has done his worst: nor steel, nor poison,
Malice domestic, foreign levy, nothing,
Can touch him further.'

> *Macbeth*

For Friends

'Friendship is constant in all things
Save in the office and affairs of love.'

Much Ado About Nothing

'To mingle friendship far is mingling bloods.'

The Winter's Tale

'If thou wilt lend this money, lend it not
As to thy friends; for when did friendship take
A breed for barren metal of his friend?'

The Merchant of Venice

'The friends thou hast, and their adoption tried,
Grapple them to thy soul with hoops of steel . . .'

Hamlet

'Ignorance is the curse of God; knowledge is the wing wherewith we fly to heaven'

A QUIZ TO TEST YOUR SHAKESPEARE KNOWLEDGE

1. Which play was Shakespeare's first tragedy?

A *Macbeth*

B *Titus Andronicus*

C *Romeo and Juliet*

D *Cymbeline*

2. What is a 'sennet'?

A a royal page

B a remark directed at the audience which other characters can't hear

C a line of verse with four feet

D a trumpet blast

3. What did Shakespeare leave his wife in his will?

A four of his manuscripts

B a mourning ring

C nothing

D his second-best bed

4. Which Shakespearean character says 'If music be the food of love, play on'?

A Richard III

B Malvolio

C Orsino

D Cymbeline

5. **How does Antigonus in *The Winter's Tale* die?**

A hands and head cut off
B mauled by a bear
C multiple stab wounds
D hanged

6. **What is Hand D?**

A additions to the play *Sir Thomas More* believed to be in Shakespeare's handwriting
B the unnamed character who fatally wounds Julius Caesar
C the compositor who made most mistakes in the First Folio
D one of the 'mechanicals' in *A Midsummer Night's Dream*

7. **Who is considered the writer who most contributed to the development of Shakespearean tragedy?**

A Aristotle
B Christopher Marlowe
C Ben Jonson
D Raphael Holinshed

8. **What are foul papers?**

A the Master of the Revels' requested cuts to plays
B Timon of Athens' credit notes
C a playwright's first draft
D the witches in *Macbeth*'s written spells

9. **Who said 'I have a kind of alacrity in sinking'?**

A Ajax in *Troilus and Cressida*
B Thurio in *Two Gentlemen of Verona*
C Falstaff in *The Merry Wives of Windsor*
D the Nurse in *Romeo and Juliet*

10. Who was responsible for the death of James I's mother?

A Robert Cecil
B the Earl of Essex
C Elizabeth I
D Richard III

11. Which of the following is not commonly considered a Romance?

A *Romeo and Juliet*
B *The Winter's Tale*
C *Cymbeline*
D *Pericles, Prince of Tyre*

12. The First Tetralogy covers which conflict?

A the Thirty Years War
B the Franco-Prussian Conflict
C the Norman Invasion
D the Wars of the Roses

13. What religion was Shakespeare officially?

A Roman Catholic
B Lutheran
C Anglican
D Jewish

14. What was Yorick's profession in *Hamlet*?

A gravedigger
B jester
C student
D Lord Chamberlain

15. **What is the name of the forest the characters inhabit in *As You Like It*?**

A Arden
B Nottingham
C Roussillon
D Ephesus

16. **Hamlet is NOT responsible for the killing of which of the following?**

A Polonius
B Rosencrantz
C Laertes
D Gertrude

17. **What was the central source for the Roman plays?**

A *A Mirror for Magistrates*
B Seneca's *De Brevitate Vitae*
C Plutarch's *Lives*
D Virgil's *Aeneid*

18. **Cultural-materialist criticism focuses on:**

A historical context
B Marxist economic Theory
C gender dynamics
D semiotics

19. **Which group of plays commonly involves complex verse, lost children and themes of reconciliation?**

A Problem plays
B Comedies
C Romances
D Histories

20. What do Don John in *Much Ado About Nothing* and Edmund in *King Lear* have in common?

A they are widowers
B they owe money
C they are illegitimate
D they have claims to the throne

21. Akira Kurosawa's samurai film *Ran* about a retiring warlord is based on which play?

A *Hamlet*
B *Macbeth*
C *King Lear*
D *Othello*

22. George Bernard Shaw thought Shakespeare was:

A an uneducated genius
B a fraud
C a poet who couldn't write pentameters
D overrated

23. Who helps Prospero and Miranda survive when they arrive on the island in *The Tempest*?

A Gonzalo
B Sycorax
C Jupiter
D Caliban

24. What significant event occurred when Shakespeare was twenty-four years old?

A   the Reformation
B   the Accession of Elizabeth I
C   the defeat of the Armada
D   Publication of Copernicus' theory that the earth orbits the sun

25. What does *Henry IV, Part 1*, Q2 mean?

A   the second act of the first part of *Henry IV*
B   Queen Elizabeth's copy of *Henry IV*
C   the second quarto version published of the first part of *Henry IV*
D   *Henry VII*

26. What is enjambment?

A   the sense running over into the next line of verse
B   lines of verse with an extra unaccented syllable at the end
C   two rhyming lines in a row
D   punning

27. How does Antony die in *Antony and Cleopatra*?

A   asp bite
B   in a fight with Octavius
C   stabs himself
D   takes poison

28. What connection does Edward de Vere have to Shakespeare?

A   he is a minor character in *Henry VI, Part 3*
B   he acted Othello more often than any other actor
C   he is thought to be the 'Fair Youth' of the sonnets
D   he is considered by some to be the true author of the plays

29. *The Rape of Lucrece* is written in:

A blank verse
B rhyme royal
C sonnet form
D prose

30. Who took over from Shakespeare as house playwright for the King's Men?

A John Fletcher
B Thomas Middleton
C John Webster
D Thomas Dekker

31. Who is the eponymous Merchant of Venice?

A Shylock
B Antonio
C Bassanio
D Lorenzo

32. Who starred opposite Kenneth Branagh in his 1993 film version of *Much Ado About Nothing*?

A Kate Winslet
B Judi Dench
C Emma Thompson
D Claire Danes

33. Who was Thomas Thorpe?

A Shakespeare's first patron
B The 'Fair Youth' addressed in the sonnets
C The first black actor to play Othello
D The publisher of the sonnets

34. In *Othello*, what pattern appears on Desdemona's fateful handkerchief?

A poppies
B strawberries
C horses
D doves

35. How many plays comprise Shakespeare's First Folio?

A 12
B 24
C 28
D 36

36. What is the name of the island on which *The Winter's Tale* is set?

A Sicilia
B Britannica
C Corsica
D Elba

37. Which of the following is NOT one of the seven ages of man in the famous speech from *As You Like It*?

A Infant
B Soldier
C Pantaloon
D Cuckold

38. In *Titus Andronicus*, how many sons does Titus have before losing most in battle?

A 5
B 7
C 13
D 21

39. How old was Shakespeare when he died?

A 38

B 49

C 51

D 62

40. In *King Lear*, Goneril's husband is:

A the Earl of Gloucester

B the Earl of Kent

C the Duke of Cornwall

D the Duke of Albany

41. Even the most 'knotty-pated' of students knows that Shakespeare's plays were most famously performed at the Globe Theatre in London's Southwark. But which of the following other venues also provided a stage for his work?

A Monument Theatre

B Blackfriars Theatre

C Marylebone Theatre

D Bow Theatre

42. In poetry, what is meant by the term 'volta'?

A a sudden charge of excitement

B a sudden change in mood or argument

C the last six lines of the poem

D the first eight lines of the poem

43. In Shakespeare's time, what was a 'cozener'?

A a coward

B a cheat

C a tailor

D a coroner

44. In *Romeo and Juliet*, who is Mercutio's murderer?

A   Tybalt
B   Romeo
C   Montague
D   Paris

45. What size audience could the Globe Theatre potentially hold?

A   250
B   1,500
C   2,000
D   3,000

46. How old was Shakespeare when he married his 26-year-old wife Anne Hathaway?

A   16
B   18
C   28
D   30

47. What does the weyard sisters' 'helmeted head' apparition tell Macbeth to be afraid of?

A   Banquo
B   Macduff
C   his wife
D   trees that can move

48. Which Italian city is the setting for *Much Ado About Nothing*?

A   Verona
B   Milan
C   Messina
D   Venice

49. In *A Midsummer Night's Dream*, who is Robin Goodfellow better known as?

A Bottom
B Puck
C Oberon
D Lysander

50. What is the name of Dogberry's second in command in *Much Ado About Nothing*?

A Boyet
B Tom Snout
C Verges
D Tubal

51. What did Elizabethan actors call what we now know as the dressing room?

A the resting room
B the roaring room
C the vestibule
D the tiring room

52. How many poems appear in the sonnet sequence published in 1609?

A 98
B 154
C 198
D 302

53. What was the profession of Will's father, John Shakespeare?

A butcher

B publican

c actor

D glove-maker

54. Who utters the immortal line 'All the world's a stage'?

A Jaques in *As You Like It*

B Benedick in *Much Ado About Nothing*

c Macduff in *Macbeth*

D Tybalt in *Romeo and Juliet*

55. What animal injures Orlando as he attempts to rescue his estranged brother in *As You Like It*?

A a lioness

B a monkey

c a bear

D a snake

56. Who was the idealised lady that Shakespeare's forerunner Petrarch addressed his sonnet sequence to?

A Lavinia

B Lisbetta

c Laura

D Livia

57. In Elizabethan England, what did the word 'facinerious' mean?

A wicked

B guilty

c easy

D flat

58. How many children did Shakespeare have?

A none
B two
C three
D four

59. In *Much Ado About Nothing*, what relation is Beatrice to Hero?

A cousin
B aunt
C sister
D niece

60. During a performance of which play did the roof of the Globe Theatre accidentally catch fire, destroying it entirely?

A *Romeo and Juliet*
B *Henry VIII*
C *The Tempest*
D *Twelfth Night*

ANSWERS

1. B	16. D	31. B	46. B
2. D	17. C	32. C	47. B
3. D	18. A	33. D	48. C
4. C	19. C	34. B	49. B
5. B	20. C	35. D	50. C
6. A	21. C	36. A	51. D
7. B	22. D	37. D	52. B
8. C	23. D	38. D	53. D
9. C	24. C	39. C	54. A
10. C	25. C	40. D	55. A
11. A	26. A	41. B	56. C
12. D	27. C	42. B	57. A
13. C	28. D	43. B	58. C
14. B	29. B	44. A	59. A
15. A	30. A	45. D	60. B

Sources

We have consulted a large range of books, articles, programmes and websites in putting together this guide. Those listed below are the ones we relied on most. All quotations in the book are taken from the Arden edition but we would recommend the website http://shakespeare.mit.edu/ for quick and easy searching within the plays online.

The Arden Shakespeare, *Shakespeare Complete Works*, Revised Edition (London, 2013)

Bate, Jonathan, and Eric Rasmussen (eds), *The RSC Shakespeare: William Shakespeare Complete Works* (London, 2007)

BBC Radio 4: *In Our Time*, 'Shakespeare and Literary Criticism'

BBC Radio 4: *In Our Time*, 'Shakespeare's Work'

Bloom, Harold, *Shakespeare and the Invention of the Human* (London, 1998)

Bradley, A. C., *Shakespearean Tragedy: Lectures on* Hamlet, Othello, King Lear *and* Macbeth (London, 1991)

Bryson, Bill, *Shakespeare: The World as a Stage* (London, 2008)

Cambridge School Shakespeare, *Romeo and Juliet*

Cliff's Complete *Othello*

Crystal, Ben, *Shakespeare on Toast: Getting a Taste for the Bard* (London, 2008)

Edmondson, Paul, and Stanley Wells, *Shakespeare Bites Back: Not So Anonymous* (Stratford-upon-Avon, 2011)

Encyclopaedia Britannica

Gill, Richard, *Mastering Shakespeare* (London, 1998)

Greenblatt, Stephen, *Will in the World: How Shakespeare Became Shakespeare* (London, 2004)

Greer, Germaine, *Shakespeare's Wife* (London, 2007)

Hopkins, Lisa, *Beginning Shakespeare* (Manchester, 2005)

Jowett, John, William Montgomery, Gary Taylor and Stanley Wells (eds), *The Oxford Shakespeare*, Second Edition (Oxford, 2005)

Kermode, Frank, *Shakespeare's Language* (London, 2000)

MacGregor, Neil, *Shakespeare's Restless World: An Unexpected History in Twenty Objects* (London, 2012)

McDonald, Russ (ed.), *Shakespeare: An Anthology of Criticism 1945–2000* (Oxford, 2004)

McEvoy, Sean, *Shakespeare: The Basics*, Third Edition (London, 2012)

McLeish, Kenneth, and Stephen Unwin (eds), *The Faber Pocket Guide to Shakespeare's Plays* (London, 1998)

Mahoney, John, Letts Explore *The Merchant of Venice* (1994)

Shapiro, James, *1599: A Year in the Life of William Shakespeare* (London, 2005)

Shapiro, James, *Contested Will: Who Wrote Shakespeare?* (London, 2010)

Wells, Stanley, *Shakespeare, Sex and Love* (Oxford, 2010)

Wright, George T., 'Hendiadys and *Hamlet*', *PMLA*, Vol. 96, No. 2 (March 1981)

http://bloggingshakespeare.com

http://shakespeareswords.com/

http://www.bbc.co.uk/history/people/william_shakespeare

http://www.bl.uk/

http://www.folger.edu

http://www.nlm.nih.gov/exhibition/shakespeare/fourhumors.html

http://www.rsc.org.uk/

http://www.shakespeare.org.uk

http://www.shakespeareanauthorshiptrust.org.uk

http://www.shakespearesglobe.com/

http://www.shakespeare-online.com

http://www.sparknotes.com/

http://www.shakespeareswords.com/

http://www.nottingham.ac.uk/manuscriptsandspecialcollections/exhibitions/online/thebawdycourt/introduction.aspx

Acknowledgements

We are very grateful to: Rosemary Davidson, Katherine Fry, John Garrett, Christopher Wakeling, Julie Garvock, James Peake, Simon Rhodes, Rachel Cugnoni, Tom Drake-Lee, Lucy Luck, Kris Potter, Ceri Maxwell, Claire Wilshaw, Dan Franklin, Fran Barrie, Jonathan Patrick, Isabel Foley, Rosalind Porter, Tom Sillito, Angela Montfort-Bebb, Morgan and Emily Coates, Geraldine Coates, Marisa Capaldi and, especially, Oliver Bebb and Jack Murphy.

LIST OF ILLUSTRATIONS

INDEX

AS LUCK WOULD HAVE IT

WILD-GOOSE CHASE

BREVITY IS THE SOUL OF WIT

ALL OF A SUDDEN

GOOD RIDDANCE

FAIR PLAY

DISCRETION IS THE BETTER PART OF VALOUR